DUNLUCE CASTLE

Dunluce Castle
archaeology and history

COLIN BREEN

FOUR COURTS PRESS

Typeset in 11 pt on 14 pt ArnoPro by
Carrigboy Typesetting Services for
FOUR COURTS PRESS LTD
7 Malpas Street, Dublin 8, Ireland
www.fourcourtspress.ie
and in North America for
FOUR COURTS PRESS
c/o ISBS, 920 NE 58th Avenue, Suite 300, Portland, OR 97213.

A catalogue record for this title is available
from the British Library.

ISBN 978–1–84682–331–2 hbk
978–1–84682–373–2 pbk

SPECIAL ACKNOWLEDGMENT

The publication of this book has been facilitated by sponsorship from the
Northern Ireland Environment Agency.

Printed in Spain
by Castuera, Pamplona

Contents

Illustrations

Figures

Tables

Acknowledgments

A project of this kind invariably involves a large team of people. Thanks in the first instance must go to Emily Murray, who coordinated the QUB students on the site and is responsible for the smooth running of the excavations. Without her involvement, the project would not have taken place. Similarly, Rhonda Robinson of the NIEA has greatly facilitated the project and has been a source of constant encouragement and support throughout. Much of the genesis of what has gone on at the site arose from discussions between us.

Michael Coulter, Brian Williams, John O'Keeffe, Paul Logue, James Patience, Bob Bleakley, Mark Francis, John Cowan and John McMillan provided additional support at NIEA, while both Tony Corey and Gail Pollock came repeatedly to the site to document the excavations and produced a magnificent photographic record of the whole process. Many of Tony's photographs are contained within the text and have ensured that this is a very attractive book. He also sourced some of the older imagery, information from which aided our interpretations. Onsite supervisors included the ever present and professional Ruth Logue, along with Sarah Gormley, Cormac McSparron and Ruairi O'Baoill. Colm Donnelly provided much-needed support at QUB, as did Audrey Horning. Geophysical survey was undertaken at various times by Ronan McHugh, Sapphire Mussen, Jeremy Pyle and Chris McGonigle. Their work will be published in various sources at a later date. Colleagues who assisted this project from UU include Thomas McErlean, Wes Forsythe, Kieran Westley, Peter Wilson, Rory Quinn and Paul Montgomery. Rory McNeary undertook some sterling work with the LiDAR data and with GIS. It is hoped that we can build on this in the future. Rosemary McConkey undertook most of the drawings of the small finds. As usual, Killian McDaid made the site plans look professional with the minimum of fuss. Nigel McDowell provided some of the images here and also came to the rescue with some of the imagery. Paul Dunlop supplied the satellite image. Philip Armstrong brought the site to life with his exciting reconstruction drawings, and he continues to develop the imagery at Dunluce. It is not possible to list all the undergraduate students from QUB who undertook their training excavation at the site, but their efforts are appreciated. Gemma Reid, from the Causeway Museum Service, engaged with the project early on and contributed greatly to the success of the outreach elements of the dig. Marianne O'Connor has recently joined the project and is working with Gemma to develop its future. Jane Ohlmeyer, TCD, provided the relevant sections of text from the Depositions project before this was available online. John Raven, Historic Scotland, initiated parts of this project and continues to be involved. Thanks to Tom McNeill for his on-site comments, although I am sure he will find much to disagree with in these pages.

The farmer at Dunluce, Sean McKinley, unhesitatingly gave permission to excavate and survey and proved to be a huge help with back-filling the excavations. The McDonnell family at Glenarm were equally supportive, while Hector's enthusiasm for the site remains an inspiration. The core guide staff, including Patrick Kirkpatrick, George Pafilis and Hazel Porter, Nicole Woods, and masonry team of Tommy Campbell and Willy Dorans, work tirelessly to promote the site and protect it from the elements. They graciously lent us their facilities during the excavation seasons and gave us every support possible. A large number of people from local community groups visited the site and often gave up many valuable hours to help us excavate. Their time and engagement was most welcome. A large number of schools from the region also participated in the excavations and we hope to continue with this work into the future.

Thanks to Martin Fanning and the staff at Four Courts Press. In particular, I would like to thank Michael Potterton for his expertise and guiding hand. This book has been hugely improved by his professionalism. Thanks also to the anonymous referees who kindly read the text and provided constructive commentary and corrected a number of errors.

Finally, thanks again to Claire, Dáire and Caoimhe, who must never again want to see the walls of Dunluce Castle!

For my father, on a milestone birthday

Foreword

Dunluce Castle has stood on the north Antrim coast for well over four hundred years: it is undoubtedly one of the best known monuments in Northern Ireland. The striking cliff-top ruins and their spectacular location have combined to make this an iconic site, used to promote Northern Ireland throughout the world.

The Northern Ireland Environment Agency (NIEA) is delighted to have such a superb historic monument in its care. The McDonnell family passed the castle into state guardianship in 1928 and from that point onwards there has been an ongoing process of exposing and conserving the ruins. Since opening up the site to the public the number of visitors has grown steadily and Dunluce Castle has evolved from being an important historic monument, to also being a key site for Northern Ireland's tourism industry.

Despite almost one hundred years of conservation and presentation of the site, there have been surprisingly few detailed published studies of the castle itself. This volume is the first comprehensive work to consider both the upstanding architectural features and the buried archaeological remains of Dunluce.

NIEA was first approached by Dr Colin Breen (Centre for Maritime Archaeology, University of Ulster) in 2008, with a request to carry out some small, exploratory excavations at the castle. This presented an opportunity for NIEA to learn more about the castle, and inform our interpretation of the site for the public. At the outset, I doubt if either Dr Breen or the NIEA staff who manage the site imagined the surprising and superb results that were to emerge. Over the next four seasons of excavation, it became clear that the castle itself had a complex history of building, alteration and adaptation, but also that the early seventeenth- century town of Dunluce lay buried, but very well-preserved, in the fields outside the caste gate. This is a fascinating prospect – our own little Pompeii buried just below ground surface.

The information derived from those archaeological excavations, and contained within this volume, adds substantially to our knowledge and will be invaluable to NIEA in the future conservation, presentation and interpretation of the site and buildings. While Dr Breen initiated and led the research project throughout, it would not have been possible without with significant contribution from the Centre for Archaeological Fieldwork and the archaeology students from the Queen's University Belfast. The local community also participated, with enthusiasm, taking part in the excavations and generating a huge amount of interest in the findings. I believe that the result of that is a new-found local pride in the castle. NIEA welcomes this local engagement and looks forward to similar collaboration in the future.

I am delighted to say that, as a result of this project, NIEA has now acquired the two fields adjacent to the castle where the Plantation town lies buried. Imagine this – the excavation of a seventeenth-century village – well preserved – a time-warp of life back then. And imagine – another wonderful element of arguably our greatest natural and built heritage on the Causeway Coast.

ALEX ATTWOOD MLA
Minister of the Environment
May 2012

Timeline

1169	Anglo-Norman invasion of Ireland
1177	John de Courcy arrives in Ulster
1264	Lands at Dunluce granted as an Anglo-Norman manor
c.1500	Dunluce Castle built by MacQuillans
c.1554–5	Dunluce Castle passed to MacDonnells
1555–65	MacDonnells rebuild sections of Dunluce
1558	Sorley Boy MacDonnell becomes head of family
1585–6	Initial plantations begun in Ulster
1588	*La Girona*, a Spanish Armada ship, wrecked off north Antrim coast
1589/90	Death of Sorley Boy, succeeded by his son, James MacDonnell
1594	Outbreak of Nine Years War
1601	Battle of Kinsale. James MacDonnell dies and is succeeded by his brother Randal MacDonnell
1603	Elizabeth I dies. James VI of Scotland succeeds as James I of England
1607	Flight of the Earls from Rathmullan
1608–11	Town and manor house at Dunluce are built
1609	Official Plantation of Ulster initiated. Randal MacDonnell, son of Randal the first earl, born at Dunluce
1618	Randal MacDonnell created viscount of Dunluce
1620	Randal MacDonnell created earl of Antrim
1625	James I dies and is succeeded by Charles I
1635	Randal MacDonnell, son of first earl, marries Katherine Villiers, duchess of Buckingham
1636	Randal MacDonnell dies and his son Randal succeeds him as second earl of Antrim
1641	Outbreak of Ulster rebellion
1642	Randal MacDonnell's estate confiscated by English parliament and he is imprisoned in Carrickfergus Castle
1643	MacDonnell imprisoned for a second time in Carrickfergus Castle
1645	Randal MacDonnell created a marquis
1649	Charles I executed and Oliver Cromwell arrives in Ireland

1653   Oliver Cromwell becomes lord protector of Ireland

1660   Restoration of Charles II

1665   Randal MacDonnell restored to his estates

1680s   Both castle and town at Dunluce effectively abandoned

1683   Randal MacDonnell dies and is succeeded by his brother Alexander

1685   Charles II dies and is succeeded by James II

1688–9   James II deposed and replaced by William of Orange

1707   Union of Scottish and English parliaments

1740s   Dunluce fair ceases to exist

1928   Dunluce taken into state care

CHAPTER 1

Introduction

Dunluce Castle is arguably Northern Ireland's most iconic monument. Positioned dramatically on the north Antrim coast overlooking the Atlantic, it has been a source of fascination for antiquarians and provided inspiration for generations of artists and photographers (fig. 1.1). In the nineteenth century, it emerged as a major tourist attraction and remains the most visited archaeological site in Ulster. It is an integral part of the local cultural landscape and few of the local populace can have failed to visit it during their schooldays or as part of later family outings. It is surprising, given its popularity, that it was until recently also one of the least understood monuments in the Ulster landscape. Although much conjectural history had been written about the site, no systematic architectural or archaeological analysis had been undertaken there. In 2008, a research project was established to examine the nature of late medieval lordship in the north Antrim region. Initially, this project was to focus on the lordship of the MacQuillans who occupied an area that essentially encompassed northeast Antrim, stretching from the north coast southwards to Lough Neagh between the rivers Bann and Bush. It very quickly became apparent, however, that the surviving archaeology across the later medieval period and into the seventeenth century was far more complex and exciting than previously thought. Following initial excavations at a number of sites in 2007 and 2008, including Ballyreagh and Ballylough, it was decided to concentrate efforts on the impressive archaeology that was emerging at Dunluce. This volume describes the results of the first four years of research at the castle. This is the first of a series of publications that will concentrate on both the site and its surrounding landscape. The focus of this book is on the historical background and architectural evolution of the castle and the subsequent development of settlement in its immediate environs. Subsequent volumes will focus on the seventeenth-century town and material culture of the site. It should also be noted that this book is in many ways an interim statement on our knowledge of the castle and its evolution. Some of the interpretations contained here may be controversial and many will no doubt be revised in future years as the project develops and our knowledge of the site improves.

Location

Dunluce Castle lies on the north Antrim coast, 3km east of Portrush and 2km west of Bushmills (fig. 1.2). Standing at the cliff edge in the castle on a clear day, the visitor

has fine views of Islay to the northeast, and across the Skerries to Portrush, Magilligan and Inishowen in Donegal to the west.

Geology

The basalt stack that the castle sits on is likely to have been a volcanic vent (Wilson and Manning 1978, 38) formed by the release of volcanic gases and the upwards movement of magma 55–9 million years ago. Its current form was shaped by erosion along faults on either side of the stack. A third fault underneath has resulted in the formation of the sea cave (fig. 1.3). Scouring of the soft explosion-breccia between the stack and the mainland at the Pound has cleared this area (Wilson and Manning 1978, 56). The exposed basalt cliff face to the east shows compound lava flow formed of thin and impersistent flow units (Wilson and Manning 1978, 20, pl. 8). Sections of the inter-basaltic bed have been exploited in the past as a source of bauxite or aluminium ore. In the mid-nineteenth century, a series of mining operations were initiated on this bed and a number of mines for iron ore were operating at Dunluce into the early part of the twentieth century. Immediately to the west lie near vertical Cretaceous chalk cliffs that trend west-southwest/east-northeast. A geological fault at the castle marks the start of the tertiary basalt shoreline to the east, that generally caps the Ulster White Limestone of the region. A narrow low elevation cliff-base platform runs along much of the shoreline while two cobble/boulder beaches lie at the base of either side of the castle promontory.

Topography

The topography surrounding the castle is varied (fig. 1.4). A ridge known as Gallows Hill encloses much of the southeast of the mainland immediately south of the castle and old town, the summit of which runs roughly along the 70m contour. This descends westwards into a narrow north–south running valley containing the stream known as the Dunluce Burn, which terminates at a waterfall at the Burnfoot. This is the major drainage artery in the area, but some smaller channels are to be found across the ridge. A number of springs are also present, including a well in the field east of the church. The land rises again on the far side of the stream. The soils in the area are predominantly well-drained, thin drift overlying basalt and are mostly brown earths with varying gleys. There are few trees across the local landscape, although there would have been extensive woodland coverage further west in the Bann valley during the later medieval period.

The marine area off the castle promontory is defined by a wide embayment, stretching from Inishowen to Benbane Head. It is well exposed to the north and associated wave action is significant, although the Skerries islands provide a degree

1.1 Dunluce is probably the most dramatically sited castle in Northern Ireland and has been a focus for artists, poets and tourists for centuries. Built by the MacQuillans at the close of the fifteenth century, it later became the centre of the MacDonnell lordship (image reproduced courtesy of Tony Corey, NIEA).

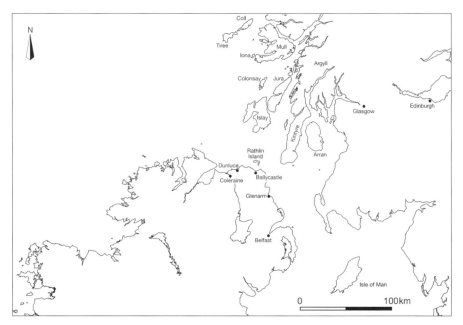

1.2 Dunluce is located on the north Antrim coast. Although viewed as peripheral today, it was once at the centre of a maritime territory incorporating north Ulster and the Western Isles of Scotland (image reproduced courtesy of Tandem Design).

1.3 The cave below the castle has been a source of many myths for centuries. It would never have functioned as a landing place, but small boats can be brought into it when the sea is very calm.

1.4 Aerial photograph of the castle looking eastwards across the castle towards Gallows Hill. The castle was originally located on the basalt promontory and gradually expanded over two centuries (image reproduced courtesy of the NIEA).

of shelter to shipping. Offshore, the seabed consists largely of sand and mixed coarse sediment deposits in places and includes a number of stony reefs. Tidal strength is up to 6 knots between Ramore Head and the Skerries, with bathymetric depths dropping quickly to 20m at the Storks and down to 165m 2km offshore (fig. 1.5).

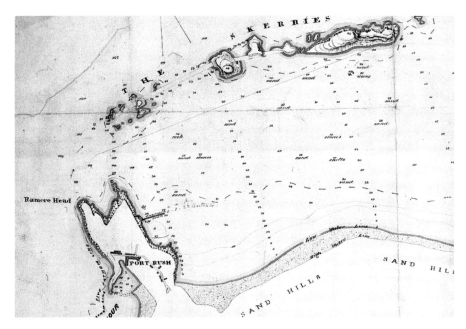

1.5 John Hawkshaw's 1859 map, showing the proposed location of a pier at Portrush and a breakwater on the Skerries with depths shown in fathoms and feet. This area served as a sheltered anchorage for vessels travelling between Ulster and Scotland.

Cultural landscape

Reconstructing the changing nature of the landscape around Dunluce in historic times is difficult because of the limitations of the cartographic evidence and the lack of landscape investigation studies. Historically, however, the area surrounding Dunluce Castle and the historic MacDonnell estates was a very varied landscape (fig. 1.6). Most of the medieval territory known as the Route was immediately east of the River Bann and ran southwards towards Lough Neagh. Positioned in a riverine valley, it is generally lowlying and consists of good agricultural land. Barnaby Rich, an Elizabethan soldier described the territory as good corn country (Gillespie 1985, 11), while Marshall Bagnal's 1586 *Description of Ulster* recorded it as a 'pleasant and fertile country'. The part of the early seventeenth-century estate lying further east, known as the Glynnes, or Glens, of Antrim, consists largely of a series of upland glens sweeping down to the coast. This is a very different landscape to that of the Route, with limited agricultural land. It would have been heavily wooded in places and this would have constituted a valuable resource in the early seventeenth century. A 1598 description of the area records the Glens as being boggy and heavily wooded (Hogan 1878), while Bagnal in 1586 describes the 'Glynnes' as 'full of rocky and woody dales'

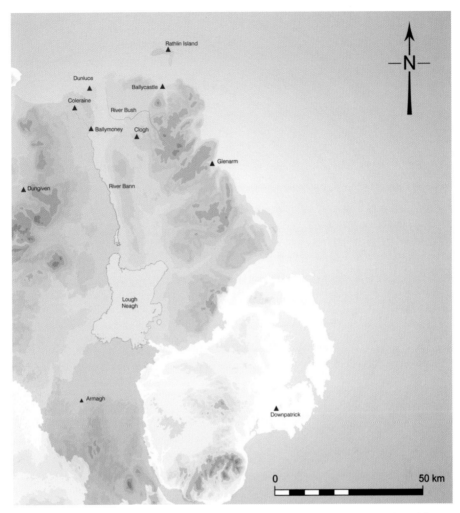

1.6 Topographic map of northeast Antrim including the territories of the Route and the Glens. These were greatly contrasting areas, with the Route incorporating good agricultural land while the Glens are mountainous and have limited lowlands suitable for agriculture.

and a place where Scottish galleys regularly land (Hill 1873). Historically, fisheries were a very important resource, in terms of both the nearshore coastal fisheries and the important salmon fisheries of the rivers Bann and Bush. Randal MacDonnell, later the 1st earl of Antrim, had originally been granted the fishing rights to the Bann in 1603, but this was contested and he later lost his grant of the tidal portion of the river in 1610 (Gillespie 1985, 16) as part of his surrender of nine townlands to planters at Coleraine. Other resources included coal near Ballycastle and an early 1639 estate lease refers to the coal mines and salt pans at Bonamargy (PRONI

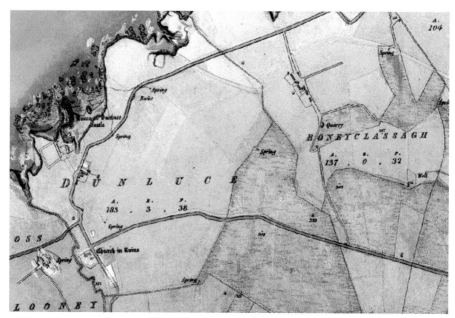

1.7 First edition Ordnance Survey map of Dunluce dating to c.1834 draped over an aerial photograph of the site. Many changes can be seen in the landscape, including the building of a new coastal road at the end of the nineteenth century. The various clachans, or settlement clusters, along the road were also abandoned by the close of that century (image reproduced courtesy of Rory McNeary, CMA).

1.8 Detail of early nineteenth-century painting of Dunluce Castle currently hanging at Glenarm Castle. The painting includes a number of important features including the well-preserved and largely intact north range along the cliff edge (image reproduced courtesy of the McDonnell family).

Table 1.1 Marine resources off the north coast of Antrim

	Common name	*Present*
Fish	Salmon	May to August
	Sea trout, pollock	June to August
	Cod, mackerel	Summer
	Ling, skate and whiting	All year
Crustacea	Crab, lobster	All year
Marine molluscs	Cockle, limpet, mussel, native oyster, periwinkle, whelk	All year
Others	Harbour porpoise, common seal, grey seal, bottlenose dolphin	

D2977/3A/2/36/1). Agriculture was the main activity throughout the estates, and it is clear MacDonnell actively supported new practices of enclosure across his lands. An early seventeenth-century poem recorded the change in the Ulster landscape at this time, with 'the mountain all in fenced fields; fairs are held in places of the chase; the green is crossed by girdles of twisted fences' (Maxwell 1923, 291). Ohlmeyer (1993) has demonstrated that in later years the MacDonnells were keen to be viewed as improving landlords through their agricultural practices and the use of long-term leases.

While the castle's location is marked on many medieval and post-medieval maps, the earliest detailed source for the area is the first edition Ordnance Survey six-inch sheet produced in the early 1830s (fig. 1.7). This shows a number of clear differences between the early nineteenth-century and present-day landscape. The primary one is the road pattern. Two hundred years ago, the main coast road ran eastwards along the Magheracross townland boundary with Clooney before meeting the junction of the Ballytober road immediately north of the church and then running north-eastwards past the farmhouse at Dunluce. By the end of the century, a new main coastal road had been constructed close to the cliff edge. This had originally been built to accommodate the Giant's Causeway Tramway that opened in January 1883, with a narrow gauge railway connecting Portrush with Bushmills and the causeway itself, before it finally closed in 1949 (McGuigan 1964). This effectively bypassed the farm to the south and cut a new route around the rocky knoll to the east of the castle. Other infrastructural change included the partial realignment of the Dunluce Burn, the course of which seems to have been partly straightened, presumably as part of the major improvement and flood relief schemes conducted across Ulster throughout the nineteenth century. In terms of other cultural features, the early OS map shows probable late eighteenth-century lime kilns at the Ballytober Junction and two further kilns associated with the clachan at Boneyclassagh to the east of Gallows Hill. An extensive limestone works formerly existed at White Rocks 1km to the west. A number of iron ore mines are also illustrated on early twentieth-century versions of the map sheet.

In terms of agricultural activity, we have very limited information relating to the practices and crops grown in earlier centuries. Flax, oats and potatoes were essentially the only produce grown in the immediate region by the 1830s (Day and McWilliams 1992, 104). Other commodities included turf for fuel consumption from the Gary bog south of Portrush, then covering nearly five hundred acres (Lewis 1837, 585), and the smaller bogs at Ballyleckan and Ballytober. Fishery resources in the area were previously plentiful, although they were subject to the various fluctuations in stocks witnessed throughout the last millennium. The salmon fishery on both the Bann and Bush rivers was especially valuable.

Previous research

In one of the first recorded antiquarian visits to the castle, Richard Pococke wrote in 1752 that

> the earls of Antrim did live in this castle and one of their ladies [the duchess of Buckingham] not liking the noise of the waves, had a house built for her just at the entrance of it, where she lived; which house is now standing without a roof (McVeigh 1995, 48).

Pococke then walked to Ballymagarry to Lord Antrim's house that had burned down 'about two years ago' (McVeigh 1995, 50). During the course of the Ordnance Survey mapping project of Ireland in the 1830s, a series of memoirs were written to accompany the maps. In September 1832, Lieutenant T.C. Robe visited Dunluce and recorded that the site 'does not exhibit any remains of architectural beauty and is now an object of curiosity merely from its peculiar situation' and suggested it might be a good position for a prison (Day and McWilliams 1992, 105). James Boyle subsequently visited the site in July 1835 and viewed it as 'striking and majestic', standing 121 feet above the level of the sea (Day and McWilliams 1992, 108) (fig. 1.8). John Stokes' memoir was far more detailed and related specifically to the antiquities and topography of Dunluce townland. He also produced a plan of the site, which, unfortunately, is no longer extant. His account contains some important information relating to the site's conservation, including the fact that one of the main hall's chimneys had fallen in the early part of the nineteenth century and that walls of the barracks [lodgings] had 'fallen in large pieces' (Day and McWilliams 1992, 113). Stokes goes on to detail his entry into the castle across the masonry arch, of which

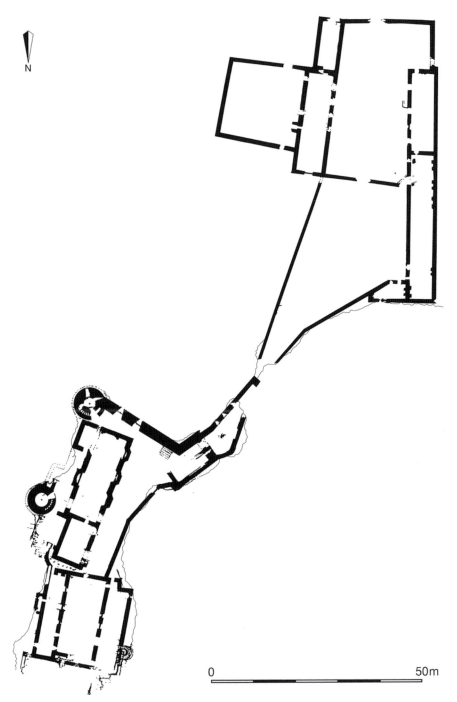

N

0 ——————————————— 50m

1.9 A redrawn version of George du Noyer's 1839 plan of the site. This very early plan shows that much of the north range had collapsed by that date, suggesting that it fell in the early part of the century. The east wall of the lodgings is also shown intact, although it too had fallen by the middle of the twentieth century.

only one side remained, into the gate-house tower, much of which had fallen down. He then entered the courtyard and noted that a large section of the western wall had given way where the large opening remains today. He entered the main hall building and noted the 'decaying human heads carved over the door' before entering the northeast tower, referred to as a dungeon and called Maeve Roe's room. Proceeding through the kitchen and into the 'second court', he recorded that the 'side next to the sea has fallen down, the foundation having slipped away' (Day and McWilliams 1992, 114). Outside of the castle, Stokes wrote that the house opposite the castle gate, occupied by a certain Widow Moore, stood on the site of the old jail and that the ruins of the 'lock-up dungeon' were destroyed when the house was built 'a number of years back'. Finally, he noted that the Dunluce fair had been held on 12 November until the latter part of the eighteenth century and that 'traces of many of the houses that constituted the town are still visible on the site' (Day and McWilliams 1992, 115). Thomas Fagan, another of the survey officers, produced a series of written descriptions of the site in May and June 1838. He was especially concerned with the church at Dunluce. He detailed the small western porch and the former presence of two doors on its southern wall. Fagan viewed the church as a chapel of ease built by the Antrim family before it ceased to function in 1822 following the construction of a new church at Bushmills. The old church here was known as Port Kammon, Bushmills' medieval name, and had been knocked in 1821. He noted an epitaph in the Dunluce church that read

> Here under lyeth the body of Florence McPhilip, alias Hamilton, late wife of Archibald McPhilip of Dunluce, merchant, and daughter to Captain Robert Hamilton of Clady, who departed this life 20th July anno 1674. Death can dissolve but not destroy, who sows in tears, shall reap in joy (Day and McWilliams 1992, 117).

Fagan also briefly mentioned Ballymagarry, to which the Antrim family moved for a short period following their withdrawal from Dunluce. Little remained of the house in 1838 aside from a section of what appears to have been a small tower and sections of an enclosing wall.

In 1839, George V. du Noyer, then working for the Geological Survey of Ireland, produced the earliest surviving architectural ground plan of the site and also drew a series of sketches (Young 1885, 133). The former is a finely executed plan and contains a wealth of pertinent information relating to the site at that time (fig. 1.9). He recorded the foundations of a house where the modern toilet block now lies and shows that the 'Pound' was fully enclosed at this time. The southern wall had later fallen and was rebuilt in the twentieth century. A masonry bridge crossed the deep chasm to the promontory, leading through what he termed the 'Barbican'. Internally, the general arrangement of the buildings is accurate, but the large accumulation of building debris masked features like the loggia, souterrain and parts of the kitchen,

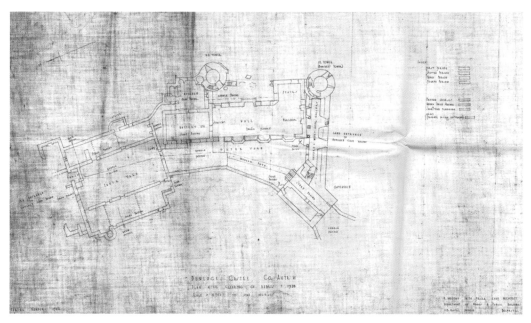

1.10 A plan produced in 1928 by the Department of Works and Public Buildings. This accurate plan was drawn after the clearance works undertaken in that year.

1.11 Early twentieth-century photograph of Dunluce Castle. The castle had by this date become a major tourist attraction (image reproduced courtesy of the National Library of Ireland).

all uncovered in 1928. He also labelled the southeast tower 'McQuillan's Tower' and called the northeast one Queen 'Maive or Mab's [Maeve] Tower' indicating that the residual memory of the original castle builders still survived at this time. Interestingly, the range at the edge of the cliff had gone at this date, indicating that it had fallen sometime in the 1820s, given that it is shown standing on a number of early nineteenth-century paintings. The architect Robert Young later published du Noyer's drawing and wrote an accompanying article for the *Journal of the Royal Historical and Archaeological Association of Ireland* (Young 1885). In a very informed insight, Young suggested that the earliest building horizon was early sixteenth century, an observation that seems to have been dismissed by later writers. Subsequent antiquarians proposed that the castle dated to the Anglo-Norman period. Bigger (1905, 154), for example, writing in the early part of the twentieth century, stated that the early part of the castle dated to the early thirteenth century and was rebuilt in the sixteenth. The architect W.H. Lynn (1905) drew on supposed comparisons between Dunluce and Dunstaffnage Castle to support a construction date in the thirteenth century. Much of the detail in his essay became the basis for all subsequent interpretations and written descriptions of the castle.

When the castle passed into state care in 1928, a major programme of conservation and site clearance was undertaken. An unpublished government report dating from 1929 provided a remarkably detailed account of these excavations for the time and remains an important source of archaeological information (the full text of the report is included as Appendix, below). R. Ingelby Smith, chief architect to the Department of Works and Public Buildings, produced a detailed plan of the castle in the same year to accompany this report (fig. 1.10). The *Preliminary survey of ancient monuments in Northern Ireland* (PSAMNI 1940, 2) ascribed the initial building phase of the castle to Richard de Burgh, earl of Ulster, or to one of his followers about 1300. Jope (1951, 36) recognized the Scottish architectural influences at the castle, including the turreted gate house, loggia and incised galley, all of which he dated to the sixteenth century, but in an unpublished note on DOE files reiterated his belief that the earliest sections of the castle were built in the thirteenth century. As castle studies developed across Britain and Ireland in the 1970s, Dunluce received only passing mention in the literature. McNeill (1983, 104) in his seminal article on the stone castles of north Antrim, understandably omitted discussion of Dunluce on the basis of its complexity and state care status. Hector McDonnell has taken an active interest in the castle and has published on aspects of its history and architecture. He published a seventeenth-century inventory from the castle, first noticed in the Public Record Office in London by Jane Ohlmeyer, and later published a comprehensive guide to the castle and its history (McDonnell 1992; 2004). This original 1651 inventory provides a valuable insight into the nature of the furnishings of the 2nd earl's home and household.

Throughout the twentieth century, conservation and landscaping were under-taken at the site on a near continual basis, some of which was successful, other parts

1.12 A sample of artefacts recovered during the car park excavation in the 1970s. The artefacts recovered across the site are representative of a range of domestic, industrial and religious activities that would have taken place in the seventeenth-century town.

far less so (fig. 1.11). Some of this work resulted in the loss of valuable archaeological material such as during the construction of the car park on the site in 1972. Artefactual material was collected during the course of this construction but no excavation took place, resulting in the probable loss of a seventeenth-century house site (fig. 1.12). Other conservation work in the castle's interior resulted in the loss of original features, coupled with poor reconstruction work, most of which took place without proper recording. The first scientific excavation at the site was undertaken by Nick Brannon, then of the DoENI, in 1987 in advance of the construction of a visitor centre in the southwest corner of the surviving mainland complex of castle buildings. A series of seventeenth- and eighteenth-century features were uncovered, including pits, cobbled and paved surfaces and walls. The results of this excavation will be dealt with in greater detail in later chapters. By the close of the twentieth

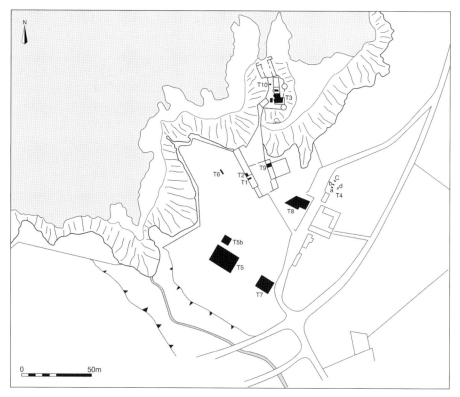

1.13 From 2008 to 2011, a programme of research excavation was undertaken across the site. This plan shows the location of the areas excavated during this period. Investigations are ongoing, and it is hoped that large portions of the excavated areas will be permanently exposed.

century, our knowledge of the site had progressed little since Young's observations in the 1880s and the exciting findings of the 1928 clearance work. There was then a pressing need to develop this knowledge base and to allow for the significant re-evaluation of the site's history and archaeology. It was against this background that a project was initiated in 2008 to address the castle's cultural development.

The present project

The work at Dunluce is one module of a larger project addressing the later medieval archaeology of north Ulster and the Western Isles. While the broader work examines settlement, communication and society across the greater region, the specific research aim of the Dunluce component of the project was to examine the historical cultural development of Dunluce Castle and its immediate environs. A research project was developed incorporating an integrated landscape investigation approach, examining the landscape cultural history of the site from the thirteenth through to the seventeenth century. This was designed to be an inclusive project and represented a research partnership between the University of Ulster and the Queen's University, Belfast, operating under the guidance and licence of the Northern Ireland Environment Agency, DoENI. The project has also drawn on the expertise of the Causeway Museum Service to work with the local community to both engage with and further develop aspects of the project. Community engagement has been a central tenet of the module and a large number of community groups, schools and other interest parties have visited and actively participated in the excavations and other aspects of the site's operations.

Excavation commenced in 2008 and has continued for four years to date. Twenty weeks have been spent excavating, while the landscape survey and architectural analysis in the field have taken eight weeks. The trenches, areas excavated and surveys undertaken are summarized below (table 1.2; fig. 1.13). All excavation has been undertaken by hand using non-mechanical means and standardized archaeological recording practice.

Table 1.2 Summary of annual fieldwork, 2008–11

Year	Excavation	Licence no.	Location	Survey
2008	Trench 3 (2 x 3.5m)	AE/08/30	Manor house external	Architectural analysis
2009	Trench 1 (1 x 3m)	AE/09/103	Stables	Architectural analysis
	Trench 2 (3 x 1m)	AE/09/20	Lodgings	
	Trench 3 (8m²)		Manor house	
	Trench 4 a, b, c, d, e		internal	
	(4 3 x 1m; 12 x 1m)		Eastern section	DGPS topographic
	Trench 5 (18 x 12m)		of west field	survey of town field
	Trench 5b (6 x 8m)		Town field	
	Trench 6 (2 x 1m,		Town field	Resistivity survey
	1 x 1m)		Gardens	of town field and
				outer castle ward
2010	Trench 7 (12 x 11m)	AE/10/86	Town field	Architectural analysis
	Trench 3 (20m²)		Manor house	Lidar survey
	TP1 (1 x 1m)		internal	Drawn survey of
			Church field	castle
2011	TP2 (2 x 1m)	AE/11/14	Outer grass area	Architectural analysis
	Trench 8 (187.5m²)	AE/11/	Outer masonry	
	Trench 9 (5 x 2.5m)		structure	
	TP3 (2 x 1m)		Brew-house	GPR survey of
			Cobbled courtyard	castle environs

Book layout

This book is divided into nine chapters that trace the history and architectural development of the castle chronologically, and contextualise the site within its contemporary society and landscape. Following this introductory chapter, chapter 2 examines the earliest evidence for human settlement at the site during the early medieval period. It then looks at the impact of the arrival of the Anglo-Normans in the thirteenth century and the establishment of a manor at Dunluce. There was no castle here at that time, but a series of buildings were constructed in the immediate environment. Chapter 3 turns to the pivotal role the MacQuillans, not only in building the castle but also in the establishment of the lordship of the Route across the region. They were involved in the refurbishment of a number of castle sites and the foundation of a friary at Bonamargy outside Ballycastle. In the 1540s, the MacDonnells, originally from Islay, arrive in north Ulster and chapter 4 details the extensive impact they had on the territory of the Route and Dunluce. The later sixteenth century was a period of almost continual turmoil and reinvigorated English expansionism, and the MacDonnells demonstrated both ingenuity and stealth in maintaining their newly acquired territories. Randal MacDonnell assumed the headship of the family in 1601 and chapter 5 outlines his significant expenditure at Dunluce, including the building of a fine Jacobean residence and a town outside the castle walls as well as the development of his estates across Antrim. Chapter 6 examines in detail the archaeology of the town founded in the opening decades of the seventeenth century, focusing on its architecture and material culture. Following the revolt of 1641, the site's fortunes began a significant downturn and chapter 7 provides an historical overview of how Dunluce was intrinsically linked to the events of that year and what was later to come. Following the Cromwellian period, the site was briefly reoccupied before being abandoned in the 1680s. A fair was held in the ruins of the town during the eighteenth century before being stopped because of excessive rowdiness. At the end of that century, the site began to attract the interest of antiquarians, and chapter 8 examines how it became a tourist attraction and magnet for artists before being taken into state care in 1928. An overview of subsequent conservation efforts is outlined. Finally, chapter 9 provides a brief overview and summary of findings and contemplates the future of the castle.

CHAPTER 2

Anglo-Norman background

We have little historical or archaeological information relating to the Dunluce area on the eve of the Anglo-Norman invasion of Ulster. For much of the later centuries of the first millennium AD, the northeast Ulster coast and a large part of western Scotland were at the centre of a maritime kingdom (fig. 2.1). Towards the end of the fifth century AD, the Dál Riada initiated increased cultural and political interplay between the two regions, with a number of sites emerging as major centres of power, including Dunadd in Argyll and Dunseverick on the north Antrim coast (Lane and Campbell 2000). Dunluce was outside the territories of this entity, but anybody living in the region would have been subject to its cultural and political influences. During the seventh century, the site was within the territory of the Mag nEilni, a relatively small area between the rivers Bush and Bann (Charles-Edwards 2011, 41). In Tírechán's account of St Patrick's travels through Ulster, the saint first visited the small kingdom of Eilne in the lands of the Cruithni immediately west of Cúl Raithinn, or modern Coleraine, where their principal church lay (Charles-Edwards 2011, 44). Interestingly, Charles-Edwards (2011, 58) has shown that the kingdom of Eilne was not listed in *Lebor na Cert* (Book of Rights), an eleventh- or twelfth-century tract, and suggests that the Dál Riada had subsumed the kingdom. It appears likely that a fortified headland existed at the site during this period. All traces of previous defences and settlement were eradicated by later castle building, but the discovery of a souterrain (see below) is a clear indicator of settlement activity during the early medieval period (fig. 2.2). The current excavations have also recovered isolated sherds of first-millennium pottery in the disturbed upper levels of the trenches on the promontory. Lawlor (1935–7, 310) tentatively asserted that the site referred to as Durlus in the Annals of the Four Masters under the year 660 equates to Dunluce, but no other writer has supported this claim.

Souterrain

Souterrains are essentially subterranean structures that can be tunnelled, of drystone construction or built using a composite set of constructional techniques. Controversy continues as to their actual function, which is variously ascribed to storage, refuge or even burial, but it is generally accepted that they date to the later centuries of the first millennium AD into the first quarter of the second (Clinton 2001, 209). There is a concentration of rock-cut souterrains in the northeast of Ireland, with a distinct

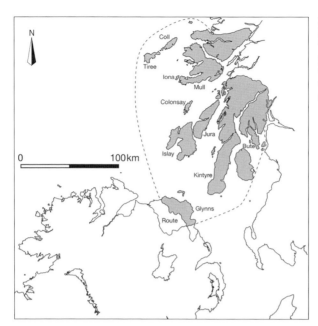

2.1 Map of the territory and kingdom of the Dál Riada. Throughout the early medieval period, this was a strong and vibrant maritime territory, witness to extensive cultural and political interplay.

2.2 A small souterrain, or underground passage, was located on the castle promontory during the clearance works in 1928. Long abandoned by the time the castle was built, these passages would have been used for storage and possibly refuge (image reproduced courtesy of Tony Corey, NIEA).

cluster along the north Antrim coast (Clinton 2001, 5). A number of these were built into exposed cliff and bank faces and their builders may have been exploiting existing natural caves or cavities. The Dunluce example was identified early in the twentieth century. During the course of the clearance work in 1928, the workmen uncovered a *c*.1.3m deep 'hollow' adjacent to and underlying the northeast tower. Upper sections of the hollow had been packed with clay and 'rubbish' in the seventeenth century to create a leveled area for new cobbling where previous subsidence had taken place. Burnt wood, bones and shell were subsequently recovered from deposits at the base of the souterrain, as well as a quantity of pottery. The faunal evidence included bones from ox, sheep and cat. This assemblage had been lost by 1950 (Ant002:003), but was identified as early medieval souterrain ware in various notes on unpublished government files. The structure consists of a narrow rock-cut passage, averaging 60cm wide, with a varying height of 1–1.5m, and an overall length of just over 13m (fig. 2.3). It is not clear where the original entrance was, but two rounded recesses are present along its length.

The interpretation of this feature is difficult. It may have been used for the storage of foodstuffs, weapons, tools or other items of value. It would have been difficult to access, however, making ease of retrieval difficult. This would of course have worked to the occupants' advantage if they needed to hide or discourage the recovery of items placed in the tunnel. Neither can we take the recovery of the animal bone and artefacts from the structure in 1928 as proof of its original function, as we do not have the contextual information relating to the finds. It may be, for example, that this material had been inadvertently placed into it as packing or had been carried in during the process of siltation. Alternatively, the structure may have been used as a refuge. It does appear that the original construction included an exit on the eastern cliff face, and the structure could easily accommodate a number of adults and children, albeit uncomfortably. It has been pointed out that attackers could easily smoke the hideaways out, if they could locate the entrance (Mallory and McNeill 1991). We need also to bear in mind the nature of conflict at the time, which largely consisted on lightning raids conducted by small bands. A hideaway that could offer even temporary refuge may have been adequate until the raiding band dispersed or friendly neighbours could come to their aid. Interestingly, a number of small souterrain-like structures have been found across the Hebrides and have been mostly interpreted as refuges, both in folklore and by contemporary researchers. The small underground chamber at Dún nan Nighean on Islay was partially stone-lined and measured 1.7m in length with a roof height of 75cm. It resembled the small souterrains at Beinn Tighe on Canna (RCAHMS 1984, 25). Similarly, a partially excavated souterrain at Kilellan on Islay consisted of a 6.4m-long trench lined with upright slabs and varied between 1 and 1.5m in width and was 90cm deep (RCAHMS 1984, 142). Ultimately, the presence of the souterrain on such a naturally strongly defended promontory is indicative of a site of some importance at Dunluce during the early medieval period.

Place-name

A separate piece of evidence that is indicative of earlier occupation at the site comes from its place-name (table 2.1). The actual interpretation of the name has been controversial, with many commentators only mentioning its later English name, Dunluce, widely adopted from the late sixteenth century onwards. Both this and its Gaelic name, *Dhúinlis*, or 'fort of the fort', bear little relation to the names used in earlier centuries. Admittedly, these earlier names refer to the parish or church at Dunluce and not to the castle. The prefix 'Dun' is widely associated across Ireland with early fortified sites varying in date from the Iron Age into the early medieval period. Its usage at Dunluce from at least the thirteenth century is a clear indicator that the promontory had been fortified prior to the arrival of the Anglo-Normans. Kay Muhr, in an unpublished note on the SMR files, speculatively raises the possibility that the earlier names may be connected with a saint associated with the church before its dedication to St Cuthbert by 1609. Unfortunately, it is unlikely that the place-name problem will ever be satisfactorily dealt with, but the 'dun' element does remain an important indicator of early settlement.

Table 2.1 Place-names associated with the castle, parish and church at Dunluce (source: partly from an unpublished note by Kay Muhr on DOE Dunluce SMR file ANT002:003)

Name	Date	Source
Dundilipsi	1264	CDI
Ecclesia de Dunkelisp	1306	CDI
Dundelipsi	1308	IMC
Caislen Duin-libhsi	1513	AU
Caislen Dhúinlis	1513	AFM
Dhúnlis	1585	AFM
Dunluce	1586	Fiants Eliz.
Sancto Cuthberto Dunlups	1609	Reeves, 1847
Ecclesia Sancti Cuthberti de Dunlippis	1615	Reeves, 1847
Dunliffsia	1645	Colgan, 1647

The Anglo-Normans

Some historical clarity emerged in the late twelfth century with the arrival of the Anglo-Normans. Following his incursion into Ulster in 1177, John de Courcy took the area east of the Bann over the following years and probably established an outpost

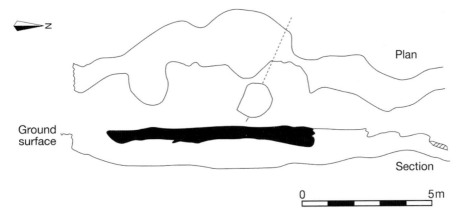

2.3 Plan and section of the souterrain (after a plan in DoENI file SM7–ANT–02–03).

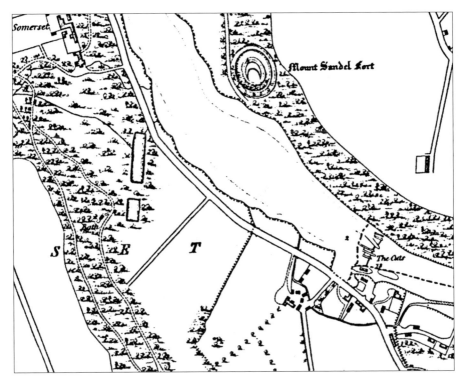

2.4 Detail of the 1831 first edition six-inch Ordnance Survey Londonderry map, sheet 7, showing Mount Sandel fort on the eastern bank of the River Bann. This enigmatic mound has puzzled archaeologists and antiquarians for decades. It appears unfinished, as the centre of the mound contains a large depression. An early Mesolithic site was excavated to the east of the mound in the 1970s by Peter Woodman.

castle at Mount Sandel immediately south of Coleraine (McNeill 1980, 6) (fig. 2.4). Hugh de Lacy took the Ulster lands in 1204 following his defeat of de Courcy at Downpatrick and was created earl of Ulster in May of the following year. It remains unclear why de Courcy was removed from Ulster, but it may have been that he was perceived as a threat by the crown or perhaps he fell out with the other lords. A number of families that were to feature strongly in medieval Ulster society now arrived in the north, including the de Mandevilles, who followed de Lacy north and established themselves as his tenants, while the Bissets also arrived, having established themselves politically over the previous decades in Scotland. Duffy (2004, 41) suggests that it is from this point that they began to establish themselves in the Glens of Antrim, supported by their association with de Lacy. Worried by the developing autonomy of de Lacy and his support of William de Braose, King John arrived in Ireland in 1210 and expelled him from the earldom. A new series of grants were given out to loyal subjects in an attempt to further undermine de Lacy's holdings and reward those followers of John who had supported him in his campaign against the earl. In 1212, Alan, lord of Galloway, was granted by the king an estate of 140 knights' fees, including much of north Antrim, Rathlin and parts of north Derry (Duffy 2004, 38). An area centred on Mount Sandel was given to Alan's brother Thomas, who built a castle at Coleraine with material from 'all the cemeteries, fences and buildings of that town, save the church alone' (McNeill 1980, 15). Alan's grant was confirmed in 1215 with additional lands in Glenarm and 'the bounds of Dalriada'. Duncan, earl of Carrick in greater Galloway, also received territory in Antrim centred on Larne and Glenarm (Duffy 2004, 37). There are questions about the authenticity of the original grant document and a number of later charters, but they are indicative of land ownership at this time.

By the early 1220s, Hugh de Lacy had returned to Ireland intent on getting back the earldom and proceeded to cause considerable turmoil across Ulster. He was eventually pardoned by Henry III and regained his position in April 1227, holding it until his death in 1243. During his tenure, de Lacy granted lands to Robert Savage in Dalrod (Dál Riada) and it is likely that both Henry de Mandeville and John Bisset were also granted their lands by him as they are in position by 1247 (Duffy 2004, 46). Both were close allies of de Lacy and clearly benefited from this relationship. Orpen (1920, 256) recorded that both Walter Bisset and his nephew John were granted lands in Glenarm, Carncastle and Ardclinis and on Rathlin, former Galloway grant lands. It was also during this period that the territory of Twescard, from the Gaelic *Tusaisceart*, meaning 'north', was subdued (fig. 2.5). This area along the north coast incorporated the Bann valley and stretched eastwards from Coleraine past Dunseverick. It is of great importance to the present study and will be referred to regularly. In 1260, Twescard county included fertile lands producing £240 per year and included an area from Coleraine to Dunseverick and Armoy to the east and south to Loughguile (McNeill 1980, 22). Following the earl's death, the earldom once more

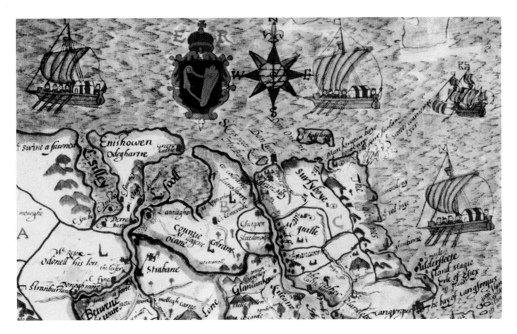

2.5 Detail from Francis Jobson's late sixteenth-century map of Ulster, showing the north coast. Note the 'Scots warning fire' at Torr Head in the northeast, which would have been used as a means of communication between northeast Antrim and Kintyre during times of crisis
(TCD MS1209/17; image reproduced courtesy of Trinity College Dublin).

reverted to the crown. This was to be a difficult period, with Gaelic power in Ulster beginning to reassert itself. The justiciar, John Fitz Geoffery, built a castle at Drumtarsy (Killowen) in Coleraine and erected a bridge across the Bann in 1248 in response to these threats (Orpen 1920, 268). Brian O'Neill of Tír Eóghain, in particular, rose to prominence and led an incursion into Ulster in 1260. In response, Henry de Mandeville, by now sheriff of Twescard, was granted monies to guard the castles in Twescard, namely Coleraine, Drumtarsy (on the west bank of the Bann at Coleraine) and Lochkel (Loughguile). Significantly, neither the castles at Dunluce or Ballylough are mentioned in this list. Accounts for Ulster survive for the period 1260–2 under Prince Edward, but Twescard was a separate administrative entity under the seneschal Nicholas de Dunheved (Orpen 1920, 278). Henry de Mandeville's accounts for Twescard survive for four terms, ending in November 1262 (McNeill 1980). Rental from manors mentioned in the text include Dunluce, returning a rent of £26 (our first confirmation that while there may not have been a castle at Dunluce there was settlement in the vicinity). Portrush returned £40, Dunseverick returned £17 and Porkaman (Bushmills) returned £20. Elsewhere, rents are returned from Bally Agherton (Portstewart), Drumtarsy, Loughguile, Ballyclogh, Armoy and Mount Sandel. The 'burgages' of Coleraine returned £23, while a number of mills and fisheries on the Bann, including the Cutts, were also listed. The total returned was £464 (Orpen 1920, 290). It is clear from these accounts that Twescard was a profitable region that was secure with a well-established Norman presence.

It was primarily as a result of the Gaelic resurgence that the earldom was revived in 1264 and granted to Walter de Burgo, lord of Connacht. We now get a more detailed record of Dunluce relating to a manor established there by that time. The lands of *Dundilipsi* (Dunluce) were granted in 1264 by Edward I as lord of Ireland to Robert de Beaumes, who then granted them to his brother Hugh de Beaumes (*CDI*, II, nos 1782, 1976). The Irish memoranda roll of 30 Henry VI (1310) contained an enrolment of two Mandeville charters on membrane 12d. One is dated at Carrickfergus 10 May Edward II (1308), by which Robert de Beaumes (whom Nicholls suggests must be heir to the Hugh of the 1264 grant) granted to Sir Henry Cougan and his heirs the manor of *Dundelipsi*, which had formerly belonged to 'Hochageran' in Ulster, with its appurtenances: one hundred messuages, three mills, two hundred carucates of land, one hundred acres of meadow, five hundred acres of wood, a thousand acres of pasture and the liberty of a free fishing boat on the water of the Bande, with its 'ketil' and other devices necessary for fishing, witnessed by Roger de Holywood (*de Sancto Bosco*), Roger Haket, Nicholas de Cruse, Hugh de Lacy and Thomas Furnys (Nicholls 1985, 5–6). A second charter is identical to this and was witnessed by the same people except it is a conveyance and was dated at *Dundelipsi* on 7 April in the third year of King Edward son of King Edward (1310) from Richard de Cougan to Sir Thomas de Mandeville and his heirs. There are a number of problems with these documents. Nicholls suggests the enrolments in the memoranda roll were based on genuine originals with some fabrication in the versions actually presented. Nevertheless, it would appear that at this date there were at least three mills operating in the immediate area and that income was derived primarily from pasture and from fishing on the Bann, where fishweirs were in operation.

The earl subsequently appointed Sir Henry de Mandeville, vassal of the de Burghs, to the office of seneschal. He was later removed from this post and William fitz Warin took Twescard. Conflict arose between the two and war was declared in 1272–3, lasting a number of years. Both the O'Neill and the O'Cahans sided with de Mandeville, while the O'Neills of Inishowen sided with fitz Warin (Otway-Ruthven 1968, 203). This level of internecine conflict and shifting alliances of the Gaelic groupings was to be a feature of the political landscape across this region over the next four hundred years. The conflict also took place against broader developments in Britain and Ireland. Henry III died in 1272 and was succeeded by his son, Edward I, lord of Ireland since 1254. A further period of turmoil emerged across western Ireland, but the historical sources are relatively quiet about the north Ulster coastal region. The Savages were well established in the region by this date and in 1276 their lands were subject to inquisition at Portkaman (Bushmills) following the death of Henry Savage, Robert's son (*CDI*, II, no. 929). Richard Savage was later called to parliament in 1310 holding one and one sixteenth of a knight's fee at Ballylough (Loghton), and it is likely that Ballylough Castle was built by the family by the early part of the fourteenth century at least. The men of Portkamen were referred to as burgesses in this inquisition document, indicating that a rural agricultural borough settlement existed there at that time. The men of Portrush were also referred to as burgesses, reflecting the settlement's status as a focus for fishing, port trade and agricultural activity.

Ballylough Castle

Ballylough Castle is intrinsically linked to Dunluce (fig. 2.6). Previous studies had suggested that the remains at Ballylough probably represent a late medieval tower house (McNeill 1983, 117) that was of subsidiary importance to Dunluce. Recent excavations at the site, however, have shown that the castle was built during the high medieval period (thirteenth to fifteenth century) and was, until the sixteenth century, the dominant fortified site in the area (Breen and Raven, forthcoming). The castle is 2.5km south of Bushmills, just under a kilometre from the River Bann to the west and immediately north of a former lake that was drained in the eighteenth and nineteenth centuries. The lake now consists of wet marshy ground fringed by trees and vegetation. Prior to drainage, the castle would have been positioned on a promontory or raised land projecting southwards into the lake. This original position is not immediately visible due to the extent of landscape change that has taken place over the past three centuries. A high ridge on a north–south orientation passes to the east of the site, rising to a height of *c.*55m OD. Further east, at a distance of 1.5km, lies the parish church of Billy.

Only a small section of the castle now stands. It consists of two walls forming an 'L'. The masonry structure stands over 11m in height and appears to represent the remains of a former three-storey structure. The structure has been subject to extensive refurbishment, probably in the first decades of the nineteenth century, when Archdeacon Traill was noted as having carried out alterations to the building. In particular, he underpinned the northeast end of the projecting northern wall, refaced and repointed much of the outer masonry work and built a thin pointed arch doorway in the inner face of the west wall. It is likely that a dovecote was inserted at first-floor level at this time. A domed alcove is present at ground floor level in the northwest internal corner of the site and appears to represent an oven. The ground floor includes a north–south orientated western wall, 2.4m in thickness and an east–west return. Two western side angles of former windows are apparent at first- and second-floor levels in this return. The nineteenth-century sources suggest that an entrance was present at this location before Traill underpinned this wall with a large masonry base. This entrance may once have been a window, given the significant

2.6 Ballylough Castle was built at the close of the thirteenth century and later refurbished by the MacQuillans. It was remodelled in the early nineteenth century by the Traills, landowners of this demesne, just south of Bushmills.

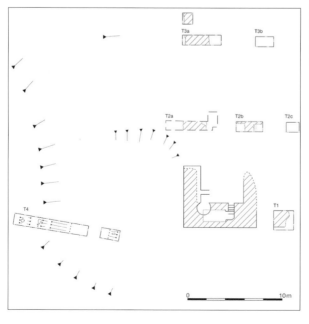

2.7 Excavations were conducted at Ballylough in 2009. Evidence for an early medieval enclosure was found immediately to the north of the castle.

change in ground level over the centuries. A window is also present on the western facing wall at second floor level.

Excavations have demonstrated that in the late thirteenth century a substantial fortified masonry structure was built at the site (fig. 2.7). This dating evidence is provided by numerous sherds of Ulster coarse medieval pottery dating from 1250–1400 (C. McSparron, pers. comm.) as well as a number of sherds of high medieval glazed and non-glazed pottery (which dominate the ceramic assemblage in the primary contexts). Sherds of Ham Green wares dating from the mid-twelfth to thirteenth century were recovered, as well as a sherd of Scottish reduced medieval grey ware likely to date to the fourteenth or fifteenth century. It is apparent that much of this structure was levelled in late medieval times and was further impacted upon during building works in the post-medieval period. The foundation of a substantial wall was located running east–west from the standing remains through Trenches 2 and 3, measuring over 22m in overall length and over 2.5m in thickness. It is important to state at this juncture that the excavations did not define the overall ground plan of the original castle and what we are left with here is conjecture. It does not appear that this wall represents the full length of a central keep, hall or castle building, but rather represents an enclosing or curtain wall running from and in line with the front wall of the castle. This may have originally enclosed a courtyard or served as a defensive wall cutting off the promontory. The wall is absent to the west of the castle and would not have cut off the complete promontory. Originally, we can speculate that the central building, possibly a hall castle, would have been represented by a square block measuring approximately 12m x 12m, with an internal division at the southern end of the building. This castle then dominated the local area during the fourteenth century.

Dunluce excavations

At Dunluce, evidence for thirteenth- and fourteenth-century settlement activity is less tangible. It is clear from the historical sources that a manor had been established here by the end of the thirteenth century, but associated archaeological evidence is limited. This is partly due to the excavation strategy adopted on the site, where layers below the later medieval contexts were not investigated, so as to ensure the preservation and integrity of the surviving structural remains. It may also be due to the limited nature of the surviving remains associated with the earlier periods across the site. Evidence for high medieval activity was located in the greenfield area southeast of the castle and south of the original roadway and contemporary farmhouse. Here, an area of relatively level ground survives before dropping steeply into an east–west running hollow to the south below Gallow's Hill. This area was targeted for investigation in advance of the possible construction of a car park. Four small trenches (4a–d) were excavated to assess this area's archaeological potential.

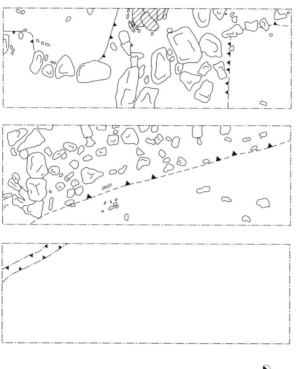

2.8 During initial trial excavations at Dunluce, evidence for Anglo-Norman activity was found in Trench 4. It is clear from the documentary sources that a small settlement was established here in the thirteenth century, but we still have limited information relating to the nature of it.

2.9 Photograph of a sherd of high medieval pottery recovered from Trench 4 at Dunluce (image reproduced courtesy of Tony Corey, NIEA).

In 4a, the upper surface of a stone-filled trench was uncovered (fig. 2.8). This ran on an approximate east–west line with a narrower north and south angle running from it. The trench had been cut into the natural subsoil and the feature appears to date to the high medieval period on the basis of a basal sherd of pottery recovered (fig. 2.9). This has been provisionally identified as Redcliffe ware, dating from the later thirteenth to the fifteenth century. It has a sandy hard wheel-thrown fabric, creamy buff in colour, with external yellow to mid-green glaze, now barely visible. A slate box-like feature was also exposed. As with other features across the site, these contexts were not removed and further investigation will be required to clarify their original form and function. A further cut feature was located on the western side of Trench 4b, running diagonally across to the bottom southeast corner of the trench. A mixture of high medieval ceramics and seventeenth-century artefacts were recovered from these contexts, indicating the mixed nature of contexts in this area. Trench 4c was featureless aside from possible narrow 'plough scars' cut into subsoil in the northeast corner. Some small seventeenth-century ceramic fragments were recovered from the trench. The other trenches were featureless.

Aerial remote sensing survey (LiDAR) across the site highlighted a number of linear features running southwards from the existing road that provides access to Dunluce House and the castle entrance (fig. 2.10). These can be interpreted in a number of ways. The most straightforward explanation is that they constituted boundaries associated with the seventeenth-century properties lining the original road. An alternative suggestion is that they are earlier and represent boundaries associated with the thirteenth-century manor. While the former interpretation is favoured, the discovery of thirteenth-century ceramics and structures in this location does open up the possibility that high medieval boundaries survive across the site. These await further archaeological investigation.

Church

The church at Dunluce is first recorded in the ecclesiastical taxation of Ireland, 1302–6 (*CDI*, V, 209). Under a listing for the diocese of Connor and the deanery of Twescard, the church of *Dunkelisp* was valued at 47s. 4d. Further churches were listed at Portrosse (Portush) at £25 4s. 8d., Portkaman (Bushmills) at £8 10s. 8d. and Bile (Billy) at £36. There is currently no evidence to suggest that this site pre-dated the thirteenth century and it is probably, therefore, an Anglo-Norman foundation. The enclosure surrounding the site is irregular and has been rebuilt. It could not be classified as circular, a feature that is generally taken as an indicator of an early medieval date in Ireland. Neither are there any surviving architectural features in the building that are suggestive of an early building horizon. As it stands, the church appears to have been completely rebuilt late in the sixteenth or early in the

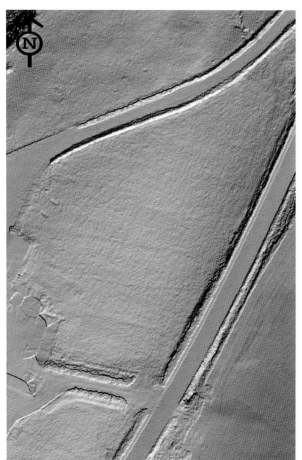

2.10 A series of linear features are just visible in this LiDAR plot of the south-eastern farm field. This light sensor technology captures high-resolution 3D imagery of the landscape and is very useful for mapping earthworks (image reproduced courtesy of Rory McNeary, CMA).

2.11 Archaeologist John Raven excavates a small test pit in front of the northern boundary wall of the church. The church was probably established in the thirteenth century and rebuilt in the closing decades of the sixteenth century. Further refurbishment took place in the opening years of the seventeenth century. Some Scottish settlers are buried in the graveyard.

seventeenth century, by which time it was known as St Cuthbert's (fig. 2.11). It is unclear whether this was also its medieval dedication. This is an unusual name in Ireland (the only other example being the later nineteenth-century rededication of the church in Bushmills), and is related to Cuthbert from Northumberland in the northeast of England.

CHAPTER 3

The MacQuillans, lords of the Route,
1300–1555

Dunluce Castle was probably first built at the close of the fifteenth century. Originally constructed by the MacQuillan family, it quickly became the centre of lordly power across the north coast of Ulster. The MacQuillans by this date controlled the lordship of the Route, a territory encompassing much of northeast Antrim, and had established themselves as one of the most powerful family groups in the region. Engaged in almost perpetual conflict with surrounding groups, their story is one of ambition, power and warfare. This chapter examines the emergence of the MacQuillans and the subsequent construction of the castle. Excavations in its interior have uncovered important evidence of early structures associated with the castle and its earliest builders. Other important secular and ecclesiastical sites were also developed across this landscape by branches of the family, including alterations to Ballylough Castle and the probable construction of Bonamargy Friary, which was to remain intrinsically linked to Dunluce over the centuries.

The MacQuillans

In 1280, Richard de Burgh was appointed earl, with Thomas de Mandeville made seneschal of Ulster at the same time. The alliance between these two families was now well established and was a dominant feature of the Ulster political landscape. Elsewhere, the Bissets were firmly in control of the Antrim glens. By the early fourteenth century, John Bisset's son's (also John) lands were located in the townlands of Droagh, Ballytober, Ballyhackett, Carncastle and Corkermain in the barony of Upper Glenarm (Duffy 2004, 49). John also held the castle of Glenarm and the Glens of Glencloy and Glenariff, Rathlin Island and the barony of Cary. A key development in the context of this study occurred in 1310. That year, Seonac MacQuillan, a mercenary seemingly working for the earl's cousin in Connacht, was retained as part of the bonnaghts of Ulster by William de Burgh. These 'satellites', later known as 'bonnaght', consisted of groups across Ulster who held their lands through the maintenance of kerne or armed groups that owed service to the earl in times of war. The McQuillans would later establish themselves as the dominant family in the area (Webb 1860), but their origins are contested. It has always been unclear as to whether they were of Anglo-Norman descent, de Mandeville stock or

3.1 Albrecht Dürer's 1521 drawing of Irish soldiers (image reproduced courtesy of Kuperferstichkbinett, Staatliche Museen zu Berlin).

3.2 Dunyvaig Castle was the primary McDonald castle on Islay by the close of the fifteenth century. Built in the fourteenth century, it was occupied into the seventeenth century by various families and garrisons.

Scottish mercenaries. The suggestion here is that they were mercenaries who became embedded in Irish society and reinvented themselves as a Gaelic lordship across the territory of the Route in the later part of the fourteenth century (fig. 3.1). Certainly, MacQuillans were present in western Scotland in the fourteenth century, but do not appear in the Irish annals throughout the thirteenth century. Nicholls (2007, 88) is clear that they were Anglo-Norman in culture, as evidenced by their use of names and through the usage of the French term *route* to describe their mercenary force. How they managed to achieve this position in society is complex and intrinsically linked to the gradual collapse of the Anglo-Norman order across north Ulster and the resurgence of Gaelic power. By 1323, the then earl, Richard de Burgh, handed command of the bonnaght to Henry de Mandeville, then seneschal of Ulster 'the intendance of all satellites of our bonnaght in Ulster ... as at any time they did to William McHulyn [MacQuillan]' (Otway-Ruthven 1968, 216). The two families were clearly separate entities at this point.

The Red Earl of Ulster died in 1326 and a year later an agent of the de Burgh family wrote of emerging serious issues across Ulster associated with the Bruce Wars and the disloyalty and self-interests of a number of Anglo-Norman vassals including Richard and Henry, now seneschal, sons of Thomas de Mandeville. In response, young William de Burgh was rushed to Ireland and knighted. Henry was arrested, having been implicated in the earl of Desmond's conspiracy, and Stephen MacQuillan (Esteuene MacHoulyn) was appointed as 'constable of the bonaght' in November 1331, having paid £200 to the earl of Ulster (Nicholls 2007, 89). Curtis (1938) links the de Mandevilles and the MacQuillans at this point on the basis that this was a hereditary post, but such a linkage does not bear scrutiny, given that the de Mandevilles were clearly out of favour and that the MacQuillans were again listed as a separate family. Earl William was assassinated in July 1333 by the de Mandevilles and the Logans, and war developed across the Ulster territories. Robert Savage established himself as a leading political figure in Ulster following the earl's murder, serving as senseschal in 1333/4 and 1343, having previously been appointed as sherrif of Twescard in 1327 (McNeill 1980, 80). It is clear that since the 1270s the Savages had been involved in the extensive acquisition of land centred on Ballylough Castle and Portrush and were now among the major landholders in north Antrim. The Irish chiefs also moved to consolidate their increasing hold over Ulster and create a broad coalition under Henry O'Neill. Peace was negotiated by 1338, but north Ulster was now firmly under the political control of a number of disparate family groupings. Economic activity continued and the interplay between the Western Isles and Ulster carried on unabated. Coleraine was listed as having trade with Gascony in 1317, while the port at Portrush was listed as being active in the Western Isles trade in the 1330s and 1350s (McNeill 1980, 92). Likewise, the MacQuillans clearly enjoyed a privileged position in the Ulster hierarchy at this time and were an integral part of the political composition of the region. The death of

Jenkin MacQuillan, high constable of the province of Ulster, was mentioned in the Annals of the Four Masters in 1358 (*AFM* 1358). Ten years later, Slevny MacQuillin, then constable of the province of Ulster, also died (*AFM* 1368).

The death of Robert Savage in 1360 marked the beginning of a period of significant change and the gradual erosion of Anglo-Norman landholding across the region. Various groupings engaged in an ever-changing jostle for power and a number of important groupings began to play a more active role in Ulster. In 1365, Brian MacMahon of Oriel organized the death of Sorley MacDonnell, heir to the lordship of the Isles and high constable of Ulster, having attempted to create a marriage alliance with him (*AFM* 1365). MacDonnell's death was avenged over the following years by the O'Neills of Ulster, demonstrating the relationship between the two and the central role that Scottish gallowglasses now played in Ulster. A year later, Randal MacDonnell arrived from the Western Isles to assist O'Neill against the O'Donnells of Donegal. MacDonnell's engagement with Ulster was not a new thing, however, and can be traced back at least to the early part of the century from the time of the 'Bruce Invasion' and the battle at Faughart in 1318 (Kingston 2004). It gained far more permanence from 1390, when Eoin (Iain Mór) Mac Domhnaill, brother of Donald of Harlaw, arrived in Ulster through marriage to Margery Bisset, gaining seven territories in the Glens (Kingston 2004, 50). By the early 1400s, Eoin Mór is referred to as 'lord of Dunevege and the Glynnis' and gained his lands of Antrim formally through indentures with Henry IV by 1403 and, against opposition, replaced the Bissets. His son Domnall Ballach's control of the territory is later referred to as the 'seven proportions of the Glens' (Kingston 2004, 69), but he also retained lands on Islay centred on Dunyvaig Castle (fig. 3.2). It was around this time that the MacQuillans appear to have developed a firmer footing in north Antrim, probably as a result of their relationship with the Savages. This is difficult to substantiate, however, as it is not absolutely clear where they were positioned geographically during the first decades of the fifteenth century. Jenkin MacQuillan was in the pay of Edmond Savage, seneschal of Ulster, in 1395 and remained as chief of his family through the first half of the fifteenth century (Nicholls 2007, 89).

The primary problem is that the Annals of the Four Masters, the principle source for this period, appear to place the MacQullians in two geographical areas. In 1418, when Niall O'Donnell banished O'Neill, he did so across the Bann to MacQuillan (*AFM* 1418). The difficulty here lies with where exactly MacQullian was located east of the river. It is tempting to suggest that at this stage he was already established in north Antrim, but the extent of his territories is unclear. Complications arose a number of years later, when MacQuilllan appeared to be located in Dufferin in north Co. Down. Of course, it is possible that the annals were referring to different branches of the family, but the fact that they refer to MacQuillan in the singular implies that they were referring to the group head and his territories. The key point here is that we should not regard the MacQuillans as a traditional Gaelic lordship at this date. They were relatively recent arrivals into the region and did not have the same extensive lineages or family history that the O'Cahans, O'Donnells or O'Neills had. Instead, we must regard them as an extended warrior grouping consisting of a few dozen men with followers and associated family. They should not be regarded as a settled 'nation' in the same way we regard other Gaelic lordships of this time. They would have had a high degree of mobility and shifting political allegiances and were not tied to a particular geographical area by historical association. In 1433, O'Donnell brought his forces to Dufferin to assist MacQuillan, who appears to have been located there at this time. Owen O'Neill pursued both and engaged the help of the Scottish MacDonnells, who attacked the armed followers of MacQuillan and Robert Savage. MacQuillan was ultimately banished and eventually took refuge with Savage on the Ards. By 1442, it seems that MacQuillan was back in north Antrim, as a conflict broke out that year with the O'Cahans, which strongly suggests a cross-Bann geographical setting, given the historical location of the O'Cahan grouping. It is suggested here that MacQuillan had earlier been granted by the Savages an estate focused on the area of Dunluce. Certainly this area became a centre for their lordship by the end of the fifteenth century and such an estate would account for their interest there.

The MacQuillan–O'Cahan feud was to escalate throughout that decade. MacQuillan had the support of the O'Neills during this conflict and retained it in 1450 (*AFM* 1450). They collaborated in 1454, when they came to the aid of Donnell O'Donnell, who had been imprisoned by Rory O'Doherty in Inch Castle (fig. 3.3). Is it possible that the MacQuillans had fallen out with the O'Neills earlier in the century and had moved southwards to be accommodated by the Savages. Once they had repaired their relationships with the former, were they then allowed to return to north Antrim? Certainly, Savage power across the north was seriously waning at this date and appears to have collapsed by 1469. The families appear to have fallen out by this time, as an alliance of Patrick White, Henry O'Neill and MacQuillan banished the Savages from Lecale and MacQuillan assumed the overlordship of the territory in 1469 (*AFM* 1469). All of this movement suggests wide flexibility and mobility on behalf of the MacQuillans, who appear to have been in control of the former Savage lands in Twescard, while also maintaining a strong presence in Down. Henry O'Neill again came to the aid of MacQuillan of Dufferin in 1470 against a branch of the O'Neills and the MacSweeneys, and MacQuillan was given Sketerick Castle (fig. 3.4) following their successful campaign.

Ballylough Castle

Archaeological work is now beginning to detail the settlement patterns of the MacQuillans across Antrim. Most specifically, there is evidence that they took Ballylough Castle in the middle of the fifteenth century and refurbished it initially as their primary residence before transferring to Dunluce at the end of the century.

3.3 Detail from Blaeu's *Atlas novus* (1654), showing Inch Castle on Inch Island at the southern end of Lough Swilly, Co. Donegal. Note how both Malin Head and Inishowen are incorrectly shown as islands.

3.4 Sketerick Castle, Co. Down, on the shore of Strangford Lough. The castle was variously occupied by the Savages, the MacQuillans and the earl of Kildare (image reproduced courtesy of the NIEA).

3.5 Wicker-centring at Ballylough Castle, which likely dates to the MacQuillan refurbishment of the fifteenth century. When arches were being constructed, wooden frames were built to support the arch and wicker mats were used to shape the feature. When the mortar dried and the frame and mat were removed, impressions of the wicker remained.

3.6 Ulster medieval coarse pottery recovered from the excavations at Ballylough Castle. This type of pottery would have been produced locally and used primarily for domestic purposes (image reproduced courtesy of Tony Corey, NIEA).

Ballylough was certainly occupied into the sixteenth century and, with the departure of the Savages, only the MacQuillans were in a position to take this residence as their own. We have seen that the castle itself was probably constructed at the close of the thirteenth century, but it underwent a refurbishment phase later in the fifteenth century, following MacQuillan occupation. The insertion of a rough wicker-centred vault over the mural passage at second-floor level could be seen as a Gaelic building technique (fig. 3.5), and such features are commonly considered to be later medieval (McNeill 1997). More Ulster medieval coarse pottery was recovered from the later medieval levels during the excavations at the castle compared to the high medieval deposits (fig. 3.6). This in itself cannot be taken as an indicator of a change to Gaelic ownership, but is reflective of the collapse of the Ulster earldom and an increased social emphasis on the increasingly gaelicized world of later medieval Ulster.

Renewed conflict

MacQuillan was again in conflict with the O'Cahans in 1472. Both Con O'Neill and Godfrey O'Cahan entered the Route to engage the MacQuillans on their own territory, but Godfrey was killed by a javelin thrown by Rory MacQuillan. A day later, the MacQuillan, Cormac, was killed and Rory took the title. A parley was called for and Rory crossed the Bann in a small cot but was attacked and drowned by a number of O'Cahan's people (*AFM* 1472). What is important in this reference is the assignation of the territory of the Route to the MacQuillans (fig. 3.7). As previously stated, this area encompassed the land east of the Bann to beyond the River Bush and southwards past Loughguile towards Lough Neagh, corresponding roughly to the Anglo-Norman territory of Twescard. The Route had been mentioned in previous annalistic entries, but these referred to the warrior grouping associated with the MacQuillan areas in Down. Regardless, by the 1470s the MacQuillans were now firmly established in this north Antrim territory and had come to be regarded as a distinct lordship. Periodic conflict continued over the following decades, with the MacQuillan killed in a fight between the O'Donnell and O'Neill in 1483 and Felim MacQuillan, son of Rory, killed at Antrim in 1490. Hugh Roe O'Donnell had also ravaged the Route during harvest time a year earlier. The O'Cahans and MacQuillans were again at loggerheads in 1492 when a number of leading members of each family were killed, while a year later the son of Rory MacQuillan and a 'great number of his foot soldiers' were killed by the O'Cahans (*AFM* 1493).

Relationships had not improved by the opening decade of the sixteenth century. Thomas O'Cahan raided eastwards across the Bann into the Route and killed Walter MacQuillin, son of Jenkin, as well as a number of O'Haras, O'Boylans and O'Quinns, bringing back herds of cattle and horses as booty (*AFM* 1506). Two years later, in 1508, there was considerable infighting among the O'Cahans, while John Mac

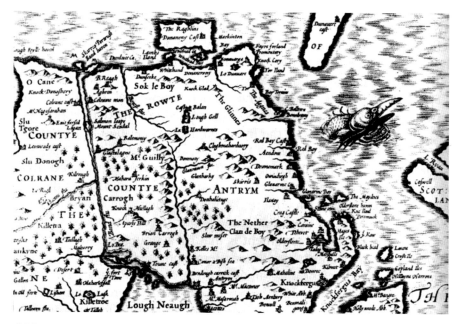

3.7 Detail of John Speed's early seventeenth-century map of Ireland showing the territory of the Route. Many of the details, including the personal names, were outdated by the time he produced the map and show that he lifted many of the details from Jobson's late sixteenth-century map.

Donnell Gorm was slain by MacQuillin. By 1513, Richard MacQuillan, son of Rory, and a group of Scots were slain by Art O'Neill following his incursion into the Glens. In this year, Dunluce Castle is first mentioned specifically by name, when it was taken by O'Donnell from the sons of Garrett MacQuillan and given over to the sons of Walter MacQuillan (*AFM* 1513) (fig. 3.8). This event is recorded in a number of different annals and is important from different perspectives. It firmly associates the MacQuillans with Dunluce, but also shows how gaelicized they had now become, given their internal disputes and strategic alliances with the surrounding groupings. This year was not to be without further upsets, as Alexander, son of Walter MacQuillan, was hanged by Domnall O'Cahan in Coleraine. O'Donnell appears to have been the leading figure in the region at this time, as he is recorded as having destroyed the O'Cahan castle of Coleraine following a disagreement with Donnell O'Cahan. Donnell was killed by the people of the Route in 1523, an act presumably carried out by the MacQuillans.

Bonamargy Friary

At the turn of the century, the MacQuillans were at the zenith of their power. They had taken Ballylough Castle and had now built a centre for their lordship at Dunluce.

3.8 Dunluce Castle, with Islay just visible on the horizon. The inter-visibility of these places highlights the sense of maritime connections that this region had in the past.

Theirs was very much a Gaelic lordship embroiled in the wider social and political life of Ulster. As with other Gaelic lordships across the country, they also engaged in the patronage of the church, specifically with the foundation of a Third Order Franciscan friary at Bonamargy, immediately northeast of Ballycastle (fig. 3.9). There are no specific details as to its foundation date but it is generally accepted that it was established around 1500 by Rory MacQuillan for the First Order before being transferred to the Third Order (Gywnn and Hadcock 1970, 269; Ó Clabaigh 2012, 312–13). Architecturally, the site consists of the main church building with a north range later added (Bell and McNeill 2002, 108). The north wall of the church and the west wall of the range made up a two-sided cloister. The south range was added by the MacDonnells in the seventeenth century. Sections of an enclosure are visible to the east of the site and a small masonry gate lodge also survives (fig. 3.10). A second Franciscan friary had earlier been established at Glenarm in the Glens of Antrim, possibly in the 1460s by the Bissetts (McDonnell 1987). Little now remains of that site.

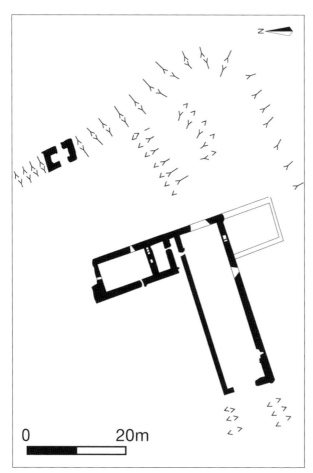

3.9 Plan of Bonamargy Friary, Ballycastle, Co. Antrim. Probably built in the sixteenth century by the MacQuillans, it was later extensively remodelled.

3.10 Photograph looking westwards at Bonamargy Friary. The gate lodge can be seen at the right of the picture, with sections of the enclosure visible to its left. The later MacDonnell mortuary addition can be seen on the extreme left.

The Ulster lordships

In the opening decades of the sixteenth century there was a renewed Scottish interest in northern Ulster. Alexander, head of the Clann Ian Mhór branch of the Clandonald, based in Islay and Kintyre, took the MacEoin Bisset territories in the coastal glens of northeast Antrim (McDonnell 2004b, 265) (fig. 3.11). This re-engagement with Ulster led directly to increasing MacDonnell mercenary involvement with this region that was to have a significant political impact later in the century. Throughout this period there was a rising degree of anxiety within the English monarchy towards Ulster and the ever-increasing power of both the O'Donnells and the O'Neill. The king's chief governor was now Garrett, earl of Kildare, whose father, the 8th earl, Garret Mór, had sided with the O'Donnells and the Maguires against O'Neill in 1498. Kildare again turned his attention to Ulster in 1524, when he led an army into the province in support of Con O'Neill against O'Donnell. The MacQuillans and a large group of the MacDonnells from Scotland sided with O'Donnell, although a peace was negotiated before large-scale conflict arose. In the aftermath, Cormac MacQuillan and the son of John Dubh MacDonnell were wounded and taken prisoner following skirmishes associated with O'Neill activity. Soon after this event, significant infighting broke out among the O'Cahans, when Rory O'Cahan is somewhat unusually labelled as being from the Route, indicating that he may have been living east of the Bann or was closely aligned to the MacQuillans. An unusual event occurred later in 1532, when Walter MacQuillan, son of Garrett, and Conor O'Cahan were both killed when the church of Dunboe burnt down (fig. 3.12). What lay behind this is unclear.

On a national scale, events were changing considerably. Lord Deputy Grey had engaged in widespread harassment against the Ulster lordships in 1539 in an attempt to subdue and undermine them. His strategy lost him the support of his king and, more traumatically, his head. He was replaced by Sir Anthony St Leger, who believed in a policy of appeasement and diplomatic persuasion coupled with an element of force when necessary. As part of this new approach, Henry VIII became king of Ireland, and the Ulster clans were encouraged by a strong hand to submit to him and in turn were regranted their lands. MacQuillan duly obliged and, under his submission in the Dublin Council Book, it is recorded that he desired to be regarded as an Englishman as his ancestors were (Hill 1873, 125). The lord deputy duly noted him as an Englishman and Roderick MacQuillan signed himself as captain of his nation and of the Route. St Leger further wrote of MacQuillan to the king that

> his country lies far from aid of your English pals, which hath been a great cause of his long rebellion, beyond forced to adhere to some Irishmen for his defence against some other of them; and as he confessed, none of his name, since the first conquest of their land, beyond captain, have died in their beds, but all slain by Irishmen (*CSPI* III, 281).

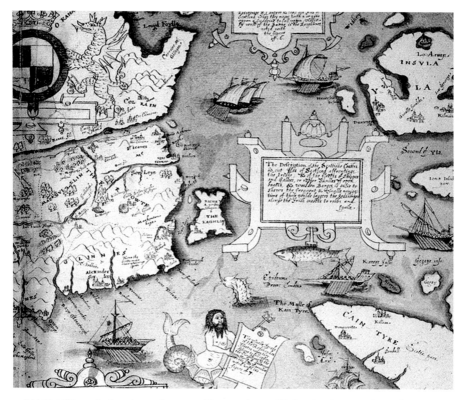

3.11 Detail from the late sixteenth-century Dartmouth map 25, showing the general area that would have incorporated the territories of the Clan Ian Mhór, including the Antrim Glens, Islay and parts of Kintyre (image reproduced courtesy of the National Maritime Museum, London).

The historical record has been taken as an indication of MacQuillan's origins and ancestry either as Welsh or English (Curtis 1938). MacQuillan is also listed as a 'Welshman of the English conquest' in 1538 in a report on the state of the realm of Ireland (*CSPI*, vi, p. 40). He was noted as a Welsh adherent of O'Neill when he sought pardon from the lord deputy (*CSPI*, x, p. 63). However, the fact that he asked to be regarded as an Englishman was surely little more than political opportunism. This form of self-promotion and protectionism was a feature of nearly all of the lordships at this time, when the maintenance of their position and lands was of primary importance and overshadowed any sense of nationhood or perceptions of identity. The assignation of Englishness also came after nearly two hundred years of residence in Ulster, making any historical linkage with an English or Welsh past tenuous at best. Highlighting this contradiction, MacQuillan was swearing allegiance to the king at the same time he was also paying due tribute to the Scots. Sir Thomas Cusack wrote that 'when the Scots do come, the most part of Clandeboy, MacQuillan and O'Cahan must be at their command in finding them in their countries'

3.12 Photograph of the ruined church of Dunboe, north of Coleraine.

(*CCM* I, 243). He went on to state that it was very difficult to prevent them landing, given the multitude of landing places from Rathlin to Carrickfergus.

Despite a number of the Gaelic lords pledging loyalty, a number of others (including O'Donnell) were more cautious (fig. 3.13). In 1542, O'Donnell, Brian O'Rourke and Manus O'Cahan marched against Rory MacQuillan (*AFM* 1542). When they reached the Bann, Rory had assembled his forces on the opposite bank, supported by a body of English troops. Large numbers of the forces from the west of the Bann managed to cross into the Route and engaged in extensive raiding across the territory. MacQuillan was forced to capitulate and make peace with O'Donnell. Subsequently, Rory MacQuillan and the son of MacDonnell raided O'Cahan land, with Manus O'Cahan and MacSweeney gallowglasses in pursuit. An engagement took place in which Alexander MacDonnell and a number of Scots were killed, but MacQuillan managed to escape across the Bann. He again attracted English support and made a second incursion into O'Cahan territory, taking their castle in the Roe Valley. He then returned to his own country before engaging the services of a number of the MacSweeneys (*AFM* 1542). This appears to have caused a degree of resentment among the MacDonnells who had fought with MacQuillan and a number of his own people. This group conspired against the MacSweenys and attacked them as they left MacQuillan's town (Dunluce?), killing the son of MacSweeny Banagh and the son of Murrough MacSweeny as well as numerous others (*AFM* 1542). 1542 proved then to be a highly volatile year, when the enmity between the two Bann groupings reached a critical level.

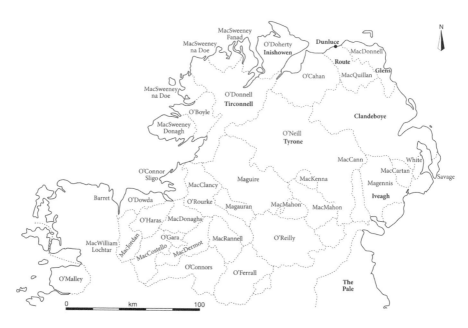

3.13 Sixteenth-century Gaelic lordships in the north of Ireland. The O'Neills and the O'Donnells were the leading families of western Ulster, while the O'Cahans and the MacQuillans were in near perpetual conflict.

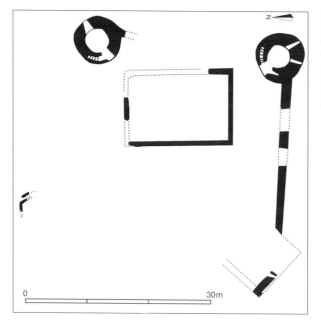

3.14 Plan of the surviving early sixteenth-century architectural features at Dunluce. The earliest castle was constructed on the headland and consisted of a central rectangular building surrounded by corner towers and a high wall.

Castle architecture

The original enclosure castle was probably built by the MacQuillans after 1490 and prior to 1513. There are no historical records that suggest an earlier date and the architectural features associated with the earliest levels are strongly suggestive of a construction date sometime in this two-decade period. Architectural analysis and an interpretation of its structural development are complicated by a number of factors. Firstly, the castle was almost continuously occupied over a two-hundred-year period during which it underwent a number of changes of ownership and significant phases of refurbishment. Secondly, following its abandonment in the 1680s, the castle quickly fell into a state of disrepair. Subsequent conservation efforts were often unsympathetic and were rarely systematically catalogued. As a result, it has often been difficult to separate out recent repair work to the walls and original masonry. Many original features have also been altered, adjusted or even, in some cases, lost or removed further hindering interpretation. Nevertheless, a provisional development sequence is presented in this book.

During the first half of the sixteenth century, the site consisted of an enclosure-type castle with a gate house, a number of corner towers and an enclosing curtain wall (fig. 3.14). Only the ground floor of the original gate house survives. This would have been a roughly rectangular building, but only the inner face of the southern wall remains, as well as possible basal sections of the western side-wall (fig. 3.15). The southern section survives to a height of 2.35m and is 2.8m wide internally. A clear difference between this earliest phase and later construction of the upper sections can be seen in differing masonry styles. This ground-floor section is marked by the use of smaller stone sizes that are rectilinear in form and laid horizontally in courses. A blocked-up loop embrasure is visible on the eastern side of this wall, measuring 82cm wide internally and 65cm high. It is internally splayed and would originally have provided flanking cover to the original gate-house entrance immediately to the east and across the general entrance area of the promontory. The outer face of this section was refaced later in the sixteenth century.

A 4.5m-high section of curtain wall ran from the gate house to a tower at the southeast corner of the castle (fig. 3.16). This was originally over 1m in thickness but was greatly thickened later in the century. It was probably accessed by a stairwell east of the castle entrance and at first-floor level from the corner tower. The two wide central embrasures were also a later addition. A further section of curtain wall survives on the western side of the promontory, but this was heavily modified and rebuilt in sections into the twentieth century due to subsidence and associated conservation work.

The southeast corner tower has been known as MacQuillan's Tower for much of the post-medieval period (fig. 3.17). This indicates the survival of the original builder's name through the centuries and provides a further piece of dating evidence.

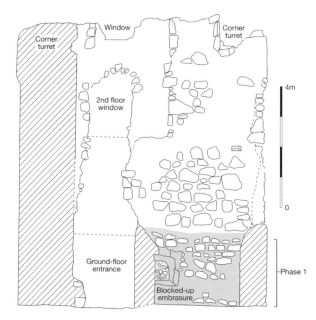

3.15 Elevation of the internal face of the gate tower. A masonry section of the earliest phase of the tower survives at ground-floor level, shaded grey on the plan. The upper levels were rebuilt in the middle of the sixteenth century.

While the tower was heavily modified in the later sixteenth century, the primary building phase dates to the late fifteenth or very early sixteenth century. Only sections of its ground floor remain from this primary constructional phase, with a small section of the first floor remaining intact. The tower would originally have been a two-storey structure with probable access to the roof level. It was constructed using rough basalt blocks and is roughly circular with wide walls over 2m in thickness. It sits on top of a basaltic outcrop, so its entrance would originally have been accessed by wooden steps. The doorway is centrally placed in the western side and has a curved arch above, which may be a later addition. A small entrance passage or lobby, 2.15m deep, lies immediately inside the doorway, from which a clockwise flight of steps leads to the first floor. On the southern side of the passage, a small 'guard-chamber' is accessed, measuring 95cm wide, 1.65m high and 1.15m deep. It has a linteled roof and contains a small splayed loop in its western side wall covering the original tower entrance. The ground floor has an internal diameter of 3.15m and is roughly circular. Two loops are visible; one large example on the southern side is a splayed linteled loop measuring 78cm wide internally and narrowing to less than 10cm at its opening (fig. 3.18). This loop covered the bridge crossing and may have been designed for an individual to lie in or for a long-barrelled weapon to be deployed. A second, smaller, loop is present on the east wall, covering the ground below the castle to the east. It was heavily disturbed by the insertion of a window. Two further loops are visible at first-floor level, with one positioned in the mural staircase facing north, and a second on the east wall facing the higher ground outside

3.16 Photograph of the curtain wall, looking from the southeast tower towards the gate tower.

3.17 Early twentieth-century photograph by Robert Welch showing the southeast and northeast towers (image reproduced courtesy of the Ulster Museum).

3.18 Photograph of a gun-loop covering the southern bridge approaches to the castle. The presence of this type of architectural feature shows that the tower was built in the late medieval period, following the introduction of firearms to this region.

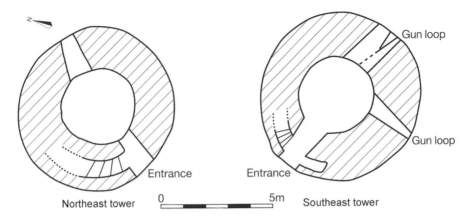

3.19 Plans of the two corner towers. Both were built in a similar style, but the southeast tower has a series of gun-loops.

the castle. The remainder of the upper-floor sections were heavily altered at a later date.

The presence of these loops is probably the most important piece of early architectural dating evidence that we have. These are primary architectural features and have not been inserted into the tower. In parts of Ireland, the insertion of gun-loops is usually taken as a clear indicator of a sixteenth-century date. In Cork, for example, the Archaeological Survey of Ireland has clearly shown that the introduction of gun-loops is a later sixteenth-century phenomenon on west Cork tower houses and castles (Power et al. 1992, 321) and this has been conclusively demonstrated for the tower houses of Beara and Bantry (Breen 2005). Recently, O'Keeffe (2000, 55) has questioned gun-loops as an indicator of late date, as the use of pistols has been recorded in Ireland in the fifteenth century. Indeed, the earliest record of a gun being used is in the latter part of the fourteenth century in Carlow (de hÓir 1982–3, 77–9). Their widespread use and consequent effect on architecture can only really be securely dated to the late fifteenth century at the earliest, however. The inclusion of gun-loops in many of Scotland's west-coast tower houses and castles is very much a sixteenth-century trend. The combination of historical sources and built evidence therefore strongly suggests that this tower dates to the earliest architectural horizon at Dunluce Castle, in the years either side of 1500.

A second tower to the northeast is known as Maeve's Tower after the legend of the sixteenth-century Maeve Roe MacQuillan being locked in the structure for refusing to marry Rory Oge O'Cahan. She was later drowned while attempting to escape with her O'Cahan lover and her ghost or banshee is still said to haunt the tower (Arlincourt 1844). It is constructed in a similar manner to the southeast tower, but is less overtly defensive and its earliest building horizon is better preserved than its southern counterpart (fig. 3.19). The tower is roughly circular, with walls nearly

3.20 Photograph of the northeast tower from the south.

3.21 Photograph of the internal area of the ground floor of the northeast tower.

2m thick that have a slight external base batter (fig. 3.20). It was partly as a result of this batter that some early commentators suggested a thirteenth-century construction date for the tower. It is more likely that the tower belongs to the same building horizon as the southeast example and also dates to *c.*1500. The entrance to the tower is positioned centrally on its western side, leading to an entrance lobby 1.95m deep. A mural staircase rises in a clockwise direction on the northern side of the passage leading to the first floor. A second doorway would have provided access into the ground floor apartment. Four jambs on the southern side of this feature consist of fine punch-dressed blocks, while one similarly dressed block survives at basal level on the northern side. A wicker-centred vault survives at ground-floor level and four beam-holes, which would have carried two supporting beams, are present 1.9m above the present floor level (fig. 3.21). The centre of the vault is 2.4m above the floor. No loops were built, but a single window embrasure is present in the east wall that has a slight internal splay and measures 1.4m wide, 1m high and *c.*1.9m deep. The absence of loops is unsurprising, given the naturally defended nature of this tower, perched as it is on the cliff's edge. Any loops would have been largely ineffective. Most of the upper sections of the tower were radically altered at the end of the sixteenth century and little survives from the earliest building phase. The dating for this structure is slightly more problematic in that its surviving features are fairly generic. McNeill (1997, 203) has commented that features such as wickerwork-centred vaults and punch-dressed stone jambs are common in late medieval buildings such as the friaries and tower houses established across Ireland in the fifteenth and very early sixteenth centuries. This general dating, combined with the more solid dating for the second tower, must also place the initial building of this structure at *c.*1500.

Excavations

Excavations were conducted in the central area of the inner ward over three separate seasons. Initially, in February 2008, a small 2 by 3.5m exploratory trench was opened up 70cm to the west of the external southwest bay window of the manor house (fig. 3.22). Unfortunately, this area had been completely disturbed in 1928 during clearance of the castle down to bedrock. The finds included seventeenth-century ceramics and internal plasterwork, but came from heavily disturbed contexts associated with the removal of deposits from the interior of the manor house. Two sherds of medieval Ulster coarse pottery were recovered, as well as a fragment of a glazed seventeenth-century North Devon ridge tile. Bedrock was reached at a maximum depth of 25cm at the northern end of the trench and 2cm at its southern end. The 1928 report records work in this area as follows:

> The levels of these pavings were adopted for the level of the grass with which the unpaved area has now been covered. Soil from other clearing was used for filling, and a system of field drainage was laid in the hollows with the dual object of reducing percolation through the rock-stack, and keeping the new lawn in condition. The excavated material [from the hall's interior] was riddled and the soil used to fill the hollows in yard outside … Preparation has been made for grassing this area next spring. A system of field drains will be laid between floor level and the rock surface below (appendix, below).

One of these field drains was located in the northeastern section of the cutting and consisted of a narrow trench just under 30cm wide cut into the bedrock containing a series of interconnected red earthenware pipe sections covered by loose slating. The extent of disturbance in this area was disappointing, but the recovery of the plasterwork and samples of material culture provide important elements of the architectural and material cultural story of the castle.

In 2009, a second trial excavation was conducted in the southeastern internal corner of the manor house. Initially, a 3 by 1.5m trench was laid out, but this was expanded to follow a structural feature that was found at the base of the trench. A gravel layer had been laid out across all of the interior in recent years by the DOE to facilitate visitors in this area of the castle. This has been replenished every few years. A loose sandy mortar deposit up to 20cm in thickness across much of the trench contained slate, bone and ceramic fragments. It was found in the 2010 excavations to

3.22 Excavations underway in the manor house. Note the foundations of the earlier sixteenth-century structure in the foreground. This was levelled later in the sixteenth century, while the manor house itself was constructed in the early seventeenth century (image reproduced courtesy of Tony Corey, NIEA).

cover the entire interior of the manor house and appears to be a levelling deposit associated with the clearance of the interior in 1928. Removal of these surface layers exposed a small area of burning in the extreme southeastern corner of the building, directly abutting the northern wall. This sat directly on top of the bedrock and had a distinct linearity to it. The shape and orientation of this shallow deposit strongly suggest that it represents the burnt traces of original floorboards. The 1928 report confirms the identification of burnt floorboards when 'a trial excavation along the inside of walls traces were found of scraps of decayed wood flooring adhering to plaster at base of walls' (appendix, below). No finds were recovered from this deposit, aside from a number of intrusive bones from small birds and rodents. A foundation trench with a maximum depth of 30cm underlay this mortared deposit and contained the mortared basal core of a wall. This consisted of a rubble foundation of angular stones with a 10–30cm size-range set in compacted mortar bonding and with an average width of 80cm.

In 2010, the excavation strategy was adapted in an attempt to follow this feature and ascertain further details relating to its morphology and function. A series of exploratory trenches were opened across the interior and additional sections of the foundation were traced (fig. 3.23). It was evident in each of the trenches but had a varying width and depth. It appears that the builders created a relatively level platform in this area of the headland and then cut a shallow foundation trench to accommodate the walling. This shallowness is not surprising, given that the builders were engaged in construction on bedrock providing a very solid base. Indeed, this location was fortunate in having a bedrock base, as many later medieval structures in Ireland were constructed using only limited foundation trenches. In one section of the foundation, an associated retaining masonry feature was located in the mid portion of the western run of the wall. This consisted of a single line of mortared cut-stone blocks running along the inside face of the feature. This would have been the bottom course of the basal section of a foundation plinth. Overlying this foundation was a later destruction layer. This consisted of a hard compacted deposit mostly of mortar, associated with the deliberate demolition of the building in the latter part of the sixteenth century. Again, this was of varying depths across the site and blended in places into the 1928 levelling works and later deposits of sand and chipped stone from the 1980s conservation undertakings.

The foundations uncovered during the 2009–10 seasons may constitute the original foundations of a late medieval structure. The masonry building had an overall length of approximately 14.8m and width of 11m. Internally, it would have measured 13 by 8.5m. It is impossible to know how many storeys this structure would originally have had, but it is likely to have had a slated roof, given the presence of slate fragments in the fill of the foundation trench. This remains a tentative suggestion as the slate may be intrusive material from the later Jacobean structure. It is highly unlikely that a building of this type would have had a thatched or wooden roof,

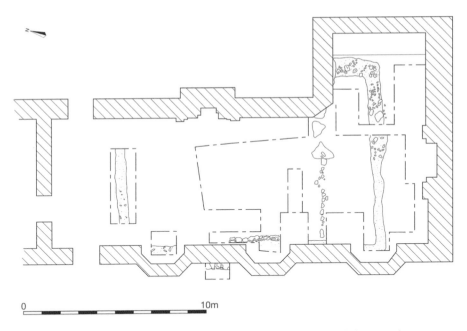

3.23 Plan of early to mid-sixteenth-century structure discovered beneath the manor house.

3.24 Dunstaffnage Castle, Scotland. Excavations here have shown that the castle was built in the thirteenth century and refurbished in the sixteenth and seventeenth centuries (image reproduced courtesy of Nigel McDowell).

however, given its exposed location on this headland. The building certainly pre-dates the seventeenth century, considering that the Jacobean house was constructed in the opening decades of that century. It must also pre-date the 1580s, as the loggia is late sixteenth century and functioned as a sheltered walkway overlooking an open space. The building uncovered during the course of the excavations could not then have been standing when the loggia was built, as it would have fronted onto an open grassed or yard space and must consequently pre-date the 1580s. No artefactual dating evidence was found associated with the structure, apart from a single small sherd of thin brown glass. This is markedly different from the green-tinged early seventeenth-century window glass recovered across the site and is likely to be late medieval.

The positioning of the structure is also of intrinsic interest. It has been clearly shown that the corner towers represent the earliest architectural horizon on the headland and the building uncovered during the excavation was clearly sited to respect their position. In terms of each of the corners on its eastern side, the building would have lain between 2 and 4m from the towers. As such, it would have been centrally placed within the fortified complex that existed on the promontory. Would there then have been a further corner tower(s) combined with an earlier gate-house complex to the west? Certainly it would have been unusual to place corner towers on the eastern flank and ignore the western wall. Having said that, there was far less of a defensive requirement on the west side, as the gate tower protected the entrance and the sheer cliff militated against the need for a further tower. We need to be cautious about saying too much about the uncovered structure, given the paucity of surviving architectural information associated with it. Its dimensions are indicative of a medium-sized hall within the broader context of Britain and Ireland. A central hall at the high medieval hall house at Aber in Caernarfonshire measured 11.2 by 8m, while a late fourteenth-century hall at Lewknor in Oxfordshire measured 10.3 by 8.8m (Fletcher 1975). These measurements are broadly comparable to the admittedly later hall at Dunluce. The identification and relative dating strongly suggest that this was the main hall of the MacQuillans, who occupied this site from at least the start of the sixteenth century. It continued to be utilized before being knocked in the late sixteenth century, firstly to be replaced by a small garden or open yard and later by the Jacobean house in the early seventeenth century.

Only sections of the earliest castle survive, but what would the original structure have looked like? The reconstructions of the site produced in the nineteenth and early twentieth century by Lynn and Bigger and others were fanciful and bear little resemblance to the actual appearance of the early sixteenth-century site. Entry across the promontory was probably via some form of drawbridge before the visitor arrived at the gate house. This may not have been a drawbridge in a true structural sense, but may have consisted of planks supported on masonry supports that could easily be drawn across the chasm or removed when the site was under threat. It is probable that the gate house itself was at least two storeys high and was accessed through a narrow ground-floor doorway. Internally, the visitor would then have proceeded into a courtyard area with a large centrally placed rectangular building within the walled enclosure. The two eastern corner towers would have protected the eastern flank and it appears that these were the only two towers present. Geophysical work along the western curtain wall highlighted a localized area of disturbance in the northwest of the courtyard that was initially considered to be a potential third tower lying westwards of the northeast tower. Excavation quickly showed that this was not the case, however, and that the disturbance was related to later sixteenth-century building and the levelling of uneven bedrock in this area. It is also possible that cliff erosion or later building work has eradicated all traces of a third tower, but this now seems unlikely. Should we be surprised that there is not another tower at this location that would provide a sense of symmetry to the castle? The short answer is probably not. Considering the architectural character of the existing two towers, there is probably no need for a tower at this location. The gate house would have provided sufficient flanking cover from a western attack, similar to the function served by the southeast tower. The northeast tower has much more of a functional feel to it and there was no need for a third tower that would have replicated its functions.

Comparative sites

As already noted, many earlier writers have compared Dunluce with a number of the enclosure castles on Scotland's western coast (Lynn 1905; Bigger 1905). A cursory examination of some of these structures does suggest similarities, but detailed comparative analysis quickly disproves any contemporary link. Dunstaffnage, for example, is an enclosure castle, but its corner towers are more substantial and excavation has shown that it was constructed during the thirteenth century (Lewis 1996; Breen et al. 2011) (fig. 3.24). Other sites, including Sween and Castle Tioram, are all thirteenth-century constructs with later refurbishment and additions (Tabraham 1997). The construction of Dunluce post-dates the initial construction of these buildings by at least two hundred years. Threave Castle in Galloway was built around 1370, with a central great tower. It has been suggested that in the mid-fifteenth century a curtain wall with three drum towers was erected in order to significantly enhance the castle's defences (McGladdery 2005, 166). The excavator has alternatively suggested that these fortifications may have been erected at the end of the century or in the opening years of the sixteenth century (Tabraham and Good 1981), dating them far more closely to Dunluce. A curtain wall with four corner towers, each containing gun-loops, was erected at Craigmillar Castle in the mid- to late 1400s (Tabraham 1997). It was later to develop along similar lines to Dunluce, with the addition of domestic ranges and outer yards in later centuries. While it is not necessarily suggested that these sites were a model for the later developments at Dunluce, it does highlight that this morphological layout was utilized across the broader region at the time in recognition of the increased use of artillery. What Dunluce also shared with a large number of Scottish sites was its dramatic location. Right across the coastal mainland and Western Isles, castles were sited overlooking the sea in highly visible and often very defensive locations. Many were located on rock outcrops or coastal promontories and each made a powerful statement relating to power and control of the seaways. This overt sense of power and defence was clearly in the minds of the castle builders at Dunluce and a formidable statement was certainly made. Structural analogies are also found on the island of Ireland in the form of later medieval enclosure castles. Thirteenth-century Liscarroll Castle in north Cork, for example, has a number of corner flanking towers that were still used into the sixteenth century while the O'Connors continued to occupy Roscommon Castle (Murphy and O'Conor 2008). Carrigogunnell Castle in Limerick was also extensively rebuilt by the O'Briens in the middle of the fifteenth century. Dundrum Castle, Co. Down, was apparently extended by the Magennises, who added the outer yard wall and refurbished the upper parts of the central tower in the sixteenth century, while the O'Dohertys in Donegal made further additions to Greencastle (McNeill 1997, 194–6). Each of these examples illustrates that the Gaelic Irish were actively engaged in castle building or refurbishment during the later medieval period. In building Dunluce, the MacQuillans were exhibiting the same mindset and deployed similar building techniques, such as the wicker-centred vault and gun-loops.

Summary

In summary, the MacQuillans began to play a significant role in the politics of north Ulster from early in the fourteenth century. By the end of the fifteenth century, they had established themselves as the dominant family grouping in the region, controlling the territory of the Route. They refurbished Ballylough Castle, provided patronage for the establishment of a friary at Bonamargy and built a significant new enclosure castle at Dunluce, which they established as their lordly centre from the early part of the sixteenth century. Their gains were not easily come by and for decades they were involved in almost perpetual internecine conflict with the surrounding Gaelic groupings. By the middle of the sixteenth century, their territories remained intact but they were on the eve of encountering a new threat from the Western Isles of Scotland. Their tenure as lords of the Route was about to come to a violent end.

CHAPTER 4

The MacDonnells, 1544–98

The story of Dunluce Castle from the middle of the sixteenth century is firmly associated with the MacDonnell family. We have seen that this branch of the broader McDonald clan referred to as the Clan Ian Mhór had taken much of the glens from the Bissets in the fifteenth century. They retained their primary power base at Dunyvaig Castle on Islay. By the 1520s, Alexander Canochson of Dunyvaig was viewed as a close ally by the Ulster MacDonnells,[1] led by Alexander Carrach, and Canochson facilitated the provision of many of the Gallowglasses fighting in Ireland (Caldwell 2008, 79). Having briefly risen in rebellion in 1529 following the potential loss of his lands on Islay, Alexander Canochson submitted to King James in 1531 and the Clan Ian Mhór regained their lands on Kintyre and presumably on Islay. Alexander died in 1536 and his son James Canochson assumed his father's mantle and also claimed the title of Lord of the Isles. As with his father before him, both he and his brothers, Coll and Sorley Boy, took an active interest in Ulster. They quickly established themselves as a formidable mercenary force and focused much of their efforts in north Antrim and Donegal. By 1553, English sources were reporting that James had taken much of north Antrim with seven thousand men (Caldwell 2008, 86), although this figure is probably inflated.

North Ulster in the 1540s

It was against this background of almost incessant internecine conflict in Ulster and enhanced Scots ambitions that the English forces under St Leger continued developing mechanisms to subdue Ulster and bring it into line. In a tripartite agreement signed in May 1543 by the lord deputy, Rory MacQuillan and Manus O'Cahan, MacQuillan and O'Cahan agreed not to interfere with the king's tenants accessing the Bann for fishing and to allow John Travers, the king's farmer at Coleraine, and his fishermen to use the castle in the town and to salt fish and draw their nets on land there (*CCM*, I, 202). They were also required to maintain the fishermen during the season, for which they would receive £10 annually. A number of hostages were given to ensure that the agreement was conducted properly. In July

---

1 For ease of reference, the branch of the Clan Ian Mhór who settled in Ulster are referred to as the MacDonnells throughout this book, while those of the broader Clan Donald in Scotland are referred to as McDonald.

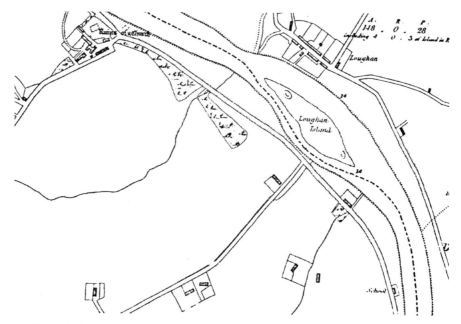

4.1 Detail of the 1831 first edition six-inch Ordnance Survey Londonderry map, sheet 7, showing Loughan Island on the River Bann. Note the two earthworks at either end of the island that probably represent the remains of the sixteenth-century fortification.

of the same year, a memorandum was drawn up in an attempt to settle the differences between the O'Donnell and MacQuillan (*CCM*, I, 209). In compensation for MacQuillan's aggressions, O'Donnell was to receive a hundred cattle. This attempted agreement clearly did not work, as O'Donnell led a large force into the Route and took the MacQuillan 'wooden castle ... [of] impregnable fastness' on Loughan Island on the Bann and gave it to O'Cahan (*AFM* 1544) (fig. 4.1). Although O'Laverty (1887, 154) referred to two earthen fortifications surviving there in the nineteenth century, the island is now extensively covered in woodland that serves to mask the surviving earthworks. The Bann drainage scheme also deposited a large amount of sediment on the island in linear banks that further confuses any interpretation of the remains. It does appear that two discrete earthworks at either end of the island represent vestiges of the former fortifications, but excavation is required to elucidate further information. On the same 1544 Loughan Island expedition, O'Donnell took the castle of Ballylough, seizing weapons, armour, copper, iron, butter and other provisions from both places. He then moved on and took the island sites or crannogs on Loughaverra and Lough Lynch before returning home. No mention is made of Dunluce, which presumably was too strong to take at this time. In response, MacQuillan engaged the services of James and Colla MacDonnell, who took back Loughan Island, killing Brian O'Cahan and others. O'Cahan then hired the gallowglasses of Rory MacSweeney and attacked MacQuillan near the Bann,

4.2 Photograph of Kinbane Castle from the south, looking north towards Rathlin Island. Islay is just visible on the far horizon to the left, while Kintyre is to the right.

although on this occasion he escaped with his life. Following this prolonged period of hostilities, a degree of peace settled, presumably strongly influenced by the presence of the MacDonnells in the area.

Kinbane Castle

It has long been held that Coll MacDonnell, brother of James and Sorley Boy, built this castle in the 1540s (fig. 4.2) and that the site represents the first attempt by the MacDonnells to establish a base on the north Ulster coast. Having arrived in the region during the early part of the decade, they required a base from which to operate. This bridgehead into Ulster was provided by Kinbane, positioned strategically at the coastal interface between the Glens and the Route and easily accessible by sea from Islay. Its primary function was as a maritime gateway and this explains its unusual position at the base of steep cliffs. A river that runs to the immediate west of the site also marks a parish boundary and may have delimited the extent of the territory of the Glens at that time. The strategic placement of a fortification between an area of traditional Scottish settlement and Gaelic Irish lands is interesting, and demonstrates expansionist ambitions among the newly arrived islanders. The castle itself was sited on a dramatic promontory of white chalk and consists of a small two-storey tower with an enclosure wall along the edge of the headland. Its entrance, protected by a small angle tower, was on the southern curtain wall. No other buildings survive in the interior, but an excavated hollow and area of cleared foreshore may be associated with a landing place and boat naust (shelter) to the west of the site. In 1551, James Croft initiated a military campaign to lessen the emerging power of the Scots forces in the north, and Kinbane was targeted. Thomas Cusack, chancellor of Ireland, wrote an account of the movements of Lord Deputy Croft, and Kinbane was mentioned as follows:

> … and also Coll McDonnell, second brother to James, had a strong castle built upon a rock, with a strong bawn of lime and stone, over the sea, named the castle of Kinbane, which my lord caused to be defaced, and broke much part thererof, so as now it is not defensible, which I am sure that never had for so much more displeasure done to them (*CSPI*, III, 116).

This episode does not seem to have displaced Coll, as he was still in possession of, but possibly not living at, the site in May 1558, when he died either at the castle or nearby. Tradition has it that Coll *Ciathach* was married to an O'Cahan (wife also known as McNeill) of Dunseverick (Hill 1873). He had three sons: Gillespig or Archibald; Alexander or Alister; and Angus. Gillespig died in 1570, with tradition stating that he was gorged by a bull outside Ballycastle (McDonnell 2004, 141). The castle is again referred to in 1574 in a list associated with an ill-fated and ultimately un-acted upon plan to bring English gentlemen adventurers to Ulster. The reference states 'Whitehead, whereupon standeth a castle, not appointed', indicating that the castle was never granted to anyone (Hill 1873, 418). It remains speculative as to whether this means that the castle was not occupied at this date or that potential occupants remained daunted by taking on a site that could almost be considered inaccessible and remained strongly associated with the still rebellious Scots.

At the end of the sixteenth century, the McDonald manuscript refers to the MacAlisters of Kinbane, where they sided with James MacDonnell and his 'highlanders' against a MacQuillan incursion into the Route in 1589/90(?) (McDonnell 2005, 144). Many years later, in 1636, the MacAlisters of Kinbane were confirmed in their holdings by Randal MacDonnell. Neither of these latter references needs to be taken as proof of seventeenth-century occupation, and the excavations that have been conducted on the site indicate that the site ceased to be actively

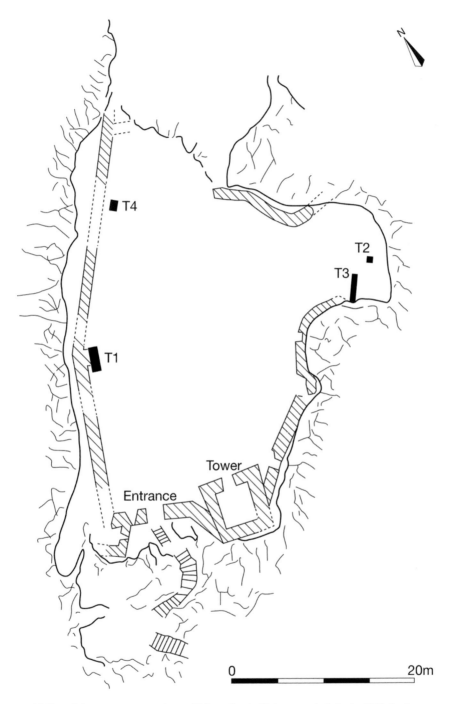

4.3 Plan of the excavation trenches at Kinbane Castle. Kinbane was built in the 1540s by the MacDonnells, but appears to have been occupied for a short time only.

occupied in the sixteenth century. At Easter 2011, a number of small test trenches were excavated in the castle's enclosure in an attempt to ascertain the nature of the surviving archaeology and to gain some insight into the castle's settlement history (fig. 4.3). Two of the trenches on the eastern elevated side of the enclosure produced no cultural stratigraphy. Trench 1, midway along the western enclosure wall, was excavated against a stone abutment that probably originally supported steps leading to a wall-walk. Domestic faunal refuse, including cattle and sheep bone, was found, but no dating evidence was recovered. A second trench (T4) uncovered a linear stone feature that may be collapse associated with the curtain wall, with an overlying burnt deposit that could be associated with the destruction of the site. This may also be a foundation deposit of a building (the burning constituting an occupation deposit), although this interpretation appears less likely. Sherds of Ulster coarse medieval pottery were found associated with the burnt deposit. These were heavily burnt but are very similar to other examples found across Ulster. Ivens (1988) described a sherd from an everted rim body found at Eskeabouy near Lough Macrory in Tyrone that had a hard fabric, black core and thin red/brown surface layer, gritted with fine mica/quartz chips with small angular quartz. This sherd was similar to examples recovered from Tullyliss rath, Dungannon and from the Rath of Dreen, Antrim. The sherds from Kinbane appear to fall into MacSparron's Category B of late medieval coarse pottery. What is also interesting from the excavations is the complete absence of seventeenth-century or early modern artefactual material. This absence, combined with the historical evidence of castle defacement in 1551, is indicative of a very short phase of occupation before the site was ultimately abandoned after the middle of the sixteenth century. The departure of Coll's descendants to Colonsay and the entrenchment of the MacDonnells in other sites across the north coast militated against the need for the castle at Kinbane and it seems to have fallen out of everyday use, remaining only as a site of symbolic importance in the landscape.

MacDonnell ascendency

Returning to the emerging broader regional story, MacQuillan of the Route was listed as one of the 'chief Irish of Ireland' in 1549 (*CCM*, 623, p. 222), while a year later both he and O'Cahan were to be encouraged to serve the king more diligently (*CSPI*, II). It was becoming increasingly apparent that the MacDonnells were no longer content to remain as minor players in the region and subservient to the established septs. By the early 1550s, they had effectively settled in north Antrim and began to flex their muscle. In doing so, they raised growing concern in Dublin. The lord justice supported an expedition in 1551 against them and sent four ships to Rathlin, where James and Coll were now based, presumably having withdrawn to the safety of the island from Kinbane. The Scots repelled the small armada and obtained

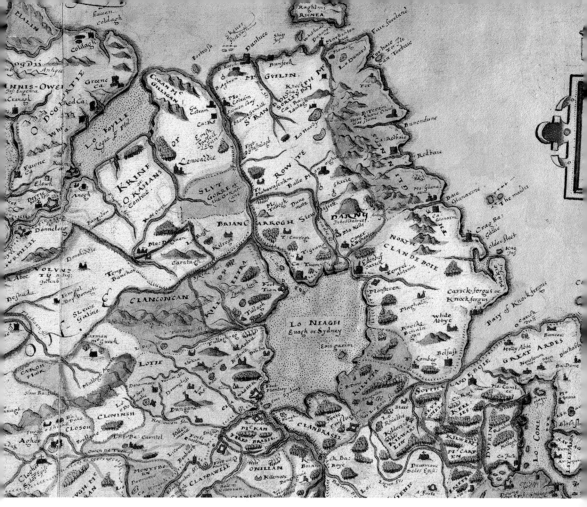

their brother, Sorley Boy, back from Dublin, where he had been imprisoned in exchange for prisoners (*AFM* 1551). Thomas Cusack, lord chancellor of Ireland, wrote to the earl of Warwick in September 1551 that the Scots now effectively controlled all of the lands from MacQuillan's house (Dunluce?) to Belfast (Hill 1873, 47–51). He also made reference to Coll MacDonnell's castle at Kinbane, although his assertion that it was no longer defensible was an exaggeration made to cover the fact that the English forces failed to take the site from the Scots during this expedition. Cusack again wrote of Ulster in 1553 in a report on Ireland to the duke of Northumberland. He described the area under study here as follows:

> The country of Clanneboye is in woods and bogs for the greatest part, wherein lieth Carrickfergus; and so to the Glynns where the Scots doth inhabit. As much of this country as is near the sea is a champion country of 20 miles in length and not over 4 miles in breadth, or little more … Next to the Glynnes is MacQuillans country, adjoing by the sea, and so to the Banne, a country of woods, and most part waste by their own wars and exactions of the

4.4 Details from Norden's late sixteenth-century *General description of Ulster*, showing the territory of the Route (image reproduced courtesy of the National Archives of Ireland).

Scots, and may not make past 12 horsemen; but they were wont to make 80. When the Scots do come, the most part of Clanneboy, MacQuillan and O'Cahan must be at their commandment in finding them in their countries; and hard it is to stay the coming of them, for there be so many landing places between the high land of Rathlin and Carrickfergus ... The water of the Bann cometh to Lough Neagh which severth Clanneboy and Tyrone and MacQuillan and O'Cahan's country. (*CCM*, 603, p. 235)

It is clear that by this date the MacDonnells had taken effective control of the north coast. It is also apparent from a number of references in the early 1560s that they had taken Dunluce from the MacQuillans sometime in the middle of the 1550s or possibly earlier. Tradition records that the castle passed into their hands through the marriage of one of the MacDonnells to the daughter of MacQuillan (McDonnell 2004a), but this remains unsubstantiated. It would certainly have constituted normal practice at this time, but it is also likely that the MacQuillans had little choice in the matter, given their significantly reduced military capacity and their essential subjugation by this date. The MacQuillans retained a portion of their lands, but they were increasingly forced further south to the southern boundaries of the Route (fig. 4.4). The increasing strength of the MacDonnells was viewed with considerable trepidation from Dublin and, following St Leger's departure, a new lord justice, Thomas Radcliffe, earl of Sussex, was appointed. Sussex was considerably more aggressive than St Leger and immediately began a number of campaigns to subdue the Scots (*AFM* 1555). He was supported in these efforts initially by the O'Neill, who shared the administration's concerns about the MacDonnells. An initial hosting had little effect and Sussex withdrew. In a description of his journey through Ulster in 1556, a number of important details relating to the study area are given. He initially camped by Mount Sandel and reference is made to a 'castle' at Loughan, which was associated with James McHenry in MacQuillan's country of the Route (*CCM*, 621, p. 257). Sussex further recorded that in the monastery of Coleraine an ancestor of MacQuillan was buried on the left hand of the altar and a picture (effigy?) of an armed knight lay on the tomb (Hill 1873, 125). The party then went onto Ballymoney to the Bishop MacGenniss', consisting of a 'castle and church joined together' before returning to Coleraine. Sussex then travelled from Coleraine to Glenarm, passing MacQuillan's castle at Loughguile and passed over a gravelled way, which Hill (1873, 195, n. 6) notes as part of a roadway known as the Black causeway that could be traced through moorland at the 'head of Glenariff ... about seven feet in width', formed of broad flat stones. Dunluce seems to have been avoided, probably due to fears of it as a place of strength at the time. It is also interesting to speculate that MacQuillan had by this date decamped to Loughguile and the MacDonnells were firmly established at Dunluce.

4.5 Photograph of the front elevation of the gate tower. This was built in a very typical Scottish style, with corner turrets. Here, the builders were effectively displaying their ancestry through the architecture of their building.

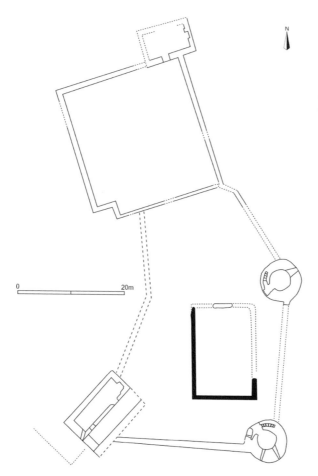

4.6 Plan of Phase 2 features across the site. The MacDonnells added significantly to the castle in the middle of the sixteenth century, with the rebuilt gate tower and the addition of a walled enclosure at the northern end of the promontory.

MacDonnells and Dunluce: Phase 2

Once the MacDonnells had taken Dunluce they undertook a major refurbishment of the castle in the closing years of the 1550s and early 1560s. The most visible expression of this was the heightening and rebuilding of the gate tower. This was done in a very typical Scottish style, with the addition of the two corner turrets (fig. 4.5). Here, they were adopting the architectural traditions that they were accustomed to and were expressing their own sense of identity through their fortified buildings. This MacDonnell rebuild, or Phase 2 in the castle's development, can be clearly traced in the standing masonry. This phase is marked by the use of large angled basalt stones sourced from the Giant's Causeway, set on edge, and used in the facing of the walls. Its masonry expression is most obvious in the gate tower and in the outer walls of the inner enclosure (fig. 4.6). One of the first elements of the

4.7 Photograph of the funnelled approach to the gate tower.

restructuring was the creation of a walled defensive funnelled passageway across from the bridge access. The angled walls would have covered the 11.5m to the gate tower door, narrowing to 1m at the bridge. Both walls were faced with large Causeway stone and were double-faced, with a rubble core and were 95cm thick. They survive to a height of just over 3m in places. Two low angled embrasures are visible on the eastern wall that would have overlooked the pound area (fig. 4.7). Large sections of both walls have been rebuilt and the ground surface has been re-cobbled, although a section of original cobbling survives against the gate tower wall in the northwest section. The gate tower itself is a rectangular block standing four storeys high, faced with causeway stone. Originally, the entrance was at the eastern side of the ground floor, but this has largely been destroyed. It would have been 1.5m wide and possibly up to 3m high with fine sandstone jambs. Three windows at each upper storey would originally have been present above the entrance.

Internally, the structure was much altered from Phase 1 under the MacQuillans, with the introduction of a covered 9.3m-long passageway leading through the gate tower on its eastern side and the construction of a chamber on the western side. A series of joist-holes are visible at first-floor level on the eastern wall (fig. 4.8). The chamber had two entrances and was possibly divided internally by a wooden partition. Its southern door was narrow (76cm) and had fine sandstone jambs. Three courses survive, standing 1.15m high. Three angled window embrasures along the west wall would have lit this chamber(s) with the best preserved southern example

4.8 Photograph of the eastern internal wall of the gate tower.

4.9 Photograph of the ground-floor fireplace in the gate tower, with the manor house in the background.

measuring 92cm wide internally. The chamber has an overall internal length of 8.3m and a width of 2.7m. A 1m-wide ground-floor fireplace was set into the northern wall. It was built with sandstone surrounds immediately on top of a section of basaltic bedrock (fig. 4.9). This chamber must have functioned as a guardroom for the castle's warden, who may have had living quarters at first-floor level. Two floor joist-holes are present 1.96m above present ground level at the northern end of the western wall adjacent to the fireplace and the northern angle of a widow embrasure is visible above these. A note of caution about the dating of the internal elements of the chamber should be made at this stage. While the use of the Causeway stone is a clear indicator of Phase 2, the use of decorative sandstone surrounds is linked elsewhere to Phase 3, or later sixteenth-century developments on the site. It may be that features such as the fireplace and door belong to this later phase.

The gate tower ground-floor passage leads to a 2.2m-wide doorway that exits into a courtyard. Originally, this was both paved and cobbled in places and was re-cobbled in the 1970s with sections of paving being removed and the surface grassed over. Immediately to the east of the gate tower, a small rectangular structure could be accessed that would have housed stairs leading to the wall-walk of the southern curtain wall (fig. 4.10). Currently in a ruinous state and only surviving at basal level, the building was constructed on the same orientation as the gate tower and had an entrance at its northeast. Internally, original paving covers the floor and a small guard chamber to the west measures 1.4m wide and 1.5m deep. The original stairwell

4.10 Photograph of structure that would have provided access to stone stairs in the sixteenth century, looking west towards the Skerries.

turned clockwise to the west, providing access to both the curtain wall and the upper floors of the gate tower. A second wall break at ground floor level in the eastern wall leads to the base of the curtain wall, but this has been heavily tampered with and is unlikely to have originally served as a door.

The second major element of this building phase was the erection of a large enclosure wall around a yard at the northern edge of the promontory. Originally measuring approximately 28m by 25m, and enclosing an area of roughly 700m2, the wall was again built using large Causeway stone as facing (fig. 4.11). It ranges from 70 to 80cm in thickness and stands to a height of over 3m. Sections of the wall are masonry topped and sloped in the same manner as the walls adjacent to the bridge. The first-floor levels and chimneys are of a later sixteenth-century date and would not have been present when the enclosure was first constructed. Four beam-holes are visible 1.65m above present ground level on the inner face of the southern wall. These indicate that some form of wooden structure ran along this range. The existing central breach in this wall section is later. There may have been a narrower entrance here originally, but at some later stage the gap was crudely widened. An original narrow doorway was probably present at the eastern end of the wall where a further section of walling of identical construction runs southeastwards towards Maeve's Tower. Portions of this have collapsed and were rebuilt in the twentieth century. Significant sections of the original enclosure wall were also knocked or rebuilt, including missing elements at the northeast, where a later range was erected. One section of earlier masonry, probably dating to Phase 1, survives in the southwest of the enclosure where the Phase 2 wall abuts sections of an earlier wall.

The surviving masonry also suggests that there was a projecting tower or rectangular building at the northeast corner of the enclosure wall (fig. 4.12). While the western side of the northern range is a seventeenth-century construct, the presence of Causeway stones in the facing of the eastern side is of a different masonry build and is identical to the enclosure wall. This structure would have been entered through a doorway in the northeastern corner of the enclosure. Each side of the doorway has sandstone chamfered jambs with a large flat sandstone threshold. The lower steps were constructed in the 1990s. The original door opened northwards and provided access into a rectangular chamber c.7m long and c.4m wide internally. While there is currently no above-ground expression of the western end wall, a large boulder is present in the southern side wall that would have served as a substantial basal corner stone. A wall is also shown on the 1928 plan extending northwards at this location. The northern side wall is no longer present, but its eastern return is also shown on the 1928 plan for a distance of at least 2m. A 1m section of this wall was still present in the 1990s before succumbing to erosion late in the decade. The identification of this corner element to the enclosure is unsurprising and its presence is typical of the type of corner towers visible on the bawn walls of many sixteenth-century tower houses across Ireland and Scotland.

4.11 Photograph of north-facing section of southern cross wall.

4.12 Photograph of projecting feature at the northeast of the sixteenth-century enclosed yard. This was likely a rectangular building, possibly a small corner tower.

The Scots menace

As the MacDonnells became firmly ensconced at Dunluce, their status as mercenaries continued to rise. In a late sixteenth-century poem dedicated to Turlough Luineach O'Neill recording a hosting he made at Armagh, the MacDonnells were mentioned as allies (McLeod 2007, 710):

> [Warriors] of Clann Domhnaill come to him
> What battalion is more battle-worthy?
> A fierce-bladed battalion from the eastern land,
> Their smooth strong hands around their sword-hilts.

A second poem as part of an address to Brian O'Rourke described the group in similar glowing terms:

> Clann Domhanill will be with him in their full strength,
> Like oaks towering above the groves,
> An excellent and wondrous band of the soldiery of Fódhea,
> The mercenaries of Islay.

In a highly symbolic move, James MacDonnell appointed his brother Coll to the lordship of the Route in 1558. This lends further credence to the hypothesis that occupation of Kinbane was shortlived, as Coll would now have taken up residence at Dunluce. Unfortunately, he died that May, a mere few months into his tenure, and Sorley Boy eventually took up the position (Hill 1873, 123). While the Scots clearly felt that they controlled the Route, this was not a position the administration in Dublin and London readily accepted. For example, the original 1543 agreement relating to what were by now Queen Elizabeth's fishing rights on the Bann following Henry VIII's death was restated in 1559 between the MacQuillans and the O'Cahans without reference to the MacDonnells (*CCM*, 603, pp 288–90). The English administration, however, had a greater worry in the ascent in 1559 of Shane O'Neill, who began a highly aggressive series of campaigns across Ulster. He moved against the O'Reillys and the O'Donnells and penetrated far south beyond Ulster's borders. O'Neill was more guarded in his view of the Antrim Scots and seems to have viewed them with a mixture of worry and respect. He appears to have brought many of them to his side and certainly large groups of Scots were fighting with him during his early campaigns, although Art Mael MacMahon had been slain by Scots in the territory of MacQuillan in 1560 (*AFM* 1560). In the following year, James, of Dunyveg, was appointed to the 'captainship' of the Route for a period of twenty-one years (Ohlmeyer 1993, 19). The earl of Sussex left from Dublin to counter the threat from O'Neill, but met with little success in the same year. The queen's grant to the MacDonnells must be seen in the context of appeasement across the northern

4.13 Dunseverick, Co. Antrim, was the chief centre of the Dál Riada on the north Ulster coastline during the early medieval period. A small tower and other buildings were constructed on the headland in the sixteenth century. These appear to have been occupied into the middle of the seventeenth century (image reproduced courtesy of Nigel McDowell, UU).

regions (Bardon 1996). Elizabeth now invited him to come to London to try and negotiate an accommodation in January 1562, after which Shane was recognized as 'captain' of Tyrone. The meeting did not result in any real peaceful outcome and O'Neill plundered much of the O'Donnell, O'Reilly, O'Hanlon and Maguire territories on his return. Both O'Cahan and MacQuillan had effectively sided with O'Neill and were listed as his allies in July 1562 (*CSPI*, vi, 200). Sussex again moved against O'Neill in 1563, but this was also ineffective. O'Neill was now encouraged to move against the Scots of Antrim in 1564, by elements of the English administration and also through his own ambitions for the area. He wrote to the lord justice from Coleraine in September 1564 that the Scots were involved in an uprising in

MacQuillan's territory and that he was moving against them (*CSPI*, xi, 245). In order to facilitate this, he refortified the old castle on the west bank of the Bann at Coleraine and sent a detachment of men across a flooding river in small coracles to defend the monastery on the east bank. A series of engagements ensued before O'Neill withdrew, unable to break the hold of the battle-hardened Scots. By Easter of the following year, he again moved against them more successfully, resulting in a final battle on the slopes of Knocklayd, where James MacDonnell, referred to by the Four Masters as a 'paragon of hospitality and prowess, a festive man of many troops', was fatally wounded. O'Neill now moved across north Antrim and took Dunseverick and Dunluce, referred to by O'Neill's secretary as Sorley Boy's 'chief castles' (Hill 1873, 135–8) (fig. 4.13). These losses were to prove temporary and the MacDonnells quickly regained Dunluce and their other lands through some form of agreement with O'Neill. His forces were later thoroughly routed by the combined strength of the O'Donnells and MacSweeneys in 1567, with Shane retreating to the MacDonnells in the Glens, where he quarrelled and fell out with them before being killed.

By November, Sorley Boy had returned to the north coast and the Glens with nearly seven hundred Scots with the tacit support of both the MacQuillan and Rory Og MacQuillan (*CSPI*, xxii, 350). Their arrival caused considerable anxiety in Dublin and once again the political structure of Ulster began to be reconfigured. Turlough Luineach was now the O'Neill and shared Dublin's concern about the power of the islanders. He had originally written to the earl of Argyle, encouraging him to attack the MacDonnells, but Rory Og MacQuillan had interfered with the messengers (*CSPI*, xxii, 352). Captain Malby wrote to the lord justices on 19 December, confirming Rory MacQuillan's assistance to the Scots. Sorley Boy now reassured Malby that he would return to Scotland once the weather improved, a promise he duly kept in late January, although he left most of his force in Ulster with MacQuillan. Interestingly, the dean of Armagh wrote in January 1568 that Sorley Boy had only gone as far as Rathlin and that he had left his people 'manuring the land' (*CSPI*, xxiii, 361). He is subsequently recorded as fortifying Rathlin in February. Rory Og was now in formal alliance with the MacDonnells, but had also married the daughter of Turlough Luineach, an arrangement that reconfigured the political landscape. It also appears that MacQuillan and the Scots had accepted Turlough and owed direct allegiance to him. Members of the Clan MacAlister from Kintyre, close descendants of the Clan Donald, had come with Sorley Boy and were now left in Ulster in Cary and Glenarm. This was to be a busy year of intrigue and political games. In February, Nicholas Bagenall wrote that the earl of Argyle had promised O'Neill help. A week later, Malby wrote to Lord Deputy Sidney that Ulster was now in a perilous state and that Rory MacQuillan was the leading protagonist of the upheaval. MacAllister left Glenarm, but vowed to return with many more Scots. A number of minor skirmishes took place in early March and Rory MacQuillan was injured. Between the 11th and

18th of that month, Turlough O'Neill was in O'Cahan country and fortified Dunalong, 'a new castle' on the eastern shores of the Foyle. Malbie now wrote that O'Neill was liable to follow the course of his predecessors into widespread conflict. O'Neill for his part was engaged in attempts to bring the MacQuillans and the MacAllisters to him, while the lord justice complained bitterly that Rory MacQuillan should have brought his complaints to Dublin and should not have acted as aggressively and independently as he did in seeking to sort out his grievances. By April, word was also spreading that Sorley Boy intended to return on the 27th and had 1,200 Scots with him. An already tense situation was by now getting significantly worse and the region was moving towards all-out conflict. Dublin now sponsored a hosting into north Ulster in order to undermine the holdings of Rory MacQuillan and the MacAllisters. Bagnall recounted details of this incursory force into the Route and stated that Ballylough Castle, 'old MacQuillan's house', was empty (*CSPI*, xxiv, 377). The force under Lord Justice FitzWilliams also stopped at Dunluce, which appears to have been still under English control, following Sorley Boy's departure, and under the guardianship of Captain Malbie. By June, it was noted that old MacQuillan (Rory's grandfather) and Rory MacQuillan had fallen out, with the former siding with Sorley Boy. The English force appears to have been successful in developing resentment and renewing old animosities among the various families causing widespread displacement. In the rapidly changing political environment the Scots effectively backed down from a large-scale movement into Ulster and remained in the islands. This continued state of unease was by now impacting upon the economy. Strategic decisions were made and the export of timber and boards from Carrickfergus and Wexford, for example, was scaled back considerably to prevent the earl of Argyle constructing galleys. By September, with the withdrawal of the Scots and continued infighting among Ulster's Gaelic families, the English forces had essentially been stood down and a large-scale crisis averted (*CCM*, 621, 156).

By April 1571, O'Neill wrote to the queen, stating that he had the loyalty of the MacQuillan but that others among the Gaelic groupings were causing problems. A brief proposal was also submitted that year to plant Ulster with loyal subjects and to expel the Scots and rebellious Irish. Walter Devereux, earl of Essex, landed at Carrickfergus in 1573 to undertake the conquest of much of Antrim, having sold much of his English and Welsh holdings to fund the scheme. His plan met with considerable resistance in the north from a new Gaelic alliance that had emerged between Turlough Luineach and Sorley Boy, with the support of the O'Cahans, MacQuillans and Maguires. Essex's expedition met with mixed success and in July 1575 he sponsored a fleet under the command of Francis Drake to sail north to Rathlin and engage Sorley Boy's followers garrisoned on the island (fig. 4.14). By that date, Sorley Boy had again regained control of the north Antrim coast, including Dunluce and the Glens. He had largely displaced the MacQuillans, due in no small part to the execution of Rory MacQuillan in 1575 and the poor state of health of his

4.14 Rathlin Island, looking southwards over Church Bay, with Fair Head in the distance
(image reproduced courtesy of Wes Forsythe, CMA).

grandfather. After a number of days siege, the island defenders surrendered and were duly massacred, with Sorley Boy traditionally recorded as having witnessed the deaths from the mainland. Essex's scheme petered out over the following months and he died in Dublin the following year, leaving Sorley Boy in an enhanced position both socially and militarily.

Tensions arose among the MacDonnells towards the end of 1575 about succession rights to the Glens and the Route, with both Sorley Boy and James' second son supported by O'Neill vying for control (*CCM*, 628, p. 35). The disagreement petered out, but the underlying problems remained. In 1578, Rory MacQuillan attacked Carrickfergus with the support of the McLeans and six hundred Scots in what appears to have been a short-lived attempt aimed at re-establishing himself and reinvigorating the MacQuillan lordship (*CCM*, 621, p. 147). By the 1580s, the Elizabethan administration was becoming increasingly concerned about a possible alliance developing between the Catholic Mary of Scotland and the various Scots groupings of the Western Isles and north Ulster. These groups, combined with French forces, had the potential to seriously undermine the security of England. In an attempt to thwart such a danger, the newly appointed lord deputy, Sir John Perrott, was sent north in 1584 to counter a supposed Scottish invasionary force (Bardon 1996) and undermine the expanding power of the MacDonnells. Sorley Boy had written to him in February, stating that he was willing to accept the lower or third part of the Glens, provided he was granted the whole of the Route, including the three great districts between the Bush and the Bann, known as MacQuillan's Country, as an equivalent for giving up two-thirds of the Glens granted to his nephew, Donnell Gorm (Hill 1873, 173). He was also to record that year that he and MacQuillan could no longer live in the same country, indicating the state of tension that now existed between the families. MacDonnell's pleas went largely unheeded and, by September, Perrott had engaged MacDonnell and his allies on both sides of the Bann and had lain siege using a 'culverin and two shakers of brass', to Dunluce by the 14th of that month. He was later to describe Dunluce as

> the strongest piece of this realm, situated upon a rock hanging over the sea, divided from the main with a broad, deep, rocky ditch, natural and not artificial, and having no way to it but a small neck of the same rock, which is also cut very deep. It hath in it a strong ward, wherof the captain is a natural Scot, who when I sent to summon them to yield refused talk, and proudly answered speaking very good English, that they were appointed and would keep it to the last man for the king of Scots use, which made me to draw tither. (Hill 1873, 162) (fig. 4.15)

Perrott wrote on 17 September that the castle's ward of forty men, who were mostly Scots, had surrendered and that he had taken a site named as Dunferte, 'the ward having fled; likewise another pyle by Portrush' (*CCM*, 632, p. 380). He also claimed that Rathlin, the traditional landing place of the Scots, was now the only refuge left for MacDonnell. In an ever more expensive campaign, garrisons were placed at Coleraine and Carrickfergus and a number of favours were granted to the MacQuillans, who Perrott viewed as the rightful subjects of the territory. Other sites occupied included the friary at Bonamargy (Bell and McNeill 2002).

Perrott's gains were to be short-lived and Elizabeth was furious at both the limited gains of the campaign and its associated expense. To compound matters, Sorley Boy retook Dunluce the following year (1585). There are conflicting reports as to how this was achieved, but it appears that two local men had infiltrated the small garrison of soldiers led by the constable, Peter Cary. Fourteen men had originally been stationed at the castle, but Cary, who may have come from the region, replaced them with his own men. A group of Sorley Boy's soldiers scaled the walls using ropes, presumably aided by the double agents, and attacked the corner tower, where Cary and a number of men were stationed (Hill 1873, 180; Dubourdieu 1812, ii, 611–12). This was presumably the southeast corner tower, which can be accessed from the ground, albeit with difficulty, and had been reconfigured to be more defensive. All the tower defenders were subsequently killed. The queen later granted Cary's widow,

4.15 Dunluce Castle from the south.

Catherine, and their five children a pension of one shilling per day to compensate her for her loss, her husband having been 'betrayed by some of his own, and miserably slain by the Scots' (Hill 1873, 180). Elsewhere, MacDonnell's men recovered other sites, including the fortified site at Dunineny, where a ward of nine men under a Captain Bowen had been stationed (*CSPI*, cxiv, 549).

Sorley Boy MacDonnell moved quickly to consolidate his position, departing for Dublin in an attempt to win back favour with the queen. In order to regain his possessions, he admitted rebellion and stated that he was wrong to take the crown's territories and castles in the Route (*CCM*, 632, p. 427). Lying prostrate at the feet of the lord deputy, he renounced all his pretended rights and begged for a pardon (Bardon 1996, 53). This was accepted and he was granted the tuoghs or sub-territories of Mowbray and Carey – that is, Culfeightrin, Ramoan and the grange of Drumtullagh and the constableship of Dunluce – four tuoghs of Dunseverick, Ballymoney, Loughguile and a small fragment of land between the rivers Bush and Bann (*CCM* II, 427.8). Additionally, he was granted, or essentially regained, all the lands of the MacQuillans, who formerly held these lands (Hill 1873, 181). Sorley's nephew, Angus of Dunyveg in Islay, submitted at the same time and was granted the Antrim glens (McDonnell 2004b, 265). Following the conferring of these territories, Sorley returned triumphantly to the Route and set about refurbishing and updating the defences at Dunluce. He died in 1589 (or 1590) and was succeeded by Sir James MacDonnell. MacQuillan immediately petitioned the administration in Dublin for the return of his lands, but was unsuccessful and James assumed control of the Route. Both parties approached Hugh O'Neill in 1594 to deliberate on possession of the territories, but this request was referred back to the queen.

1580s refurbishment: Phase 3

Following Sorley Boy's retaking of the castle, it appears that he undertook a programme of renovation to update it, taking into account the emerging architectural norms of the day. In particular, much of the programme of works undertaken at this date were an attempt to gentrify the site and demonstrate the MacDonnells' increasing political standing and clout. The erection of a loggia (a columned gallery) along the southern curtain wall reflected a late sixteenth-century architectural trend that was being adopted at a number of Scottish castles. Dunluce's loggia was essentially a small covered arcade, six bays long, supported by limestone columns and open to the north (fig. 4.16). Originally an Italian architectural feature, they were inset in buildings or gardens to provide an ornate space that was cooled by the winds. These features were adopted across northwest Europe in the sixteenth century, and the provision of such a feature at Dunluce is indicative of its owners' desire to be seen to adopt contemporary design. Examples are known at Castle Campbell and St Andrews castles in Scotland, while the lavish loggia and decorated wall at Crichton Castle was also a late sixteenth-century attempt to impress James VI. It is likely that the MacDonnells were attempting to make a similar impression. Such a feature seems entirely inappropriate at Dunluce, given that it would have faced into the harsh winds blowing in from the Atlantic on an almost year-round basis, in an area hardly renowned for its high temperatures or burning sunshine during the summer months. Instead, it has to be seen in the context of broader trends being adopted across this region at the time. Six columns partially survive, set 1.42m apart. Each is set on a plinth and has an ornate base. The columns themselves are made of block segments with an average diameter of 41cm. The tallest surviving column stands 1.61m. In the early part of the seventeenth century, the loggia was covered over when a building range was erected here against the south gable of the later Jacobean manor house.

Significant alterations also took place to the two corner towers. In the southeast tower, a large splayed window embrasure was built into the eastern side of the ground floor wall, partially obliterating an earlier loop (fig. 4.17). A second arched embrasure window was set into the southern side of the wall at first-floor level. The northeast

4.16 Photograph of the loggia at Dunluce Castle. This would have formed a north-facing walkway adjacent to an open yard or small lawn and were fashionable European architectural features built at various Scottish castles in the sixteenth century.

tower was extensively remodelled at first-floor level to create a roughly square floor plan, *c*.4.3m in diameter. A small window was inserted into the northwest face above the stairs and has surviving sandstone surrounds on its eastern side. In the first-floor interior, six joist-holes are visible on the north wall, 2.4m above floor level, while four joists are present on the inner south wall face. It is possible that a number of these served different structural functions, as they pierce the outer face of the wall. There is likely to have been a window in the northeast corner and another window was set in the angled corner at the southeast. A fireplace was set in the east wall between these two windows; it was 1.18m wide and 68cm deep, with finely chamfered blocks at its sides. On the southern side wall, a 1.1m-wide doorway, *c*.2m high, provided access to the eastern curtain wall, of which only a small projection survives at the base of the tower. A final angled window embrasure was inserted into the west wall, measuring 95cm wide internally, 1.28m deep and *c*.2m high. The room would originally have been plastered with a white lime plaster with gravel inclusions.

4.17 Photograph of late sixteenth-century window inserted into the southeast tower.

4.18 Photograph of the front of the 'buttery' building. This was built originally as a masonry house, but was later modified to function as a service building for the manor house.

Buttery

One of the most interesting elements of this phase was the probable erection of the 'buttery' building (fig. 4.18). The pre-existing large rectangular masonry building erected by the MacQuillans and uncovered by excavations must have been levelled once the loggia was erected. This necessitated the construction of a substantial residence for the MacDonnell chief. The buttery is a two-storey rectangular structure measuring 10.05m long internally and 6.07m wide. As with most structures on the site, this building underwent a number of changes. It was originally accessed at the northern end of the west wall. Here, a massive 4.2m-wide doorway partially survives, built with fine chamfered sandstone jambs. This was narrowed to 1.2m, with the southern side of the entrance blocked up. It is likely that this was originally a double doorway. An external set of steps was built immediately north of the door, providing access to a raised entrance. This is likely to have been a later addition (as the steps partially mask the chamfered jambs) and may have been undertaken in the early seventeenth century when Randal MacDonnell erected a substantial new house that incorporated the buttery. Two windows lit the ground floor, one 1.5m-wide splayed window in the southwest end and a second narrower 1.2m wide one in the northwest end. A third window was 2.1m above ground level on the east wall. Six beam joist-holes are visible on the east wall 2.05m above the paved surface. These were associated with a first-floor chamber that had a central fireplace in the northern gable wall with two windows either side.

It is difficult to be more precise in the dating of this building. In general terms, it must be earlier than the manor house, dated in the next chapter to 1611. It must also post-date the erection of the inner court in the late 1550s by the MacDonnells, as it is of a different masonry construction and sits very awkwardly by the enclosure wall. It is therefore most likely to date to the years immediately after 1585. Finding comparative examples across the island of Ireland is extremely difficult, given the paucity of identifiable surviving remains from this period. Certainly, domestic masonry structures of this date are known from Wales at sites such as Ty Mawr, Wybrnant and Bryn Yr Odyn, MaenTwrog. The bastle sites, or fortified houses, of the Scottish and English borders have a similar date and had similar dimensions but were far more defensive in character, with ground-floor barrel vaults, first-floor entrances and living quarters. Of course, the house at Dunluce did not require an overtly defensive character, considering its siting within a pre-existing defensive enclosure. Ultimately, when the house was first built for the MacDonnell, it would have constituted a fine building for its day. It must, however, be seen in the context of the erection of two domestic ranges within the inner court at the same date. When first built, the 'buttery' does not appear to have been overly domestic and could instead be seen as a small hall used by the MacDonnell to receive visitors. Under this guise, the building was continuing the medieval tradition of a hall separated from the private quarters of the lord and his retinue.

Inner court range

There is little surviving evidence that many buildings were contained in this area when the enclosure around the inner court was first built. During the 1580s, extensive rebuilding took place that completely overhauled the character and appearance of this part of the castle. Two new ranges were built using the pre-existing east and west walls, with the addition of first-floor domestic ranges. The northern range was added in the seventeenth century. The eastern range was a two-storey masonry structure measuring 20.37m long and averaging 3.8m wide internally (fig. 4.19). It had an 80cm-wide entrance linking it to the area east of the 'buttery' in the east corner of its southern gable. A fireplace was constructed centrally in the gable, measuring 1.58m wide and 66cm deep, with projecting sides. Only the basal sections remain of the 70cm-thick western side wall built using large basalt blocks with a rubble infill. A 1.1m-wide doorway is present 6.9m north of the gable and provided access into the courtyard area. A second 1m-wide doorway is located 12.9m from the gable and provided access into a second internal chamber at this northern end of the building, marked by the slot-trench for a wooden partition. One ground-floor window was inserted at the southern end of the east wall, suggesting that this ground floor would have been relatively dark. On the first floor, the angled southern splay of a window is visible at the extreme southern end of the west wall. The east wall has four splayed windows, with a possible fifth in the large breach at the southern end. A small fireplace was also inserted centrally on this wall, with a projecting external chimney stack. A series of first-floor joists can also be seen along this range. The so-called 'latrine' was inserted into the range in the seventeenth century, although this has also been referred to as a 'magazine' by nineteenth-century antiquarians.

The western range has a maximum internal length of 20.46m and an average width of 4.8m. It was also converted into a two-storey structure (fig. 4.20). Four doorways provided access into this range, which appears to have had three internal chambers and a passageway to an external western door, at least in its final construction phase. Only one window at ground-floor level is visible where the south angle of an embrasure partially survives on the east side wall, opposite the 'latrine'. The rest of this wall is much collapsed, but it appears again that the ground floor would have been a relatively dark space. A 1.15m-wide doorway at the southern end of the east wall provided access into an entrance chamber. This area of the castle has been heavily interfered with and it is difficult to elucidate its chronology. Sections of this wall have collapsed and have been rebuilt in the recent past, but no records were kept of the nature of this repair work. A fireplace was present in the southern end wall, now masked by later rebuilds and repair. Only a section of its eastern flue is visible behind the standing wall. On the western section of the gable, a fireplace was inserted at first-floor level. Its stack was made of fine sandstone ashlar blocks. A second first-floor fireplace with an external projecting chimney was added centrally

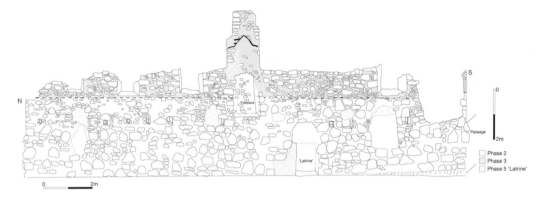

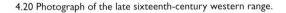

4.19 Elevation of the east wall of the cliff-edge enclosure, showing the late sixteenth-century additions at first-floor level.

4.20 Photograph of the late sixteenth-century western range.

on the west wall, while a third stack was placed over the double bread oven at the northwest end of the west wall (fig. 4.21). The ground-floor ovens are set in an 85cm-deep recess. These appear to be later additions to a 2.4m-wide fireplace with a large projecting chimney. While the northern oven is largely gone, the southern example is a large, slightly domed, stone-built example with stone flag. It is set 85cm above ground level and is nearly 2m deep and 50cm high. An earlier blocked-up doorway is present in the west wall just south of the ovens. This would originally have provided access to the external cliff edge area outside the enclosure wall. A fourth fireplace is present on the northern gable and the building would have been roofed using scissor trusses.

Nine Years War

Ulster was again beset by crisis in the closing decade of the sixteenth century. Hugh O'Neill had been appointed earl of Tyrone in 1585 and, through astute political manoeuvring, he had overcome the enmity with the O'Donnells of Tír Connell to create an important Gaelic alliance between both septs. He aided the escape from Dublin Castle of Red Hugh O'Donnell, who was proclaimed the O'Donnell in 1592, with O'Neill proclaimed as the O'Neill at Tullahogue, following the death of Turlough Luineach in 1595. Gradually, over the preceding years, O'Neill had turned against Elizabeth. Concerned at the gradual erosion of the effective autonomy of the Ulster lordships and creeping subjugation of their religious beliefs, political tension rapidly developed. Consequently, the Ulster lords, fearing the subdivision of their lands, as had happened to the MacMahons in Monaghan, initiated a programme of resistance across Ulster. Maguire initially lost Enniskillen early in 1594, but through an alliance with O'Donnell and later with O'Neill (who had originally supported the English forces) he managed to retake the town. The position of the MacDonnells in the early years of the war is complicated by internal strife and wrangling over territory and inheritance. Having originally sided with James against the MacQuillans, O'Neill shifted his favour to the latter in 1596 as James was in negotiations with the English to seek the release of his brother Randal (McDonnell 2004b, 267). Following the release of Randal, however, James again won favour with O'Neill and lent his support to the cause of the Ulster chieftains. In 1597, Sir John Chichester, governor of Carrickfergus, wrote to Lord Burghley, complaining that James MacDonnell and his brother Randal had broken down two of their castles at Glenarm and Red Bay and were in the process of fortifying themselves at Dunluce with three guns, including a demi-canon and culverin that had been recovered from the wreck of the Spanish Armada vessel *La Girona*, lost nearby off Spanish Point in 1588 (*CSPI*, cc, p. 200).

Dunluce refortification: Phase 4

There are a number of key surviving structural elements relating to this refortification. Specifically, in recognition of the widespread use of artillery by this date, the south-facing curtain wall was significantly thickened with masonry, increasing its width to over 2m. Two wide-angled embrasures were also set into the wall. Both openings are 2m wide internally with a height of 2.8m and a depth of 2.1m, with external brick surrounds (fig. 4.22). These brick features are probably later

4.21 Photograph of the double oven feature in the western range. These would have been used to bake bread and other foodstuffs.

4.22 Large embrasures apparently inserted into the curtain wall to accommodate guns from *La Girona*, wrecked in 1588 at the nearby Giant's Causeway.

seventeenth-century additions. Traditionally, these have been interpreted as facilitating the cannon recovered from the *Girona*. The demi-cannon was a medium-sized gun that would have been *c*.3.4m long, firing a thirty-two-pound shot. It had a range of 490m. The culverin was a smaller long-bored gun that fired 15–17-pound shot. While both would have fitted into these spaces, it would have been a reasonably tight fit and would have made the cannons both unwieldy and difficult to use, limiting their effectiveness. Additionally, they would have had to fire upslope, effectively over a blind summit, severely limiting their role during an attack. Their presence was probably more for visual impact than having an effective defensive role. There is no clear evidence for further defensive work, presumably masked by the major renovations undertaken in the opening decades of the seventeenth century.

More or less at the same time, James MacDonnell was displaying his keen survival instinct and petitioned the queen to make him the officer with responsibility for controlling the cross-channel trade of the northeast in return for his effective support (McDonnell 2004b, 268). Covering all angles, he also gifted James VI a cannon that had been recovered from *La Girona*. Late that year, he travelled to Edinburgh in an effort to be appointed head of the Southern Clandonald over Angus of Dunyveg. He was subsequently knighted by the Scottish king and granted a tract of land in Kintyre. James VI had recognized that James was potentially a more valuable and loyal ally and supported him in his feud with Angus. In the summer of 1598, James landed on Islay with four hundred men and, with the support of the MacLeans, took control of the island. On Kintyre, Angus was driven from his base by his son, Sir James of Knockrinsay, who had been recruited by James VI in this campaign. The Islay alliance very quickly broke down, allowing a period of internecine conflict and uncertainty to develop on the island. A similar set of uncertainties existed in Ulster as the Nine Years War drew to a close. As the tide of the war shifted, the MacDonnells were faced with a decision as to which way they would swing and how they could best emerge from the decade-long conflict. Very quickly, after the disastrous campaign at Kinsale, and having originally marched south with the Ulster Gaelic lords, the MacDonnells abandoned the cause and sought to repair their relationship with the crown. Their instinct for survival was to prove their salvation once more.

CHAPTER 5

Randal MacDonnell, Dunluce and unofficial plantations

Following the death of James MacDonnell in 1601, Randal MacDonnell assumed the headship of the family (fig. 5.1). It was under his leadership that their holdings and territories across north Antrim were consolidated and a major programme of plantation and building schemes was initiated. Dunluce Castle was radically altered and expanded, while new or rebuilt settlements were constructed both in the Route and in the Glens. Randal's ambitious schemes were paralleled in the official plantation project west of the Bann and in the lands of the Scottish settlers, Hamilton and Montgomery, in north Co. Down (Perceval-Maxwell 1973). The Ulster landscape was subjected to significant change, as a wave of new settlers arrived, new building forms developed and society underwent considerable cultural and economic change.

MacDonnell land grants, 1603–4

After James I ascension to the throne of England in 1603 following the death of Elizabeth, Randal MacDonnell was granted by letters patent the territory of the Route and Glynns (fig. 5.2; table 5.1). In making this grant, James was recognizing MacDonnell's Scottish ancestry and connections, as well as his personal friendship with the king. The original grant in May 1603 covered sixteen tuoghs and included the four baronies of Dunluce, Kilconway, Cary and Glenarm, totalling 333,907 acres (PRONI D2977/5/1/1/1; Hill 1873, 196). As part of this grant, MacDonnell was to provide '120 foot soliders, 60 to be good shot and the rest swordmen and pikemen and 24 horsemen' (*CPRCI James I*, 1603, 8), an important illustration of his military capacity at this time. This grant was intrinsically linked to the original grant in June 1586 of part of the Route to Sorley Boy MacDonnell, who had gained the territory extending from the River Bush to the Bann and three toughs of Dunseverick, Loughguile and Ballymoney, with all of the lands of the MacQuillans and the constableship of Dunluce Castle (*CCM* II, 427.8). The MacDonnells had been engaged in decades of internecine conflict with the MacQuillans before finally displacing them in the 1580s. Through astute political manoeuvring, the MacDonnells maintained their territories into the opening years of the seventeenth century and

5.1 Plan of the Antrim estates granted to Randal MacDonnell in 1603. These included all of north Antrim and Rathlin Island.

ensured their survival through their relationship with James. Problems with the original 1603 grant led to Randal MacDonnell being reissued with the grant in 1604 with the condition that he divide the territory into two-thousand-acre precincts and build a castle or manor house on each of the smaller five-hundred-acre units (*CPRCI James I*, 1604, 137). This structured approach was essentially replicated in the later official plantations across Londonderry, settlements historically examined by Curl (1986).

Lewis plantations

In granting these lands to a traditional 'Gaelic' lord, James I was not just rewarding friendship and ancestry but he was also displaying an acute understanding of the political situation in Ulster and demonstrating that he had clearly learned a number

Table 5.1 Details of Randal MacDonnell's 1603 grant, consisting of sixteen tuoghs, equating to the modern baronies of Dunluce, Kilconway, Carey and Glenarm, originally comprising 333,907 acres (PRONI D2977/5/1/1/1). The identification of the tuoghs is taken from Reeves (1847)

Territory		Description
Route	Between Bann and Bush	Included the parishes of Coleraine, Ballyaghran, Ballywillan, Ballyrashane, Dunluce and Kildollagh
Route	Dunseverick and Ballintoy	Part of Billy parish in the barony of Cary and part of the parish of Ballintoy containing Dunseverick Castle
Route	Ballylough	Part of Billy parish in lower Dunluce and the parish of Derrykeighan
Route	Loughguile	Parish of Loughguile
Route	Ballymoney and Drumard [Dromart]	Parish of Ballymoney, parish of Kilraghts
Route	Kilconway	Part of barony of Kilconway
Route	Killyquin	13 townlands in western parish of Rasharkin parish
Route	Killymurris	Concentrated on Dunloy in Finvoy parish
Route	Dunaghy	Concentrated on parish of Dunaghy, including village of Clough and Oldstone Castle
Glens	Munerie (Mowbray, Mowberry)	Parish of Ramoan and Grange of Drumtullagh, included town of Ballycastle
	Cynamond of Armoy and Rathlin	Parish of Armoy and Rathlin
	Carey (Cary)	Originally smaller than Cary barony but included Fairhead and Murlough Bay
	Glinmiconogh	The Middle Glens including Cushendall
	Largie (Largy)	Including part of Ardclinis parish
	Park	Included Tickmacrevan, Templeoughter and Solar. Name refers to the demesne of Glenarm Castle.
	Larne	Included parishes of Carncastle, Killyglen, Kilwaughter and Larne

5.2 Portrait of James I (image reproduced courtesy of the National Portrait Gallery, London).

of valuable lessons from the ill-fated Lewis plantations. Late in the 1590s, a plan had been developed to undertake a plantation of the Isle of Lewis with settlers from the lowlands of Scotland (MacCoinnich 2007). The islands had continued to pose a political problem for Edinburgh, with a number of the clan groups essentially operating semi-autonomous territories, and hinder trade and economic activity with lowland Scotland. The plantations were a concerted attempt to break the power of the islander families, while being promoted at the time as an attempt to bring civility, modernity and trade to these marginal lands. In November 1598, a group known as the 'Fife Adventurers' set out with five hundred men with the aim of establishing a burgh on the island of Lewis, initially founding a settlement at Stornoway (Dobson 2004). Almost immediately, the undertaking met with stiff resistance from the islanders and in 1601 the MacLeods took the settlers' fort. The majority of the planters left the island, although settlement continued in kind up to 1609, when the Mackenzies bought out the rights to the scheme (MacCoinnich 2007, 16). Kintyre was also proposed for settlement in 1598, but it was not until 1607 that the scheme commenced. By 1609, the earl of Argyll was encouraged to establish 'within the bounds of Kintyre' a burgh that was initially called Lochead and later renamed as Campbeltown, drawing inhabitants from Ayrshire and Renfrewshire (Dobson 2004, 12).

The Lewis settlement was clearly a failure and the Lochead scheme only succeeded due to the support of Argyll. James now appreciated the importance of gaining local support and participation in any plantation scheme. Also, the imposition of central bureaucratic control and governance of such schemes in Gaelic territories from a distance, whether that was Edinburgh or London, was impractical and never likely to succeed. When it came to Ulster, the king had a far clearer idea of what was required to develop a successful scheme on the ground. In granting the lands to MacDonnell, he was grooming an ally and ensuring the continuation of political and economic stability in an area of key strategic importance. MacDonnell's primary interest was always in the maintenance of his personal standing and the development of his estates. The MacDonnells had shown themselves to be shrewd political and social players over the previous three decades and had demonstrated a particular talent for survival. Interestingly, the architecture of their principal residence at Dunluce demonstrates this continual renegotiation of their political and social status through their sponsored architectural refurbishment of the castle, reflecting Gaelic, Scottish and finally English forms. Randal MacDonnell, in turn, was never an expansionist in the mould of Tyrone and was very much an individualist. James recognized that MacDonnell's territories would create a buffer zone between the still volatile Gaelic territories of mid- and west Ulster. He also recognized that MacDonnell would facilitate and positively encourage the future expansion of trade activity throughout the north Irish Sea region. Having MacDonnell on the king's side would also dilute the influence of Argyll across the region, as it would the local English bureaucrats governing the colonies. Consequently, the grants to Randal did not receive universal favour. In particular, Lord Deputy Chichester, who had particular designs on north Antrim himself, complained bitterly to the king about it (Canny 2001, 188). MacDonnell prevailed and in July 1610 he received a new patent confirming the original grant following his surrender of nine townlands in Coleraine to be used for the formal plantation.

MacDonnell settlements

Almost immediately following his grants, Randal MacDonnell began establishing a network of settlements across his estates. These were set up to act as centres of trade and small-scale industrial activity and were to be populated by both new settlers brought in from Scotland and existing Irish inhabitants. In May 1608, he was

Plantation of Ulster
With the ending of the Nine Years War following the Battle of Kinsale in 1601 and the submission of O'Neill in early 1603, Ulster returned to a period of terse peace. A restless O'Donnell became involved in conspiracy to aid insurrection from 1604, however, leading ultimately to the Flight of the Earls from Rathmullan in 1607. The departure of the earls left a large portion of Ulster lands open to formal plantation. Cahir O'Doherty had been granted Inishowen, but rose in revolt in 1608, taking Derry. This insurrection provided the crown with an excuse to confiscate lands of the Gaelic lords, including the O'Cahans, O'Dohertys and O'Donnells. A formal plantation scheme was initiated later that year that envisaged three classes of beneficiaries – English and Scottish undertakers with their tenants (English and Scots); servitors with settler or Irish tenants; and, finally, native freeholders. The confiscated territories were to be divided initially into precincts with a chief undertaker with estates of 2,000, 1,500 and 1,000 acres. They were also required to build a castle or fortified residence by 1613, establish an agreed number of settlers and remove any Irish still living on the land. By 1610, large undertakers were required to plant 'twenty-four able men of the age of eighteen years or upwards being English or inland Scottish'. Private financing lay behind much of the scheme. Initially, the county of Coleraine scheme was assigned to a syndicate of twelve London companies that became known as 'The Honourable The Irish Society', a joint-stock company that lent a mercantile emphasis to this settlement. By 1613, the county, by now known as Londonderry, had been granted to twelve groups of the London trade guilds with estates of c.3,000 acres. Elsewhere in Ulster, further private plantation schemes were initiated, including those led by Hamilton and Montgomery in north Down and by the MacDonnells in north Antrim.

authorized by the lord deputy to make denizens in Ireland of all the 'Scotchmen' he would require (*CSPI*, 224). In developing this network, MacDonnell was directly replicating the pattern of development in the areas of the official plantation and setting up an economic structure that would expand and compete with that of the other counties. It is clear, though, that MacDonnell was not simply copying what was happening in the western counties, but was enacting a scheme that was as innovative and in many ways as ambitious as the official schemes. Indeed, it appears that in some instances the Antrim schemes were initiated prior to those of the western counties. MacDonnell would have already had a clear idea of the type of infrastructure required for his settlements, following discussions both with the king's bureaucrats and through his personal connections and relationships with the architects of the official plantations. He was already on the ground, knew the landscape intimately and forged ahead with his schemes at the earliest opportunity. By 1606, he had been granted the right to hold a fair at Cloghmagherdunaghy [Clogh] on the feast of John the Baptist (fig. 5.3); a fair at Dunkerd in the Route on the feast St Michael; a Saturday market at Dunluce; a Tuesday market at Dunineny and a Thursday market at Glenarm in the Glens (*CPRCI James I*, 1606, p. 274). The grants were important, not only in demonstrating MacDonnell's interest in implementing economic frameworks, but also because these places were to serve as new centres of settlement and administration for the Antrim estates. By May 1608, Randal had agreed to divide up

5.3 Clogh Castle, Co. Antrim, was originally fortified in the thirteenth century but was later rebuilt and became one of the centres of the MacDonnell estates (image reproduced courtesy of Claire Breen).

5.4 An early 1930s photograph of the Jacobean house at Dunluce. Note the cobbling has yet to be laid in the yard. The structure appears in a relatively precarious state now that all of the rubble had been cleared from its base (image reproduced courtesy of the Ulster Folk and Transport Museum).

his territory as per the earlier grant and gave an undertaking to build castles and 'capital messuages' in each of the listed manors (*CPRCI James I*, 1608, 527). There is a degree of cultural continuity at each of these sites, with each having a pre-existing castle or fortification and probably small-scale associated settlement. What happened in the first two decades of the seventeenth century though represents an important break with the past. In a number of cases, the late medieval fortifications were extensively refurbished or rebuilt. This is particularly evident at Dunluce, Glenarm and Dunineny. More importantly, from a plantation perspective, MacDonnell built a number of new towns centred on these late medieval sites. They have limited associated documentary evidence, but archaeological research is beginning to elucidate important information about their morphology and settlement patterns.

Architectural change

The opening decades of the seventeenth century heralded significant societal change across Ulster. There was a movement towards adapting the new cultural norms sweeping Europe, with an emphasis on 'civility'. This phenomenon also found expression in the emerging architectural fashions of the time. In particular, architecture moved away from the accommodation of communality as previously found in the shared extended and open spaces of the medieval castle, towards a new emphasis on privacy. As the old systems focusing on the allocation of sheltered space and food provision for the sept lord, his extended family and retinue in a castle broke down, the emphasis began to move towards the centrality of the new lords and their immediate family. Private spaces were created for them within the new forms of housing, and the division between master and servant became more pronounced, with the provision of exclusive and utilitarian space. Increased emphasis was now placed on consumption, and the overt display of material wealth and gain became common among the elite within a rapidly increasing social divide. Increasingly, houses across Ireland and Scotland adopted English forms, with large bay windows and the increased use of glass as production technology improved.

Manor house

The manor house at Dunluce is a typical expression of these processes and represents one of the finest surviving examples of early Jacobean architecture in Ulster (fig. 5.4). While not technically a 'manor house' when it was initially constructed, it did essentially assume that role in the 1620s and has traditionally been labelled as such. Consequently, this label has been adopted here, primarily for ease of discussion. It was built against a pre-existing structure directly to the north known as the 'buttery' and was designed as a two-storey L-shaped building on a north–south axis with a

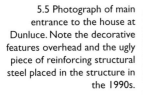

5.5 Photograph of main entrance to the house at Dunluce. Note the decorative features overhead and the ugly piece of reinforcing structural steel placed in the structure in the 1990s.

west-facing frontal façade. Originally, the building would been rendered externally with a lime-based mortar and small sections of this survive in places. It is likely that the building was also limewashed, but no evidence of this is now visible. The building's quoins are made of fine ashlar sandstone blocks, which are also present in the windows. Three tall bay windows dominate this frontal elevation, with six transomed and mullioned windows set in the bays. Each of the bays is approximately 3m wide externally. None of the window stonework survives, but a modern example was inserted into the southernmost bay by the DOE in the 1980s. Three string courses consisting of projecting yellow sandstone blocks are present at the base and top of the ground floor windows and above the first floor window set. The main entrance doorway, which is 1.6m wide, was positioned in the northwest corner of the front façade and was originally ornamented (fig. 5.5). This positioning at the effective end of a building was unusual, as the majority of entrances to early Jacobean houses are placed centrally, to convey symmetry, and reflected the ordered sense of space that architecture was striving to demonstrate. It may be that the architect was attempting to create a symmetrical connection with the buttery or was trying something different. Unfortunately, during conservation works on the building in the nineteenth and twentieth centuries, much of the stone surrounds and features of the entrance were removed. Little now survives of the original feature, apart from a number of ashlar blocks and three heavily weathered possible animal heads or natural features inset above the door.

Internally, the building measures 20.55m by 6.72m, with walls averaging between 90cm and 1m in thickness. The main doorway would have provided access to an entrance hallway that had a doorway to the left into the buttery building and access through a wooden partition to the right into the main reception chamber. This chamber would have been lit by two of the bays in the western wall and by a number of windows in the eastern elevation. An ornate fireplace was centrally placed on the eastern wall and had a projecting chimney wall to the rear. A further wooden partition uncovered during excavations in 2010 would have divided the reception chamber from the parlour, which occupied the southern wing of the house. The footings for a doorway were revealed against the angled eastern return of the internal wall. The parlour itself, measuring 11.22m by 6.2m, was lit by the southernmost bay and by a window in the eastern return of the north-facing projection. A single large fireplace, 1.95m wide, was set into the southern gable adjacent to an elevated doorway to the immediate east that would have provided access to the southern curtain range and the corner tower. It is evident from both this entrance and a second example on the first floor that there was a masonry and timber range built against the tower and the southern enclosure wall. Evidence for a former wooden stairway leading to the first floor is clearly marked in the plaster impressions on the internal face of the southern end wall and by a number of structural support holes. This would have been a private stairway providing access for the immediate family and close servants to the earl's quarters and main hall on the first floor. In keeping with the emerging trends of the time, this was a light space lit by a window on the eastern wall.

Ascertaining the original morphology and functionality of the first floor is complicated by the current state of the structure and by the interference and misguided attempts at conservation and rebuilding that have taken place in the recent past. Its floor plan is likely to mirror that of the ground floor, with a partitioned private space at its southern end lit by one of the bay windows and by a window on the northern return wall. A fireplace was positioned off centre to the west on the southern gable in order not to interfere with the main fireplace at ground-floor level (fig. 5.6). Two doorways provided access into the adjacent curtain range either side of this feature. It is probable that the remainder of the first floor accommodated the main hall in the house. This was where the lord would have entertained, with this level facilitating good vistas east and west across to the Skerries and Donegal as well as over to Islay to the northeast. The room was lit by two of the windows along the

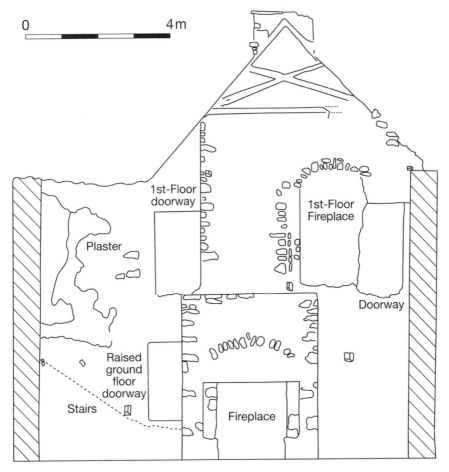

5.6 Elevation drawing of the southern gable. Doorways at ground- and first-floor levels provided access to a now-removed building range along the curtain wall. A staircase to the first floor was formerly present east of the large fireplace.

western wall and by at least two further windows at either end of the eastern wall, as evidenced by the chamfered sides of two former embrasures. A final fixed mullioned window was placed on the eastern side of the north gable. This is the only window to retain its original mullion and stanchion bar. The projecting chimney flume at ground-floor level is likely to have extended to this level and would have accommodated a centrally placed and decorative fireplace on this wall. As with the lower hall, the walls of this space would have been panelled and a number of tapestries would have adorned the space. A further door was positioned in the northern gable to provide access to the buttery and the staircase.

It is probable that there was an attic. There is adequate height beneath the roof timbers and the projected height of the first-floor ceiling to accommodate such a feature. It would have been lit by three probable dormer windows placed above the bays to retain the symmetrical format of the front façade. The roof itself was constructed using a scissor-brace technique at its southern end, the imprint of which survives on the southern gable. Each tall triangular gable was pitched at a 45° angle and would have been slated and later topped with North Devon glazed ridge tiles. Additionally, decorative stonework finials topped the gables. Short projecting chimney stacks topped the roof on the south gable and on the eastern wall. The stacks are surprisingly short in comparison to other buildings of the period. Across England and parts of Ireland, tall decorated stacks were designed to increase the visibility of the house and draw the visitor towards it. In many cases, this would have been the first element of the house seen, so they became an important feature. The setting of Dunluce worked against this, however, as the primary approaches were from the south. Gallow's Hill would then have obscured the castle, originally designed to be viewed as a maritime fortress, so its early seventeenth-century stacks were of little importance compared to other contemporary houses.

Kitchen

The kitchen of the house was contained in the space immediately east of the buttery (fig. 5.7). Originally, it would have been accessed from the door in the eastern wall of the manor house and entered through a doorway in the southern cross-wall down two stone steps that led from the cobbled yard at the rear of the house. This area would have had a pitched roof supported by wooden beams. A single surviving beam-hole and corresponding horizontal beam space are evident at roof level on the line of the original northern wall of the kitchen. During the clearance work in 1928, 'decayed wood of sills and post' were found *in situ* by the north wall of this area, providing further evidence that a building of partial timber-frame construction formerly stood here. The kitchen space itself occupied a roughly rectangular area measuring 6.6m by 5m and was roughly paved. A series of drains are visible under the northern wall and were also present along the western area of the site, where it has been suggested that the kitchen's sinks would have been. A domed oven was built against the northeast corner tower at a height of 80cm above present ground level. Internally, it has a maximum height of 88cm and is 1.4m deep. This would have been used primarily for bread making once a fire had been lit inside using sticks and allowed to die down. A small chimney flue was built, leading into the main flues above the large fireplace in the centre of the eastern wall of the kitchen. The fireplace measures 3.66m wide and is *c*.1.2m deep. A number of fine cut stones that formed part of its original surround survive on either side, while the chimney has cut sandstone on the chimney stack. Heavily fired basalt is visible at the rear of the fireplace. This would have been the main domestic cooking fireplace for Randal's household. A number of large pots

5.7 Photograph of the kitchen that would originally have served the main house. The kitchen was built in two phases, with the northern end being added later. The focus of the kitchen was the large fireplace on the eastern wall, where much of the cooking would have taken place and an oven was set into the wall of the northeast tower.

would have been hung over the fire and used for boiling. A second oven is present in a rectangular chamber immediately to the north of the kitchen area, but this probably dates to a later period in the seventeenth century, judging by the presence of red brick in its construction. It is likely that this was built at the same time as the lodgings range, probably sometime in the 1620s.

Buttery

The 'buttery' (essentially, a service room used for the storage of provisions, ale and wine) was adapted in the early seventeenth century and was incorporated into the manor house. The building had two chambers divided by a wooden partition. This division probably took place at the same time as the doorway was blocked up as the slot-trench that would have accommodated the planking lines up exactly with the reconfigured inner side of the entrance. The floor surface was roughly paved at the same time. During the building of the manor house, the pre-existing south gable of the buttery was used and the north gable of the new house built directly on top. The scar of the original roofline can be seen on the north face of this gable. Two doors were inserted into the gable at this time, providing ground-floor and first-floor access between the two structures (fig. 5.8). Tradition records that this functioned as a buttery by this date. In medieval times, butteries were usually located between the great hall and the kitchen, an arrangement that was effectively adapted here. The ground-floor entrance was blocked up by this date, considerably narrowing it from its original width of 4.2m. A first-floor doorway led from the buttery into the first floor of the manor house. During the course of the 1928 clearance, finds in this area included a broken glass stem, fragments of wine bottles and 'some diamond panes of thin greenish window glass', the typical form of early seventeenth-century window glass found across the town site.

Manor house date

The dating of the manor house has been controversial. In the 1611 Plantation Commissioners Survey led by George Carew, the report noted that Sir Randal 'had built a fair stone wall about the whole rock, within which he hath erected a good house of stone with many lodgings and other rooms' at the castle of Dunluce (Benn 1877, 677). A number of writers have linked this reference to the buttery (McDonnell 2004a; Quinn 2002), as it was felt that the Jacobean structure was a later construct. McDonnell stated that the structure is likely to have been constructed c.1620, while Reeves-Smyth (2007) ascribed a date of c.1630. This dating was guided by the development of Jacobean manor houses in the formal plantation territories across the Bann, where numerous new houses were built towards the end of the

5.8 Photograph of the southern gable of the 'buttery'. There would have been two doors providing access into the manor house at ground- and first-floor levels. The roof of the building was pitched below the window at the upper eastern side.

5.9 Detail from Thomas Raven's early seventeenth-century map of Bangor, showing the large Jacobean house and associated gardens overlooking the small coastal town. A variety of house forms were present in the settlement (image reproduced courtesy of North Down Museum).

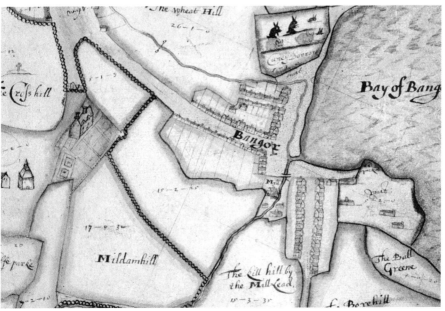

second decade of the seventeenth century. The archaeological and historical sources clearly indicate that construction of the small town was well advanced at Dunluce by the close of the first decade of the century, however, and that Randal MacDonnell was actually a number of years ahead of the building projects associated with the plantations west of the Bann. Neither is MacDonnell likely to have built such a small un-ambitious structure as the buttery when many of the merchants in the adjacent town had larger and more attractive residences. Internally, the buttery measured 10m by 6m, while the merchant's house excavated in 2009 was 10.5 by 5.9m. Similarly, the southern portion of the second house excavated in 2010 had an internal width of 5m. While it is evident that the buttery underwent refurbishment, its general morphology is not suggestive of the primary residence of an aspiring and ambitious landowner of MacDonnell's status. Additionally, the 1611 survey, for example, makes reference to a number of fine stone buildings that had already been erected by this date at Carrickfergus, including a 'strong' house being constructed at Stranmillis outside Belfast that was fifty-six feet long and intended to be 2.5 storeys high, and a large house built by James Hamilton at Bangor. This was presumably the large stone house depicted on the 1625 map of Bangor illustrated by Thomas Raven, showing a two-storey house with an attic and dormer windows and a centrally placed doorway (fig. 5.9). Furthermore, Raven's maps of the Londonderry plantation commissioned in 1622 by Sir Thomas Philips show a number of standing houses that were similar in style and format to the Dunluce house. In particular, the illustration of the house at Macosquin in the Merchant Taylor lands shows a three-storey masonry structure with a further attic and dormers fronted by a central entrance and two tall, projecting flanking bays (fig. 5.10). Plans for this house and settlement were laid out in 1615, with the ground plan of the house measuring 52 by 34 feet (15.8 by 10.3m). We have no way of ascertaining whether these were the final dimensions of the standing building, but its length is comparable to the Dunluce building (20.5m internally), given that it had three rather than two bays. Certainly, the Macosquin example was standing by 1620, but construction must have commenced by 1618 at the latest. The type of Jacobean architecture depicted can be traced to an earlier date elsewhere. At Knole in southeast England, for example, similar bay windows were erected between 1605 and 1608 by Thomas Sackville during major refurbishment of the house. There is therefore little reason to doubt that the existing structure at Dunluce was constructed by 1611.

Mainland buildings: Phase 4

Stables

During the first two decades of the seventeenth century, Randal initiated building projects on the mainland directly adjacent to the castle. These included an enclosure

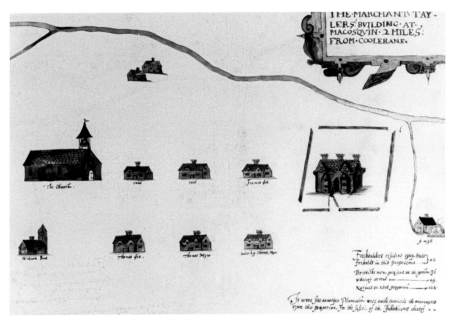

5.10 Detail from Thomas Raven's early seventeenth-century map of Macosquin. The main house had a central entrance and two bays and would have been broadly similar in appearance to the manor house at Dunluce (image reproduced courtesy of North Down Museum).

5.11 The stables block at the castle was located in the outer courtyard area and had a set of external steps that would have been used as a mounting platform.

wall and a stable block (fig. 5.11). The stable and harness room is positioned at the southern end of the western range of buildings in the outer court area. It is a plain rectangular building with an internal length of 18.8m and width of 5.62m. A single entrance is located in its eastern wall that narrows to 1.18m between the well-shaped sandstone jambs that would originally have contained a wooden doorway. A lead-lined slot for a doorway pintle survives in the northern basal jamb. Sections of a cobbled surface that appears to be original survives in the entrance. The side walls were constructed from roughly faced basalt blocks of varying sizes, with a rubble mortared core. The eastern side wall survives to waist height, rising to just over 2m above ground level at the entrance. Two possible window apertures are present at the northern end of this wall, which would have been up to 1.6m wide. The western wall is windowless, but contains eleven beam-holes on its internal face, between 50 and 90cm above the present ground surface. They are irregularly spaced, between 1.4 and 1.8m apart, each consisting of a rectangular hole averaging 19cm wide and 15cm high. It is likely that these supported wooden beams and partitions that separated each individual stall in the stables.

The building's northern triangular-headed gable survives largely intact. It originally supported a sloping slated roof. There are clear architectural indications that this building accommodated a first floor or at least an attic space. Two single windows are built into the gable at ground- and first-floor level. Both are splayed inwards, indicating that the stables were built earlier than the adjacent lodgings block to the north, as it is unlikely that a stable's window would have opened into such a block. This earlier construction date is also supported by the evidence of the external western face of both buildings, where the original end quoins from the stables have been incorporated into the later lodgings. Three of the uppermost examples are of yellow worked sandstone. A series of floor or ceiling joists are visible in the northwest corner, with eight further examples in the centre of the west wall. The ground-floor window is 95cm wide, 97cm high and is 77cm above the ground.

Stables excavation: Trench 1

A small trench, measuring 1m by 3m, was excavated in the northern section of the stables building abutting the western wall, running on an approximate east–west orientation. It was positioned here to target an area of high resistance in the geophysical data and to elucidate the function of the beam-hole on the western wall. It was assumed prior to excavation that this would have originally supported a timber partition for individual booths. The upper layers of sod and soil were heavily disturbed through both the abandonment phases and later repair and conservation work. These contexts came down onto a very uneven subsoil at the western edge of trench. No indication of flooring or any indication of the former insetting of cobbling were located, and it appears likely that the original ground surface of the stables consisted of hard-packed clay, presumably covered with straw or other bedding

5.12 Photograph of the excavation trench in the stables building showing the central drain that facilitated the run-off of waste from the stable. The ground surface of the stables would have consisted of compacted clay and was both rough and uneven.

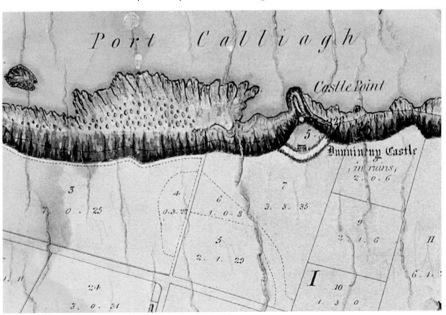

5.13 Detail of Dunineny Castle from a nineteenth-century town map of Ballycastle. Garrisoned in the later sixteenth century, Randal MacDonnell redeveloped the site in the early seventeenth century, when it served as an administrative centre within the Antrim estates (image reproduced courtesy of Causeway Museum Service).

material. A stone-lined drain was located at the eastern end of the trench in what would have been the central area of the structure (fig. 5.12). This runs north–south, and geophysical survey indicates that it then turns eastwards and runs diagonally across the outer yard before exiting on the eastern side of the complex. This feature was uncovered during Nick Brannon's previous excavations at the site and was described as follows:

> A small trench [was] cut on the other side of an adjacent wall and relocated the gully (narrow gully, up to 80cm wide ran downslope from a pit in the 'visitor building' and had a two-stage infill). Some confusion was caused, however, by the fact that the gully appeared to run underneath the wall. Analysis of standing remains identifies this as the wall of the south gable of a large building conventionally identified as the castle 'stables', and believed to be of seventeenth-century date. Since the gully, or at least its infilling deposits, must be of eighteenth-century or later date, the wall, as presently standing, must be of even later date. While its integrity in ground plan terms cannot be questioned, it is likely that this masonry is a modern version of an earlier ruin … The search for the gully in the 'stables' building involved excavation through a soil-less deposit of demolition debris up to 60cm deep. Clearly, the grassed 'floor-' level inside this building does not accurately represent an original floor level (Brannon, unpublished DOE file).

A number of things can be clarified from the 2009 excavations here. Brannon's infilling deposits occurred once the site was abandoned and cannot be used as dating evidence for the standing structures. The gully was built as a primary feature during the construction of the stables, which are dated here to the early part of the seventeenth century. Finds included horse bone (some butchered), a horseshoe and a sherd of Ulster medieval coarse ware.

Dunineny

MacDonnell also proceeded to redevelop other fortified sites, including Dunineny, a dramatically positioned coastal clifftop fort immediately west of Ballycastle in north Antrim (fig. 5.13). The site was recently excavated as part of a research project on late medieval Gaelic lordship. A rescue dig was also undertaken in association with conservation of the castle's masonry (McNeill 2004). The site has an extensive history. Initially fortified in prehistory and possibly periodically occupied at various times during the medieval period, a small English garrison was placed there in 1585. In December 1603, Hugh O'Neill received the constableship of the 'fort of Dunaneny', as part of the Antrim estate grant, a lease subsequently reissued to

MacDonnell in 1612 to include the market town of Ballycastle. The excavations showed that the surviving standing masonry and the visible internal features had been constructed in the early seventeenth century, with a castle-like gate house and a series of timber-framed structures erected in the fort's interior. Excavation uncovered two such structures measuring 6m by 3m and at least 5m by 4m respectively. Both originally consisted of timber-framed superstructures on low stone footings with windows holding paned glass. A fine external, cobbled pathway with a central drain circumvented the house platforms. Limited evidence of material culture included four sherds of everted-rim ware and two sherds of slip-ware. McNeill (2004, 193) suggests that the site functioned as the administrative centre of the barony of Cary, a hypothesis that sits very comfortably with the emerging picture of the structure and management of the Antrim estates following recent discoveries at other MacDonnell centres, including Dunluce, Ballycastle and Glenarm.

Randal, 1st earl of Antrim

The first decades of the seventeenth century saw Randal MacDonnell emerge as the dominant political figure in northeast Ulster and a significant economic player across the region. He had earned particular favour with James VI & I, who commented to Chichester in 1613 on MacDonnell's 'dutiful behaviour to the state and the example of his civil and orderly life endeavours very much of the reformation and civilizing of those rude parts ... where he dwells' (BL Add. MS 4794, fo. 233; Ohlmeyer 2004, 47). Randal, from the outset, was an astute political player and the bardic poet Ó Gnímh wrote a poem in praise of him and commented on how the MacDonnells had effectively become Irish (Mac Cionnaith 1938, 290–3). In 1617, the council book of Ayr recorded that he was admitted as a free burgess of the town (Ayr Burgh Archives, Council Books B6/11/4, fos 583v–586v), while in May 1618 he was granted the title of viscount of Dunluce (*CSPI*, 62, p. 199; *CPRCI James I*, pp 373, vii). Two years later, Randal was created the 1st earl of Antrim (*CPRCI James I*, pp 492, xviii). Over the following years, he consolidated his position and demonstrated increasing political confidence and business acumen. Much of his success, and income stream, were linked to a policy of leasing out his lands. This MacDonnell policy has been discussed in detail by Jane Ohlmeyer (1993) and many of the leases were listed by Hill (1873, 438–40). In the late 1610s and 1620s, Randal leased out significant acreage, often with mills, fisheries and woodland included in the deeds. Archibald Stewart was one of the first grantees and received 120 acres of land at Ballintoy and Ballylough as well as lands elsewhere. The MacNaughtons received sixty acres at Benvarden and a further sixty at Ballymagarry. At Drumtullagh, the Stewards were granted two hundred acres, while the McHenrys got lands at Dromore, Ballylease and Killtinny near the Bann outside Coleraine. James Hamilton leased 250 acres at Mullaghmore,

Clonghcarr, and also got the customs and pound at Ballymoney in 1625. The McHenrys were at Ballyreagh, the McDuffys leased Coulkenny, Ballybennaght and Clogher, while Mcffertry had 120 acres at Carnglassmore and Canglassbeg. Hugh Boyde's lands included Carncoggie, O'Cahan held 120 acres at Shanbally, and Brice Dunlop's leased lands included a watermill at Ballycastle.

Intrinsically linked to this was MacDonnell's interest in agricultural development and improvement. Always open to change, in 1622 the earl prohibited the use of ploughing using garrons tied by the tails and stated that all of his tenants should adopt the English fashion of ploughing (BL Add. MS 4756, fos 60v–71r; Treadwell 2006, 248). An indication of the extent of economic activity on his estates can be gleaned from the level of exports from Irish ports during the period 25 March 1621 to 25 March 1622 (Treadwell 2006, 393). During that time, the Antrim estates exported seventy-five hides, whereas 2,062 were exported from Carrickfergus and 568 from Carlingford. Five-hundred-and-forty oxen and cows were exported, compared to 454 from Carrickfergus and 773 from Dublin. Antrim seems to have a particularly successful horse trade, with 409 being exported, compared to fifty-eight from Dublin, twenty-five from Dundalk and 590 from Lecale and Clandeboy. Thirty-six barrels of beef were exported, compared to Limerick's thirty-three, with fifty-six barrels of oats and beans exported from Antrim, compared to Carrickfergus' 1,783. There were no documented exports of fish from the estates that year, but there must have been an extensive trade with Scotland.

Writing to the lord deputy in December 1625 in effect to seek further funds to improve his military capacity, he proclaimed his loyalty and stated that he had 'pikes and pieces for infantry, but no powder, lead or match', and that he had no colours and would not have his men 'go to the field like kernes' (*CSPI*, 241, p. 64). The earl's increasing independence was shown in 1627, when he put the crown bailiff in stocks and held court sessions with some of the proceedings in Irish. Concern was later raised that Antrim's son was being educated in France as a papist and that he should be returned to England and educated there (*CSPI*, 242, p. 81). None of these issues appears to have affected his economic activities. In July 1628, he was licenced to hold a fair at Ballycastle (*CPCR Charles I*, 1628, 326), and in 1629 his estates in the Route, the Glens and Rathlin were reconfirmed, excepting three parts of the Bann fishery, the castle of Olderfleet [Larne] and land in the possession of the bishop of Down and Connor. These lands were created into the manors of Dunluce, Ballycastle, Glenarm and Oldstone, alias Cloghinaghene Donaghie [Clough] (*CPCR Charles I*, 1629, 490). As a measure of his success, the earl of Clanricard noted that he 'hath good tenants and is very well paid his rents' (Ohlmeyer 1993, 25). This contrasts with Antrim's earlier statements from January 1627, when he wrote to Lord Falkland complaining about his tenants, who were mostly English, stating that they were threatening to leave his land uncultivated (*CSPI*, 244, p. 204). This incident must have represented only a slight hurdle, as his confidence was again asserted in October 1629, when he

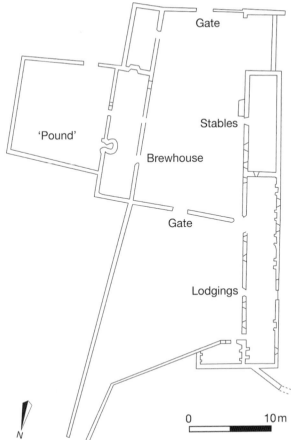

5.14 Plan of the outer range of buildings at Dunluce. This area included the castle lodgings, stables and a brew-house.

complained of his tenants having to travel to Carrickfergus for quarter sessions. The earl suggested holding two sessions at Oldstone [Clough], where his people would build a session house (*CSPI*, 249, p. 490).

Mainland buildings: Phase 5

As both the status and fortunes of the 1st earl grew, he continued encouraging investment and new building at Dunluce. In particular, a brew-house, probably operating on a commercial level, and a major new lodging block were constructed (fig. 5.14).

Brew-house

The brew-house range is located on the eastern side of the outer entrance yard (fig. 5.15). It has an overall length of 24.1m and a width of 6.2m. This would have been a two-storey masonry building, and appears to have had three discrete internal sections marked by variations in ground level. It is not known to what extent this represents the original arrangement of the building range, as twentieth-century conservation work has interfered with both the masonry and the ground levels. The southern end of the range appears to have been the domestic element, containing a fireplace centrally set in the rebuilt southern gable, 82cm wide and 95cm deep. The walls of this section are plastered, but the lower north end is not. Two windows were contained in the west wall. Five metres north of the southern gable, the south side of an angled embrasure survives, while a second angled window is present 1.7m north of the door, 1.2m above present ground surface. This 95cm-wide doorway was 7.9m north of the gable on the west wall. An opposing blocked-up doorway is present on the east wall and is 1.1m wide. This was originally brick-lined, suggesting that this range in its current form was contemporary with the lodgings block.

The lower or northern section of this range was industrial. It was entered from the upper courtyard through a 1.85m-wide entrance. There is a surviving window 2m above present ground level in the northeast end of the east wall, measuring over 1.7m wide internally. Of most interest is the keyhole-shaped masonry structure that projects into the centre of the building and extends eastwards through the side wall into the pound area to the rear. Set on a raised masonry platform, this has the appearance of a corn-drying kiln. It was originally a lower structure, however, and was built up to represent a kiln in the 1980s. Finally, the northern end of the range was well drained, with a large outlet visible in the northeast corner.

Excavation Trench 9

Excavations were undertaken in this area during June 2011. They were primarily aimed at examining the function of the keyhole-shaped structure and elucidating the nature of surviving archaeological remains. A trench measuring 6.2m by 3m was excavated across the full width of the building directly below the keyhole-shaped feature. While the trench itself was of a limited size and the deposits in the trench had been subject to considerable later interference, it was possible to discern two primary occupation phases. An earlier building had been constructed at this location as evidenced by the foundations of mortared walls (see fig. 5.16, nos 925/926) underlying both the eastern and the western side wall and a possible early flagged surface. Its morphology, composition, location and orientation suggest that this was built at the same time and in a similar manner to the stables block across the yard. This earlier wall was associated with a rough cobbled internal surface (906), made up of various stone sizes less than 28cm in diameter laid directly onto the subsoil (fig. 5.16). In its second phase, the building was converted and the side walls rebuilt. A mortared masonry plinth was built to accommodate the keyhole structure. It consisted of a two-course high flat platform (907) with an irregular flagged surface. A roughly circular post-hole or shallow pit (909) measured 58cm in width and 20cm

5.15 Photograph of the brew-house looking northwards. The large masonry feature in the foreground would originally have held a large boiling vat used in the brewing process.

Brewing

While the brewing of ale has taken place since ancient times, dedicated brew-houses only really became widespread in Britain and Ireland by the sixteenth century. Early brew-houses consisted of well-ventilated buildings with a pot surrounded by brick or stone with various other tubs and coolers (Pearson 2010, 4), with beer being the most popular beverage produced from the sixteenth century. Its consumption was far more widespread during the later medieval period than today, due in part to the scarcity of clean and dependable drinking water. The stages of brewing were straightforward and varied little. Barley was most commonly used and was initially cut, threshed, soaked and let dry while being turned. This produced malt, essentially an artificially germinated grain, which was dried on a kiln and then ground. Following this, the malt was transferred and mixed with water and soaked in a mash tun at a low temperature. This produced sweet liquid called 'wort', which was separated normally by draining through the base of the tun. The by-products were used as animal feed. Once the wort was put in large metal vessels or pots called a 'copper' or 'keeler', they were boiled with hops, and often other ingredients were added. After boiling, they were drained through a vessel with a perforated base, called the 'hop back', and the hot wort was cooled and yeast added for fermentation (Pearson 2010). The beer was drunk immediately or transferred to barrels for storage.

deep. This is probably associated with the two putlog holes in the eastern side wall. A second, larger and deeper, pit (920), 1.1m wide and 5cm deep, was cut 1.5m north of the post-hole. The function of this is unknown, but it was later used to bury a large quantity of roofing slate. A drain (905) was also inserted in this area in the late nineteenth or early twentieth century, while a pipe (913) was laid in the middle of the century. The original cobbled surface is self-draining to the north, while a two-sided angled drain is an integral part of this surface, running along the western side of the building.

Finds

The stratigraphy was heavily disturbed in this trench due to both the later insertion of the modern drains and the extent of refurbishment and later building collapse in the building. Consequently, few of the artefacts recovered were *in situ*. One bowl from a late eighteenth-century clay pipe was recovered from the upper disturbed soil, as was a small quantity of bone including teeth, that was probably carried into the trench during rubble clearance and site levelling. Nine sherds of eighteenth-century pottery were also found in these upper disturbed layers. Mixed in with the upper contexts were ten sherds of gravel-tempered North Devon ridge tile and two fragments of plain red tile. This form of tile is generally accepted to date from the mid- to late seventeenth century and is further evidence that this building was refurbished, or at least re-roofed after the first two decades of the century. The same ridge tiles were found in the manor house deposits, indicating a castle-wide programme of refurbishment. Additionally, sixteen corroded nails or nail heads were also found in the deposits, indicating the presence of wooden internal structures. Finally, part of a 15mm-wide metal band was found in the pit (920) and would originally have been the hoop of a small bucket or similar object with an approximate diameter of 20cm.

Function

Prior to excavation, the function of this building range was unclear. Architecturally, there was a strong suggestion that the southern end was domestic, with its large gable fireplace, windows and doorway. The northern end clearly had an industrial element, given the presence of the wide doorway, limited windows and internal kiln-like structure. A search of the sources coupled with the information from the site masons that the kiln was remodelled in recent years and had originally taken a different form (it was of the same height as the plinth), strongly suggest that this building was a brew-house, used for the production of ale or beer. A late medieval brew-house originally associated with Holywell Priory was excavated at Shoreditch, London, by the Museum of London archaeology section (Lewis 2010). A medieval malt and brew-house was also excavated at Castle Acre, a Cluniac priory in Norfolk (Wilcox 1980).

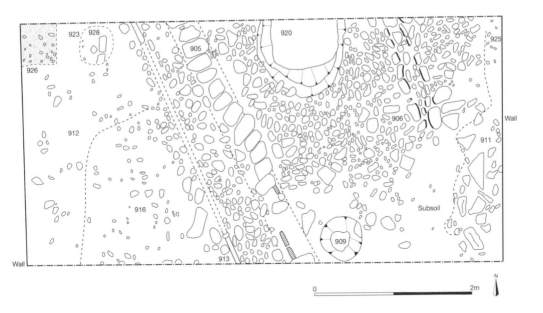

5.16 Excavation plan of Trench 9 in the brew-house. A series of drains was inserted into the cobbled surface to facilitate drainage from the brewing process.

5.17 Photograph of the southern internal section of the lodgings building. This building accommodated visitors to the castle and consisted of a series of individual guest rooms, each with its own window and fireplace.

Here, the range measured 23m by 13.7m and consisted of a combined malthouse and brew-house with a double-bottomed vat with two malting kilns. A number of these structures bear very close resemblance to the keyhole structure at Dunluce. The scale of the site in Norfolk suggested that this was a commercial brewing venture. Other brew-houses that have been investigated include one at medieval Lacock Abbey in Wilthshire, a sixteenth-century timber-framed malthouse at Church Farmhouse in Shropshire and an Elizabethan malthouse at Harvington Hall, Worcestershire (Price 2007). Elsewhere in Europe, a seventeenth-century brewery on Świętojańska Street in Gdańsk contained an identical arrangement of a keyhole-shaped structure set on a low plinth, but this was made of brick (CARARE 2012).

The keyhole structure in Trench 9 could be either the base of a malt kiln or the bottom support structure for a copper. If it was a kiln, then it is likely that the upper floor of this end of the building was used for drying, and the post-hole and pit could have provided columnar support for an upper floor. This could have been used as a maltings for drying and a storage area. The two surviving putlog holes in the east wall would also have supported some form of wooden structure. A similar arrangement at Lacock supported a long mash tun. Ultimately, more extensive excavation is required, both within and outside the building, in order to develop more clarity relating to its original layout and function.

While this complex is located within the outer ranges of the castle complex, it is also possible to identify others involved in brewing at the town. William Boyd, a merchant from Dunluce, produced a will in 1624 (Hill 1873, 389–93). He left to his wife, Catherine Mcgdmartine (*sic*), 'his houses and gardens in the town of Dunluce', while his son Adam received land, fishing rights and his 'furnished feather bed, brewing kettle and aquavitae pot'. The latter two items are of special interest and must surely have been linked to brew-house operations. Boyd was a man of some substance, and left other lands, money and goods to various individuals and gave a harp to Walter Kennedy, his son-in-law. Robert Thomson was left a black cloak and thirty barrels of oats, while David Thomson received his rapier and all the 'books of his office'. Other items included cloaks, swords, horses, saddler, silver plate and goblets.

Lodgings

The long lodgings range is the most architecturally expressive building in the mainland complex (fig. 5.17). It was clearly built at a later date than the stables as different masonry styles are utilized in the two buildings. The lodgings also use red brick, which is dated to the later phases of castle rebuilding. Another key indicator of a later date is that the north gable of the lodgings has a ground-floor and first-floor window. It is highly unlikely that a stable would have had windows opening into a lodgings block, bringing with it all the sights, smells and sounds associated with horses, and these would have been blocked up when the lodgings were built. It seems that this range dates to the 1620s when Randal redeveloped this outer area to reflect

5.18 Photograph of external face of northern end of the lodgings building, showing the beam-hole supports for a balcony above the ground-floor window. This would have allowed visitors view the gardens and was accessed through a first-floor doorway in the northern gable.

his increased economic standing. The overall range measures 36m in length and 5.8m in width internally. The range would originally have been divided into two by a screened passage, however. The southern end of the range was entered from the upper outer courtyard through a door in the west side of the high cross-wall and into a first-range doorway in the east wall, 9m north of the gable. The layout consists of a series of ground- and first-floor rooms containing a fireplace along the west wall and lit by one or two windows on either side wall. Most of the east wall has collapsed, with a portion of its southeast end lying on the ground outside the range. Architectural features such as windows and a door can still be made out in the collapse. Two angles from a window are visible at the extreme southern end of the east wall. First-floor joist-holes are apparent 2.6m above the present ground surface on the inner face of both side walls. Four ground-floor formerly linteled fireplaces survive on the west wall of this southern section. They average 1.21m wide internally, are 70cm deep and have projecting masonry sides. Two further first-floor fireplaces survive above at first floor level, offset to the north from the lower examples. Both are lined with red brick. There is a window c.70cm north of each fireplace, c.70cm above present ground level. These were originally linteled, had splayed sides and measured 1.3m wide internally and *c*.1.6m high. Traces of three narrower first-floor windows are visible. This symmetrical arrangement changes after the third ground-floor fireplace, where no first-floor fireplace is visible but two windows are present. The west wall is collapsed at this point and the fireplaces and windows are blocked up. The northern section of this overall range has an internal measurement of 21.5m, before meeting what would formerly have been a screens passage.

The passage is marked by opposing doorways set in the east and west side walls, both measuring 1.8m wide internally. The eastern door provided entry from the outer yard, while the western door facilitated access into the formal garden areas immediately to the west. A single ground-floor fireplace is visible internally on the west wall, measuring 1.25m internally, with projecting masonry sides. A second, 1.2m-wide, projecting fireplace survives at the end of the north wall. A number of ground-floor windows are also present. The north angle of a blocked-up example is visible 1.7m to the north of the fireplace on the west wall, while a second window, set 1.2m above the ground and measuring 1.37m wide and 1.14m high, is also present on this wall section. Two further windows are present on the east wall. Only the north angle of the southerly example survives, while the second is 1.3m wide internally and was positioned next to a 1.2m-wide doorway that led into the courtyard to the east. One of the most interesting features of this north range is an external balcony that was accessed through a doorway in the centre of the north gable at first-floor level. A series of eleven joist-holes, set 3.2m above present ground level, supported this structure, which would have wrapped around the northwest corner of the building range, providing views over the sea and the garden complex to the west (fig. 5.18). An additional window was present to the east of this doorway.

The lodgings building has an adjoining northeast range (fig. 5.19). This irregular-shaped building, 8.5m long and 4.16m wide internally, runs along the northern cliff edge and is contemporary with the construction of the main north–south range. This was divided into two apartments and was entered through two separate doorways in its southern wall. The eastern example is now partly blocked up, but would have had sandstone surrounds. The doorways average 1.15m in width. Two ground-floor fireplaces are present. A 1.38m-wide fireplace with projecting masonry sides was placed in the west gable, while a second, narrower example, 1.07m wide, was set in the east gable and has red brick in its construction. The narrowness of this example is reflective of the narrow gable that was restricted in terms of its size due to the fact that the building was constructed on a small bedrock outcrop. The northern wall contains one very wide window, 3.47m, at ground-floor level. This appears exceptionally wide for a window of this date, albeit that it was extensively rebuilt in the twentieth century. Old photographs and paintings do, however, suggest that this window originally had mullions, which might account for its width. Two windows are also visible at first-floor level on the north wall. The roof would have been pitched and the roofline can be traced on the west gable. This section of the

5.19 Laser scan of northern lodgings building. This survey method produces a highly detailed image of the site that can be used for both recording and future conservation purposes (image reproduced courtesy of James Patience, NIEA).

range strongly resembles the late sixteenth-century lodgings range at Dunottar Castle in Scotland, where each lodgings room had its own door, fireplace and window (Douglas Simpson 1976).

Finally, at the same time as the lodgings building was erected, the so-called funnel walls were also built. These are the two walls that run along the cliff edge at the northwest from the lodgings to the bridge and along the eastern cliff from the brew-house. The northwest wall stands to a maximum height of 3.6m and both enclose a courtyard area that the geophysical survey indicates was originally cobbled. This is probably the 'new pavement in the inner court next the drawbridge and outer gate of Dunluce Castle' referred to in the depositions taken in 1653 relating to the events during October of the 1641 revolt (TCD dep. 838024r018, fos 24r–26v). The reference to a 'new pavement' adds support to the hypothesis that the castle was refurbished in the 1620s, when the lodgings were built, and again in the late 1630s, when new roofs were added to various buildings, as evidenced by the recovery of the North Devon ridge tiles from a number of trenches. The cross-wall, between the brew-house and the lodgings, was probably also constructed during the refurbishment phase, as it is not keyed into the northwest corner of the building. It stands to a maximum height of 3.48m, is 70cm thick and has a length of 22.2m, including the area of the central breach and western doorway. Only one side of the central door or gate survives, and this is marked by a plastered rebate and sandstone footings on the western side of the 3.2m gap. The wall would have been rendered on both faces and has a drain outlet at the base of the north face of its east end.

The extreme north range at the cliff's edge in the inner court was also added at this time (fig. 5.20). This was entered through a rectangular porch at the northeastern corner of the yard and led to a two-storey building on the western side of the headland. Clearly later than the other structures in this area, it was built over and against the standing inner court enclosure wall. It is also of a different masonry construction type than the small sixteenth-century building that stood at the eastern end of this range. The northern side wall and eastern gable of this building are now gone, but the western gable stands largely intact. A large 2.3m-wide fireplace was built at ground-floor level in the gable, while a second, smaller, fireplace was present at first-floor level. The chimney is topped with red brick and brick was also used in the flue, providing a further indicator of a construction date in the seventeenth century. A small recess was located immediately south of the fireplace, 1.2m wide and 1.8m deep, leading to two windows at ground- and first-floor level respectively. Only the northern side angle survives of the upper window. Two beam-holes are visible above the lower window, with red brick inclusions. The room would have been plastered internally. Two further first-floor windows were contained in the south wall, while one ground-floor window partially survives 1.12m above ground level.

Castle gardens

The opening decades of the seventeenth century saw an increase in the development of pleasure gardens associated with high-status residences and individuals of power and authority. They were no longer utilitarian spaces for the production of food and herbs, becoming spaces of retreat specifically designed for pleasure, recreation and the appreciation of plants. In ideas adopted from Renaissance Europe, gardens developed with designs incorporating symmetry, architectural features and statues (Reeves-Smyth 1999, 103). At Dunluce, a garden complex, including a possible bowling green, was developed behind walls immediately west of the castle (fig. 5.21). This was very much a private space designed for the use of the earl and his guests

5.20 Photograph of northern cliff-side range.

5.21 Aerial photograph of the landscape setting of Dunluce Castle. The main 'town field' is immediately west of the castle, while the church and associated graveyard are in the bottom centre of the image (image reproduced courtesy of the NIEA).

exclusively. Access was gained through the screened passage in the lodgings building, with no apparent access from the town. There were three distinct components to the garden area, including a bowling green, a terrace and a set of raised beds. Bowling was a popular medieval pastime, but developed more formally in the sixteenth century, with greens becoming widespread by the seventeenth century. The interpretation of this area as a green derives from two sources: it is labelled as such on the early Ordnance Survey maps; and most of the early writers refer to it as such. While the area, measuring 75m east–west by 25m north–south, has long since lost its manicured appearance due to extensive grazing, it is generally flat, and the presence of a green would be expected in close proximity to such a prestigious residence as Dunluce.

The section of the garden north of the green is dominated by a central raised terrace measuring *c.*20m by *c.*12m and raised above ground level to a height averaging 60cm. There is no evidence of stone facing or any other stone. Originally accessed from a now blocked-up doorway in the west wall of the lodgings, it would have been the dominant feature in the gardens.

Trench 6

The platform was targeted for excavation in an attempt to elucidate its morphology and original character. Two test pits were excavated, measuring 2m by 1m and 1m by 1m respectively. The larger trench was positioned in the centre of the platform in line with the opening into the lodgings range, in the hope of clarifying the form of garden architecture at this point. The excavation showed that riddled soil had been mounded to create the raised area. A sherd of North Devon gravel tempered ridge tile found in the soil suggests that this feature was laid in the mid-seventeenth century. The smaller trench was excavated at the edge of this platform to define its border. This demonstrated that the platform had a sod-faced bank. The section showed that successive layers of earth had been laid down to create it. There was no indication that any stone architectural fragments survived. A single sherd of late medieval green glazed ware was found in this smaller test trench, having been carried in with the garden soil.

The final section of the garden consists of a series of raised beds in the northernmost area, running along the cliff edge. These beds are of varying shapes and sizes, having a maximum length of 7m. Most are roughly rectangular, but the easternmost examples are angled to reflect the shape of the headland at this point. Traditionally, these would be interpreted as flower beds, but it is difficult to know what type of flowers could have been successfully planted here in such an exposed location. There is a 3.5m-tall wall projecting northwestwards from the central part of the northern gable that runs for *c.*9m along the cliff edge before returning west along the southern side of the beds. It is unclear whether this wall enclosed the whole area. If it did, then this would have added significantly more shelter in this area. A programme of environmental sampling is required to gain a better understanding of this whole area.

Death of the earl

By the early 1630s, Randal had developed both a fine residence and an initially prosperous town at Dunluce. His estates across Antrim were doing reasonably well, even taking account of the inevitable disputes and squabbles that marked the management of such an estate and the political machinations of the day. There were signs of growing problems, however. In siting a town at Dunluce, Randal had made a number of significant mistakes. These would have a serious impact of the town's development and will be dealt with in the following chapter. On 10 December 1636, Randal MacDonnell, 1st earl of Antrim, died at Dunluce and was buried at Bonamargy. His elder son, also Randal, inherited Dunluce barony and Dunluce Castle with all its furniture and chattels, but was to prove a different and less capable man than his father.

CHAPTER 6

Dunluce town, 1608–41

One of Randal MacDonnell's most significant undertakings was the construction of a small town surrounding the castle in the opening decades of the seventeenth century. The use of the term 'town' to describe the settlement may be controversial, with some commentators arguing that it should instead be viewed as a village. Providing a definition of a town is complex and is made more difficult in this instance as this was a seventeenth-century settlement, one that we cannot usefully compare with contemporary aspects of an urban site. When we examine the usual attributes of a town, Dunluce does indeed have many of them. It was a formally designed and planned settlement containing administrative buildings such as the castle, a counting house and a probable courthouse or jail. Additionally, it had a number of service buildings including a mill, a smithy, a brew-house and a church for religious service. There was economic diversity within the settlement and it was not reliant solely on agrarian activity. It was a central place in the landscape, accommodating a market and storage buildings, and it was regarded as the administrative centre of the Antrim estates. Finally, the full range of social forms and relationships were present, as exemplified by social hierarchies ranging from the earl to the families of agricultural labourers living in the vicinity.

Population

The historical sources tell us little about the development of the site and the people who lived there. In 1611, the report on the work undertaken by servitors in the counties of Down, Antrim and Monaghan reported that the town of Dunluce consisted 'of many tenements, after the fashion of the Pale, peopled for the most part with Scotsmen', and that Randal had built 'a good house of stone with many lodgings and other rooms' (PRONI T811/3, fo. 13). This shows that construction of the town was well underway at this time and that many houses had been built, in a similar manner to those in Dublin and the surrounding area. Data from the survey suggests that there was at least forty houses in the settlement during the 1620s, indicating a minimum population of 240 individuals. We know little about the occupants and can identify only a handful of them before 1641. Five-hundred-and-twenty-one men were listed on the c.1630 muster roll for Dunluce barony (PRONI D/1759/3C/3). These were the earl of Antrim's adult male tenants of English and Lowland Scots extraction capable of bearing arms in the event of an Irish insurrection. It is not possible to

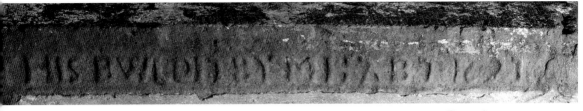

6.1 Photograph of the inscribed stone, formerly set above the doorway of Dunluce House. This reads 'THIS BWLDIT BY MH^BT 1623'.

6.2 Aerial photograph of the area surrounding the castle, showing earthworks relating to the former town.

discern who among these lived at Dunluce, but a sandstone lintel recovered from the doorway above Dunluce House had the following inscription 'THIS BWLDIT BY MH^BT 1623' (fig. 6.1). There is only one individual on the muster rolls bearing the initials 'MH' and that is Michael Henderson. 'BT' was probably his wife, so was not listed. Other clues identifying individuals include the grave memorial by the church erected to his children in March 1630 by Walter Kid, 'merchant of Dunluce' and burgess of Irvine. We also have the previously mentioned will of William Boyd from the town dated 1624.

Position

The town was developed in the immediate environs of the castle (fig. 6.2). Somewhat surprisingly, it was not established in the sheltered valley surrounding the church, but was instead built on the north-facing slopes outside the castle walls. This was an

6.3 The cave beneath the castle from the sea. Boats can only be brought into the cave in the calmest of conditions. The absence of a safe landing place at the castle was a major impediment to its development in later periods.

unusual choice from a number of perspectives. There would have been little shelter afforded to the houses, as this area is fully exposed to both northerly and westerly winds. During the winter months, this section of the Ulster coastline is battered by the elements, and the residents of the town must have felt the weather keenly. One of the most surprising elements of the location is the absence of a sheltered harbour or landing place. In perfect conditions, small, rowed vessels less than 6m in length could enter the cave beneath the castle, but these conditions are rarely witnessed here (fig. 6.3). There is no other safe place to draw a vessel ashore beneath the castle, with Portrush and Portballintrae offering the nearest relatively safe harbours. The absence of a readily accessible port would have severely limited the town's ability to grow, and was a major oversight. This was a period of strong economic growth, often centred on large bulk cargoes being transported in ships of ever-increasing size. The inability of Randal MacDonnell to feed directly into this new economic sphere would prove to be a costly mistake, preventing him from competing directly with the emerging river port town of Coleraine, less than 10km away. In siting the town where he did, Randal was essentially displaying his initial inability to break with the medieval mindset. Prior to the seventeenth century, settlement clusters were focused on castles throughout this region, but the economic structures at the time did not require formalized mercantile settlements. Trade and exchange was controlled by the lord and were largely limited to agrarian activities focused on his own and neighbouring estates. The increasingly globalized markets of the seventeenth century required far greater degrees of specialization and facilities to manage and handle the growing levels of trade. Randal may have demonstrated a keen awareness of emerging

6.4 Results of a resistivity survey of the large field to the west of the castle. The outlines of a series of houses, shown as a black rectangles, can clearly be seen either side of a north–south running street (image reproduced courtesy of Ronan McHugh, CAF).

architectural norms, but he seems to have had a limited understanding of the needs of the new economic order. His choice of position for the town meant that it was almost doomed to failure before it ever had an opportunity to expand.

Physically, the new town was bordered by the cliffs to the north and Gallows Hill to the south and parts of the east. The deep gorge through which the stream flows formed the western boundary. There does not appear to have been defences around the town, although the topography constituted a form of defence, while the castle itself would have provided adequate shelter for the earl, whatever about the remaining residents. The absence of a town wall or other form of artificial defences is not overly surprising. New plantation settlements like Coleraine engaged in extensive protective measures, including large banks, walls and palisades, to defend themselves against the native Irish. MacDonnell had few such concerns, with his family having been the dominant grouping in the area for the previous sixty years. He did not see the need for such defences and enjoyed a sense of security and entitlement unknown to the new English and Scottish arrivals west of the Bann.

Layout

Our evidence for the town's layout comes from a number of sources. A programme of topographic survey was undertaken across the area using both dGPS and airborne high-resolution LiDAR survey. Extensive areas were also subjected to terrestrial geophysical survey, including resistivity and ground-penetrating radar (GPR) (fig. 6.4). A series of contemporary and historic aerial photographs were made available to the project, which greatly aided the interpretation of the remote sensing data. Finally, excavation across the site has provided detailed insights into selected areas, with which we can extrapolate broader patterning and site development. The town appears to have been laid out in a single phase. This is evidenced by the uniformity of the plan and the single primary construction phase for the houses and associated streets found during the excavations. While the town was focused on the castle gate, its central place was a triangular area, measuring 30m by 15m maximum, outside the gate leading upslope to the present farmhouse (fig. 6.5). This surface was cobbled, with a series of drains running alongside the adjacent houses. Each drain consisted of lines of opposing inwardly angled flat stones creating a series of shallow downslope gullies. The surface was slightly convex and an element of patterning can be seen in the cobbling, marked in places by a series of stones set in small arcs within the surface. This may not have been a deliberate attempt at patterning and may instead represent the work and style of a particular mason, but is noteworthy nonetheless. Such a central place is a key feature of many medieval and later towns and continued to be a component of small Ulster towns into the eighteenth and nineteenth centuries, when such areas are known as 'diamonds'. These served as gathering places and locations where markets were held. The location of the walled enclosure, immediately to the east of the outer mainland castle yard, is also important in this context. Commonly referred to as the 'pound', this served as a compound where animals could be kept, impounded or temporarily held. Pounds were often places where a lord would keep a tenant's cattle or sheep until a fine or tax was paid. It is easy to appreciate the importance of such a place on a busy market day. The adjacent well would have facilitated easy public access to freshwater.

At the southern end of the triangle, a road passed on an east–west orientation. This would also have been a cobbled surface and was the main thoroughfare through the town. Continuing eastwards, a smaller street or laneway joined the main street halfway down the slope and veered southwards towards the well opposite the church.

6.5 Reconstruction painting of the town c.1625. A number of different styles of houses would have been present along the cobbled streets of the town, including masonry and timber-framed structures. Further buildings of a lesser quality build are also likely to have been present on the margins of the settlement. Each house had its own garden plot. A range of other buildings, including mills, a courthouse and a blacksmith's workshop, were also present (image reproduced courtesy of Philip Armstrong).

The main road led towards the base of Gallows Hill before rounding its eastern extremity and continuing eastwards towards Bushmills, running roughly parallel to the current coastal road. Back at the junction with the triangle, the main road continued westwards before joining a junction where the road swung sharply to the south. Its northern return continued northwards and constituted a second main street in the settlement, lined with merchants' houses as well as a blacksmith's workshop at the northeast corner of the junction. At the base of the merchant's road, the cobbled surface continued to just before the cliff edge before it turned eastwards and ran along the outside southern wall of the formal garden area and then meeting the castle entrance. A smaller path led from the base of the road westwards to the stream, where there is likely to have been a mill. This merchants' street consisted of a convex cobbled surface with a main drain on either side of the road (fig. 6.6). It would have been about 11m wide and contained linear stone settings that delineated

6.6 Photograph of the street surface and associated house in Trench 5. The house was occupied in the early seventeenth century by a Scottish merchant. Its walls survive to over a metre in height. Such preservation is not common in the Irish landscape, but is present here due to the protection successive earls of Antrim have afforded these fields.

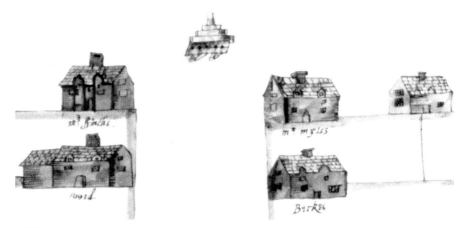

6.7 Detail of masonry houses from Raven's early seventeenth-century plan of the Drapers' settlement at Moneymore. The central market cross and stocks can be seen in the upper part of the image.

property boundaries, entrances and footpaths. A series of upright stones also acted as jostle stones to prevent carts and horses from bumping against the upstanding architecture. This road continued southwards past the church, with side returns over the back of Gallows Hill towards Bushmills and along the line of the current

Ballymagarry road. These would have been the primary terrestrial routeways at the time, as the current coastal road was developed in the nineteenth century.

Architecture

A variety of building forms were present within the town. From a combination of intensive topographic and geophysical survey, coupled with seventeenth-century illustrative sources, we can hypothesize that there were at least three primary house types within the town, including masonry and timber-framed buildings, as well as what are typically referred to as 'Irish-type' houses. Our evidence for the masonry houses is drawn primarily from Thomas Raven's contemporary plans of official plantation settlements west of the Bann and in north Down. The most common type consists of stone-built structures with dormer windows built from the roof line (fig. 6.7). These were double-gabled with chimneys commonly built into both gables. The houses had a centrally placed door with a second opposing doorway in the rear façade wall. A number of glazed windows were present either side of the doorways and in the dormer features. Slate was the most common roofing material. Timber-framed buildings were also extensively illustrated on these maps and may have had either a masonry base or were built using large basal sill beams. They were of a similar size to the masonry houses and had a similar internal arrangement. The final type was traditionally referred to as 'Irish'. Raven invariably illustrated a number of houses of varying quality and build on the periphery of the plantation settlements (fig. 6.8). These appear to be houses built predominantly using daub, with some stone examples, each with rounded corners, a central hearth, few windows and a single door. Thatch is the most commonly shown roofing material.

This tradition of illustrating the residences of the Irish as being of an inferior quality is a recurring theme and one that also featured in contemporary literature. Fynes Moryson, writing in the early seventeenth century, recorded that the Irish 'build no houses but like nomads living in cabins, remove from one place to another with their cows' (Kew 1998, 38) and referred to their lords as living in 'a poor house of clay, or … a cabin made of the boughs of trees and covered with earth'. Spenser, in his *View of the state of Ireland*, first published in 1633 but completed before 1598, made a number of very disparaging remarks about these houses. In this work, Eudox commented that an Irishman's house is more like a pigsty than a house and that the occupants lie and live together 'with his beast in [the same] one house, in one room, in one bed, that is clean straw, or rather a foul dunghill' (Hadfield and Maley 1997, 84). A number of researchers have taken these descriptions as representing the norm. Glasscock (1993, 229) described the dwellings of the Gaelic Irish as being 'insubstantial dwellings with roofs of branches, sods and thatch', while Nicholls (1993, 403) described them as 'flimsy and insubstantial' due to the fact that these

6.8 Detail of 'Irish-style' houses from Raven's early seventeenth-century plan of the Drapers' settlement at Moneymore.

people were mobile and continually on the move. These buildings are commonly referred to as 'creats' and have been defined as round one-roomed wattle-built structures (O'Conor 2002, 197). Excavations at Glenmakeeran (Site 1) in 1982 uncovered a single-room sub-rectangular house with opposing entrances and an annex with external measurements of 10.2m by 5.2m, orientated on a northwest/southeast axis (Williams and Robinson 1983, 30). A probable central hearth was uncovered and the site was dated broadly to the later medieval period on the basis of six sherds of everted-rim ware recovered in the main chamber. During the excavation, it was noted that the sod walls of the house were most likely used in tandem with cruck trusses, given their insubstantial form. Three similar houses were excavated in 1952 at Goodland and the largest of these was similar in many respects to the Glenmakeeran site (Case et al. 1969; Horning 2004). This consisted of a single-roomed sub-rectangular site with a downslope annex, opposing entrances and clay and sod walls with both everted-rim ware and glazed seventeenth-century pottery recovered. Horning (2001, 385) identified a sub-rectangular Gaelic dwelling at the Mercers' plantation at Movanagher on the banks of the Bann, measuring 4m by 7.5m with a central hearth. No such sites have yet been identified at Dunluce, but it is likely that they were present and future excavation work should identify their remains.

Masonry buildings

To date, a number of large houses have been identified through excavation and survey in the town. Before we consider the results of the excavation, the farmhouse known

6.9 Photograph of the front of Dunluce House. This farmhouse was rebuilt in the eighteenth century using the remains of an earlier building.

as Dunluce House requires discussion (fig. 6.9). While it currently has the appearance of a typical nineteenth-century Ulster farmhouse, it has undergone a number of refurbishment and rebuilding phases and originally dates to the early seventeenth century. During the 1950s, large windows were inserted and it was pebble dashed. Its general form, dimensions and surviving features including an original basement and the previously mentioned date-stone all point to its earlier origins. Tradition also labels the house as a courthouse. The 1830s OS memoirs record that 'Widow Moore's house opposite the castle gate stands on the site of the old jail. The ruins of the lock-up dungeon of that jail were razed at the erection of the above dwelling house some years back' (Day and McWilliams 1992, 115). The current house stands on the footprint of the earlier structure, and it appears that at least part of the present masonry is early. A further five structures were identified in the town-area trenches.

Trench 5

Trench 5 was located in the lower northwest quadrant of the large town field and was excavated in 2009. It consisted of a north–south orientated trench measuring 18 by 12m with a 6m by 8m extension to the east (fig. 6.10). The trench was positioned over what appeared topographically to be the basal foundations of a large rectangular building. This was clarified during the resistivity survey, which showed the

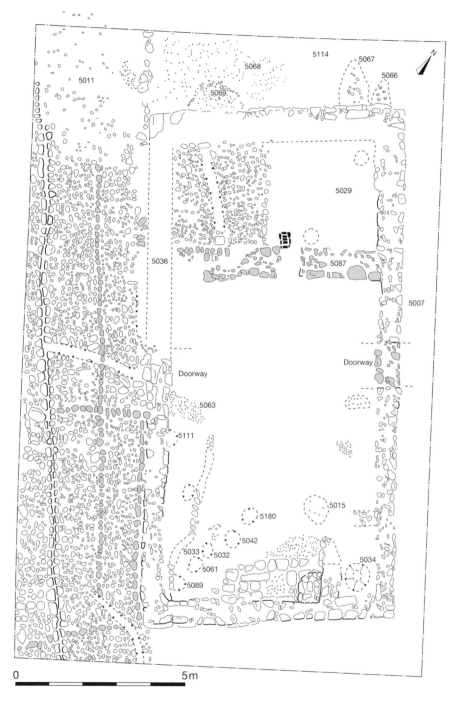

6.10 Plan of Trench 5. The early seventeenth-century building uncovered in this trench was subdivided late in the 1620s to accommodate animals.

rectangular outline of a structure as an outline of high resistance. Subsequent excavation exposed the well-preserved foundations of a house and revealed a clear sequence of events associated with cultural activity in this area. The archaeology was exceptionally well preserved, primarily due to the fact that no ploughing had ever taken place here in the recent past. Throughout the later eighteenth and nineteenth century, the earl's agents had been instructed to protect the field and to prevent removal of any building stone. As a consequence, the footprint of the town survives largely intact, with buried archaeology encountered within the sod layer and walls and features protruding through the grass. While many structures were completed by 1611, the town would have undergone continual refurbishment and building episodes over the following decades. The building exposed in Trench 5 was no different. Its excavation provided valuable information relating to its structure, layout and role within the town.

The building fronted onto a well-constructed cobbled street surface (fig. 6.11), laid down at the time the house was constructed. This initial phase of construction is evident in each of the town-area trenches excavated across the site and is indicative of a major building programme undertaken by the earl in the period 1608–11. Excavations clearly demonstrated that the street was well planned and executed. Only a portion of the eastern side of the road was exposed, but topographic survey, coupled with geophysical investigation, suggest that this was *c.*11m wide. It ran from the present road northwards towards the cliff edge before turning to the castle. Drainage was a significant consideration, given the wet climate of this region, and the street would have had two side gullies, with a slightly raised centre to aid run-off. A section of the eastern gully was exposed running northwards roughly parallel to the house. This consisted of pairs of large flat stones laid inwards to create a shallow and narrow channel. Two further shallow earth-cut drains were found at the southwest corner of the house and at the entrance on the west wall. Both were designed to carry water and other materials away from the house. Also set into the cobbled street surface were a number of lines of stones of equal size and of a slightly different hue to the main street surface. These marked the initial property boundary of the house to the south and to the southern side of the doorway. A third line ran 1m west from the west wall of the house and seems to have marked a footpath. The cobbles inside this linear feature were slightly smaller than those in the main street surface. These cobbled surfaces are reflective of the new focus of town design and would have been unheard of in previous centuries. They are indicative of a settlement that was increasingly interested in order and the imposition of civility through the separation of the pedestrian merchant's ability to easily access his house from the hustle and bustle of street traffic. A separate arrangement of stones in the street appears to have been deliberately set to act as jostle-stones, to ensure that horses and carts veered away from the house. Much of the northern area of the street was very disturbed due to quarrying. A linear feature consisting of medium-sized chalk stones partially

6.11 Photograph of excavations underway in Trench 5.

6.12 Photograph of the hearth in Trench 5. This would have been the focus of domestic activity in this house (image reproduced courtesy of the NIEA).

survived running from the northwest corner of the house to the edge of the baulk. This would have been a property boundary and illustrates the use of different and alternatively coloured stone to mark out features within the urban setting. Only the basal course survives of this feature, which may have represented the outer face of a narrow wall. Another possibility is that the earl's town designer laid out the plan for the whole site using this type of stone and that this feature represents a survival from the early design stage.

One of the first things the builders did was to create a level platform on which to build the house. This is a feature of a large number of house platforms across the site, where terracing is clearly evident in the topography. Once completed, the house would have fronted onto the street and had an external length of 16.7m and a width of 8.2m. Internally, the site measured approximately 13m by 6m. It would have been at least 1.5 storeys high, probably built with dormer windows similar to the examples shown on Raven's maps. Evidence for this came from a careful analysis of the building collapse, where the outline of the original south gable could be traced lying horizontal on the ground. This had either collapsed or was deliberately destroyed by the end of the 1660s, as no artefactual material later than that date was found underlying it. The original height of the pitched gable was over 6m. Slates recovered from the site clearly showed the form of roof that was present. No evidence of cruck construction was noted on the surviving walls. At ground-floor level, the house was entered through a central door on its western façade and the visitor would have had to take one step down into the building onto a paved threshold. The lower level of the house interior compared to that of the street level would have made drainage more difficult. It suggests that the road was laid initially and property boundaries were then marked out. When it came to the actual erection of the houses, however, terracing was required and the internal ground level was lowered. A small metalled area (5063) survived immediately inside the door, creating a hard surface. Further metalled areas were evident in front of the hearth and in two other patches, but most of the floor surface would have consisted of a beaten clay floor. A second, opposing, 1.1m-wide doorway was present in the east wall, but this was blocked up during a later phase of internal redesign. The building was of masonry construction. Its walls averaged 80cm in width and were mortared and plastered internally, although no decorative plasterwork from any ceiling element was recovered. A number of very large stones acted as foundations at the corners of the building. It was not possible to calculate the number of original windows present, but numerous shards of a thin green glass testified to the former existence of glazing. A particular concentration of glass and associated lead cames was found at the base of the external northeast section of wall, just north of the doorway, indicating that the building had rear, as well as front, windows. The glass was mostly triangular and is evidence that the original windows did not have large panes, but rather consisted of diamond-leaded lights.

A large fireplace was uncovered against the south gable, consisting of a 2.5m-wide flagged hearth with projecting masonry sides (fig. 6.12). Dense charcoal and burnt clay in the centre of the feature identified the precise location of the hearth. An arc of stones was built into the eastern side of the fireplace, suggesting that this was used as some form of oven or warm holding area during the process of food production. A further series of shallow pits, arcing internally to the west of the fireplace, contained coal and charcoal deposits, indicating that this was a working and storage area, probably also associated with the preparation of food and the maintenance of the fire. This interpretation was supported by a shallow internal drain that snaked through the area, facilitating water run-off. On the far side of the hearth, a small closet was set into the southeast corner of the house. Measuring 2m by 1m, it contained an indoor dry privy consisting of an earth-cut 1m-deep pit, probably originally lined with straw. No trace of a wooden superstructure for this feature was found, but some form of seat would have been present. Filled with highly organic soil, this feature would have been regularly cleared out by hand. There was no plumbing associated with the feature and no piping. The remnants of a masonry feature projecting from the inside of the east wall constituted the remains of the stone base for a wooden partition that would have enclosed this closet. Such close proximity between the hearth and the toilet would have led to an interesting mixture of smells, and indeed noises. While the occupants were clearly aware of new developments in polite society associated with privacy and personal hygiene, they, like the settlement as a whole, retained elements of a medieval mindset. The absence of any piping or draining mechanism and the location of the toilet near to food preparation indicate that the settlers still had much to learn about Renaissance society.

No further structural features were identified that belonged to the first phase of the occupation of the house. Sometime after the first build of the house it was subdivided with the building of a cross-wall (5087) creating a separate room at the northern end of the house, measuring *c*.3m by 7m. Clearly later than the primary construction horizon, it was built above the basal levels of the original side walls. Internally, it was cobbled on its western side, laid down with a central drain that exited through a small arched opening in the north gable. While this appears too small to accommodate cattle, it may have been used for pigs and was very clearly a byre of sorts. Heavy burning on the east side indicates that some form of industrial activity had taken place in this area. A small feature consisting of a series of red bricks laid in a small rectangle, which provided a base for a door, was found immediately inside the doorway to this end of the house. The doorway in the eastern side wall was also blocked up during this rebuild. The masonry used to block up this opening collapsed in a single intact block during the destruction of the house and was clearly identifiable during excavation. Artefactual evidence suggests that this destruction took place before the 1650s. If this was the case, then the insertion of the byre was significant and provides important insights into the economic development of the

6.13 Photograph of the 1547 coin recovered from Trench 5. This coin was minted in Vilna and is a reminder of the migration of Scottish merchants to northern Europe at that time. The coin was probably worn as a pendant by a descendant of one of those earlier merchants (image reproduced courtesy of Tom Carey).

6.14 One of the tiles recovered from Trench 5. This would have been made in the Netherlands and is an indicator of the high quality of the interiors of these houses (image reproduced courtesy of Tony Corey).

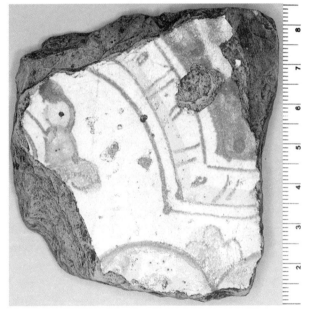

town. It points to a change in fortunes for the occupants of the house and is indicative of a reversion to subsistence agriculture, as discussed below (pp 146–8).

It is important to consider who this house was built for. Its size, construction and location are all strongly suggestive of an occupant with some standing within the town. Given that the settlement was first established as an entrepreneurial venture designed to attract Scottish settlers, it is hard to escape the conclusion that this was a house occupied by a Scottish merchant. Further evidence supports this theory. One coin minted in Lithuania in 1547 was found in the house and was worn as a pendant, as evidenced by a hole pierced through it (fig. 6.13). While the discovery of such a coin is initially very surprising in the Ulster landscape, its presence is easily explained when one remembers that there was extensive Scottish mercantile migration to northern Europe in the middle of the sixteenth century. It is easy to imagine that the coin was kept as a family memento of a relative participating in an earlier enterprise. Three Scottish James I coins dating to 1614 were recovered from primary contexts in the southwest corner of the house. A variety of ceramics were also recovered. Their significance in the context of the material culture of the house is dampened by the fact that the house was used as a drinking and eating booth during the later eighteenth-century Dunluce fair. The vast majority of the ceramic assemblage recovered during the excavations came from this later period. It was possible to identify the presence of a small number of English wares in the primary contexts, as well as a handful of local coarse wares that had been used for cooking. The adaption of these Ulster medieval coarse wares by the settlers as the predominant domestic wares is a feature of other houses across the town. It is reflective of cultural interaction between settler and Gael and the emergence of structures that facilitated economic and social engagement between them, as well as the material social renegotiation the planters underwent. Eighteen bowl fragments from clay pipes were recovered, eight of which dated to the period 1620–60, and one had the letters 'RB' incised. These are the initials of Richard Berryman, the well-known pipe maker operating in Bristol between 1619 and 1652. Only one bowl was dated to the period 1650–80, with the remaining dated examples being from later centuries. A total of 165 stem fragments were recovered.

Having established that the site was occupied by a merchant of standing within the community, why then was a byre inserted into the house at a later date? The dating evidence for its insertion comes from the ceramic evidence, which suggests a mid-seventeenth-century date. It is not possible to be more specific than this, given the general dating frameworks of the pottery recovered, including the North Devon wares. Either way, it had taken place prior to the late 1660s. What it does show is that the occupants were now reverting to subsistence agriculture and that they were no longer solely dependent on mercantile activity to sustain their livelihoods. This diversification suggests a downturn for the occupants in both a physical and a metaphorical sense. Of course, they may not have been the same occupants as those who first took up residence in the building, and we certainly know that all the merchants left at the outbreak of conflict in 1641. But this reconfiguration of what would have been a fine residence to one that also accommodated animals reflects changing circumstances. As the economic fortunes of the earls declined, so too did those of the town residents. The town was clearly not developing successfully as an

6.15 Photograph of house structure in Trench 7. This house would have closely abutted the blacksmith's workshop. It was much disturbed by later activity, so we have little information relating to its function.

6.16 Excavations under way in Trench 8.

economic centre, lacking a port and competing as it was with Coleraine. Alternative livelihoods were sought out and subsistence agricultural became more prominent. The relatively fine early seventeenth-century Jacobean interior of the house now gave way to an agricultural vernacular interior that would have been familiar to Ulster's farmers into the nineteenth century.

Excavations were also undertaken at the rear of the house. Due to time constraints, this investigation and its findings were limited. Both topographic and geophysical survey clearly showed that the house had a small enclosed yard or garden space at its rear. This was enclosed by a low-lying earthen bank and no evidence for a palisade or fence was found. A large rubbish pit was found to have had a substantial concentration of seventeenth-century ceramics including Delftware jars, Ulster coarse ceramics, North Devon ware, Black ware and Frechen stoneware. Other finds included clay pipe fragments, two Dutch 'lowland' tiles and faunal material (fig. 6.14). Ninety-three pipe-stem fragments were recovered from this extension, with nine bowl fragments, two of which dated to the period 1610–40 and three to 1620–60. A distinct concentration of slag was also found at the southeast corner of the site. The total recovered could fit into an A4-sized bag and must be related to some form of industrial process. The recovery of the tiles is of special interest and is indicative of a house interior utilizing the design norms of the day, coupled with material culture that reflected European-wide consumption combined with local interaction.

House: Trench 7

A second house was partially investigated in Trench 7 over a six-week period in May and June 2010. A 12m by 11m trench was positioned in the southwest sector of the large townfield adjacent to the castle in an attempt to interrogate the junction between the two streets identified through the 2009 geophysical survey and located during the 2009 excavation season. Initial removal of the topsoil and grass sod (7001) immediately exposed underlying cultural deposits 6–10cm below the surface. The end gable of a masonry structure was uncovered at the northern side of the trench (7015). The southern sections of its two side walls were present, running into the northern baulk, as well as the western section of the southern gable (fig. 6.15). The western portion was of masonry construction, bonded with mortar, and had three surviving courses. More substantial basal stones were present at the corner, a structural feature that this building shares with the Trench 5 house and the blacksmith's workshop. The far side wall was similarly built and also had three surviving courses, but with few traces of mortar and very substantial basal stone blocks at the corner. The gable had been heavily interfered with and it is clear that it had collapsed into the building, as evidenced by a localized compacted rubble mound with mortar concentrations. In the gable, there was no evidence of a fireplace, but this

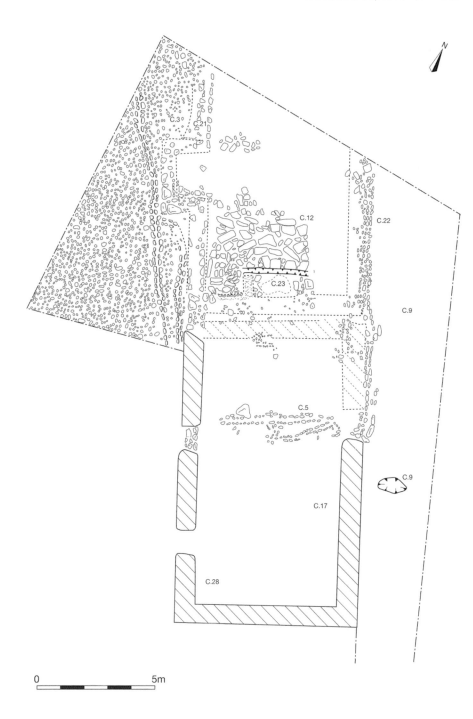

6.17 Excavation plan of Trench 8.

section of the structure had been demolished to such an extent that any trace could have been destroyed. No identifiable examples of decorative stonework such as hearth paving stones or side stonework were noted either, but these may have been removed from the site at an earlier period. Evidence for burning activity near the upper southwestern corner of the structure was uncovered when a small slot-trench was excavated against the northern baulk into the structure's western wall. This burning was very similar to the primary floor deposits associated with the hearth in the contemporary building excavated in 2009, and is indicative of the former presence of a hearth here.

Each of the walls consisted of a double row of roughly dressed and faced stones with a rubble core. On the basis of these surviving elements, it was possible to ascertain an internal width of 5.2m and an overall width of 6.8m. Its original floor surface originally consisted of a compacted clay surface, but no other internal features were found. Externally, a V-shaped gully ran alongside the eastern wall. This had been filled with small stones, was over 30cm deep and was designed as an integral feature of the building.

Trench 8

A fourth major trench was excavated in June 2011 to investigate the ruined masonry structure south of the castle walls between the gate and Dunluce House (fig. 6.16). The partial remains of a rectangular building measure *c.*15m in length and 6.5m in width internally (fig. 6.17). Its walls (8028) have an average width of 80cm and were built using roughly cut basalt facing stone with a rubble mortared core. This was made with lime combined with tiny pebbles and shell. Sections of the wall stand nine courses high in places, to a height of 2.2m above present ground level. The lower portion of an apparently featureless southern gable survives, but there was no above-surface indication of the northern gable prior to excavation. Two door openings are present on the western side wall. Entrance 1 is 2.5m from the southwest corner and is 1m wide with an internal splay on its southern side. The second entrance is 2.7m further along the wall and is slightly wider, at 1.2m, with two internal side splays. No features are visible on the east wall, but most of its north-eastern section has collapsed. There are two sections of the side walls where windows may have been present at the southeast corner of the east wall and at the northern end of the west wall, but neither of these has any definitive surviving archaeological evidence for such features. It is the unconvincing evidence for windows combined with the absence of hearths, subsequently confirmed by excavation, that makes the interpretation of this building intriguing. It clearly did not have a domestic function, yet would have been in a significant position in the town, fronting onto the large open cobbled area leading down to the castle gates. It was against this background that a large trench was

6.18 Resistivity survey of approach area to castle and outer court area. This shows cobbling covering much of this area, and a number of drains (image reproduced courtesy of Ronan McHugh, CAF).

6.19 Photograph of the excavated area in Trench 8. Here, a house and associated range of storage or retail buildings were found, fronting onto the central diamond-shaped large open space in the centre of the town.

0   40

excavated, incorporating all of the interior of the building and a large section of the open area to the north. The trench was irregularly shaped, measuring 19.5m by 15m.

Geophysical survey showed that the area immediately to the west of the building was cobbled (fig. 6.18). Once the grass sod was removed, the surface of the cobbles began to be exposed less than 15cm beneath the surface. Inside the building, however, it became apparent that this area had been extensively disturbed (8017) down to subsoil, and any archaeological stratification had been removed. A number of areas of bedding soil and sand (8010) tied this disturbance to the landscaping work undertaken early in the 1970s, as documented in the DOE files. Only two features survived in the interior, a shallow sub-circular pit (8029) 13cm in depth and 1.13m wide, and a drain-like feature (8005). No function could be assigned to the pit and it is likely to have been associated with initial construction work on the building. A second feature consists of two roughly parallel linear stone features, made up of double lines of closely set stones. The northern row is likely to have functioned as the slot-trench for a wooden partition, creating a northern room in the building. This is supported by the fact that the feature stops 1m short of the west wall, presumably to allow for an internal door. The second component of this feature likely consisted of a shallow drain that would have exited the building through a doorway in the east wall. Finally, a large stone deposit (8004) along the eastern baulk constituted collapse from the east side wall. This showed up in a 1930 RAF aerial photograph, but was spread out during the 1970s landscaping of the area. An Elizabethan coin was found in this disturbed collapse, but cannot be considered to be in situ, given the disturbed nature of its context.

An intact cobbled surface (8003) of a street or market place survives immediately west of the masonry structure (fig. 6.19). This was made up of relatively large beach cobbles of various hues. A number of circular gaps appear in the surface, but these were associated with posts that had been driven in in the twentieth century. Two drains were set into the surface. The first ran northwards along the line of the masonry structure towards the castle gate. A second drain ran inside it along the outer face of the northern building abutting the masonry structure, before veering west and joining the main drain. Both were constructed in an identical manner to those found in Trenches 5 and 7 consisting of pairs of inwardly slanted flat stones. Smaller cobbles were packed between the two drains, in contrast to the larger stone used in the main street surface. Finds were less frequent in this trench in general, but an early seventeenth-century belt buckle was found. Surprisingly, a late Mesolithic/early Neolithic axe was found lying on the surface of the cobbles. This is likely to have been lost by someone who had acquired it as a curiosity, reflecting the awareness that seventeenth-century communities had of past populations.

The foundations of a timber-framed building were located immediately north of the ruined stone building. This area had been heavily disturbed during landscaping works in the 1970s and the subsequent placement of a footpath across the site. As a consequence, most of the northern half of the building has been largely destroyed, and a large portion of the eastern side of the building removed. What survived consisted of a large fireplace inserted into the southern gable, internal paving, a section of the western wall and the footings for a bay or porch-like structure. We cannot be confident of the original dimensions of the house, considering the extent of disturbance, but it would have had an approximate internal width of 5.5m, with a minimum length of 10m. While only a small number of slates were recovered, it is apparent that this was the roof material used. Masonry foundations of the walls survive on the western side of the house only. From our investigations, it appears that neither the gable nor the eastern façade ever had stone walls, but rather consisted of timber framing on substantial sills. The line of these sills survived as impressions in the heavily compacted and levelled soil in these areas, allowing us to extrapolate the original line of the timber walls. The eastern line in particular was especially evident, as the blackened occupation deposits found in the interior were absent in the area where the sill would have been positioned directly on top of the yellowish subsoil, ensuring it was not stained. A partially surviving external drain provided further evidence for the orientation of the east wall. The surviving masonry on the western side of the structure would then have constituted a basal plinth for the timber superstructure. This provision of a masonry base is a common feature on buildings of this date, but its use on only one side is unusual. It may be that the topography required such a feature, as the house was built on a slope. Certainly, the area was initially levelled prior to construction, and a rough metalled surface was created. The most surprising element of the wall was the presence of the projecting bay or porch 3m along the line of the wall from the southwest internal corner. This projected 1.15m externally and had an internal width of c.1.5m. Its interpretation is difficult, as the feature only partially survived, but it likely represents the bay for a window or the location of a doorway. No indication of a threshold survived, but if this was a door visitors would have had to step down into the interior in the same manner as in the house uncovered in Trench 5 (see above, pp 139–48).

The fireplace was the most prominent surviving feature in the house (fig. 6.20). It was set against the southern gable and consisted of a wide, partially paved, hearth with a central fire area. A projecting masonry element was evident on its western side, but this was absent from the eastern side. Originally, the hearth had an associated masonry chimney stack, but this had collapsed. Careful excavation of the stone collapse indicated that a curved stone arch would have been present above the fireplace, although this may have been a support arch rather than a decorative feature. An area of paving was laid in front of the hearth, consisting of large stones laid flat. This would previously have been more extensive, but had been disturbed by modern landscaping work. A narrow gap was present between the hearth and paving and a number of wood branches were recovered from this context, presumably timber that was originally intended for the fire. The alcove to the east of the hearth produced a

6.20 Photograph of the fireplace and internal paving in Trench 8. This domestic space within the building appears to have been burnt to the ground in 1641. A group of heavily burnt cooking pots were found lying in a space to the right of the fireplace.

number of large sherds of Ulster Medieval Coarse Pottery. These had been used for cooking and were found with a quantity of animal bone and black occupation deposits. This area had clearly been used for domestic activity and the use of local wares is interesting in terms of the material engagement of the settlers with local populations and traditions. A number of finds from primary occupation deposits dated the occupation of this building to the opening decades of the seventeenth century. One early coin, a pipe bowl displaying the initials 'RB' and a number of sherds of North Devon ware all supported this dating hypothesis. The house appears to have been burnt to the ground, probably in 1641. A 15cm-thick deposit of burnt organic soil was found lying across the paving and was associated with a significant burning event. This fire, combined with the twentieth-century landscaping, ensured the relatively poor survival of the original form of this building.

One final feature survived at the rear of the masonry structure. This was an irregular oval pit (8009), 36cm deep. The pit had been used as a cesspit, and a sherd of a Frechen jar was found at its base. The pit fill consisted of a blackened organic soil with some charcoal.

The location, positioning and structural remains of these two buildings are interesting. Firstly, it is apparent that there was a masonry structure abutting a timber-framed building. While the latter was clearly a domestic structure of sorts, the masonry building was not. It could be hypothesized that it was a warehouse, storage

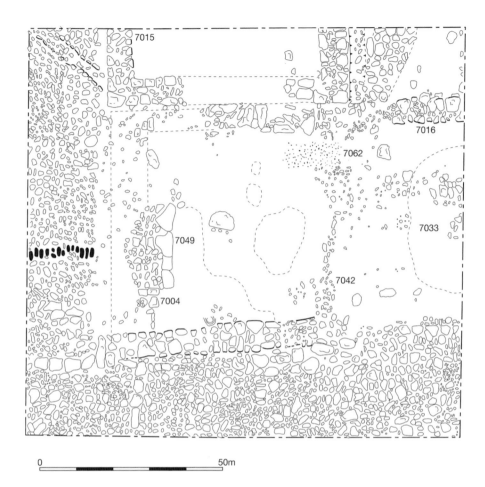

6.21 Excavation plan of Trench 7. This trench contained the well-preserved remains of a blacksmith's workshop. It was entered through large wooden doors along its eastern side and a forge was set into the western wall. Tools belonging to the blacksmith lay to the north of the forge and a mound of horseshoes lay undisturbed along the southern wall.

building or shop, while the adjacent timber-framed structure was the residence of the merchant or owner of the stone building. Unfortunately, the stratigraphy was so disturbed in the southern building that any attempt to assign function on the basis of material culture or archaeological evidence is restricted. Even so, the limited range of material culture in the wooden building is more indicative of a private residence than of a public domain. It appears far more likely that this was the home of a merchant of some standing in the community rather than a building used as an inn or for administrative purposes. The division between the buildings is also of interest. It is not inconceivable that they were linked by a common gable, but again the destruction of the southern building has militated against definitive explanation.

6.22 Photograph of Trench 7. The smithy was located at the junction of two streets at an important point of entry into the central part of the town.

6.23 Photograph of gaming pieces found associated with the blacksmith's workshop. These indicate that the smithy was a social area where people gathered to gossip and pass the time of day while the blacksmith worked.

Blacksmith's workshop

The primary structure uncovered in Trench 7 consisted of the remains of a blacksmith's workshop (fig. 6.21). While there has been a degree of disturbance associated with this structure, it is possible to elucidate the original morphology of the building. Internally, it measured 5.2m by 4.8m. The building was orientated on an east–west axis, with its western gable parallel to the northwest-running roadway (7014), and its southern side wall parallel to the east-running roadway (7002). It was therefore at the junction of these two cobbled surfaces and, as such, would have been positioned very strategically in terms of entering the town and approaching the castle (fig. 6.22). It would have been a masonry structure with a set of large wooden doors that opened out to the east. A metalled surface (7062) was positioned internally in the northeast sector of the building, indicating the presence of a smaller entrance that was incorporated into the large doors, probably in the form of an inset door. Its northern wall was heavily robbed out, but its 80cm-wide base was of drystone construction, with large stones laid flat. The corresponding southern wall was better preserved and was constructed using large angular stones with a packed core of smaller stones. Three courses remained in situ. A shallow, roughly stone-lined gully ran along the bottom of the external face of the wall. Little remained of the western gable due to later robbing and usage of this area in the eighteenth century, when the adjacent street was the location of the Dunluce fair. This wall would have accommodated the forge and an associated chimney, built off-centre on its southern section. The original masonry associated with the chimney flume had collapsed or had been deliberately pushed forward and its rough outline and form could be discerned in the stratigraphic sequence. This would have been mortared, with a tall projecting element over 4.5m in height. The base of the feature survived (7049) and consisted of a line of large stones laid flat at the front and a further packed spread of smaller flat stones laid immediately to the rear. Significant traces of burning, including charcoal and stone staining, were found on these stones and it is clear that this functioned as a large hearth at the base of the forge. A masonry structure would originally have been built up around this, but the remnants of this survived only on its southern edge, where an in-situ base of a mortar-bonded double-block wall (7004) stood three courses high. This would have served as the supporting side wall of the forge and was 1m from the southern side wall of the building. Significant quantities of clinker (7006) were spread along the base of this wall, and a small mound of four horseshoes was also found. Clinker is a waste by-product from iron production and is formed from the oxygen in the furnace and impurities in the slag and fuel. It frequently forms around the tuyère or the opening through which air is pumped into the furnace to raise the temperature.

The floor surface of the building consisted of heavily compacted clay, 5–10cm thick, that was very black due to the quantities of burnt materials that had been trodden into it and the general nature of working practices in this type of environment. A large collapsed stone block sat in a central depression 1m east of the hearth, and this may have been the position of the wooden block for the anvil. The ground surface east of this was clearer of surface deposition, and this may be indicative of an area where the smith moved more. There was a 1.9m space between the hearth and the northern wall. A chisel and a number of L-shaped hanging nails were found in this location, possibly indicative of the former position of the blacksmith's bench, where he kept his tools. A further concentration of hanging nails was found in a rough linear arrangement along the base of the northern wall, where further tools and implements must have hung.

The smithy opened onto an open yard space to the east that had a ground surface of compacted clay. This was open to the roadway and was easily accessible by passing trade. The northern side of the yard was enclosed by a wall (7016) that protruded from the baulk for 1.94m, was between 60 and 82cm wide, and had three surviving courses. This wall would have been in line with the northern side wall of the workshop, but had an opening present to allow access from this yard to the rear space of the adjacent building. The burnt remains of a wooden post and associated post-hole (7064), packed with at least seven medium-sized stones, were found in this space and are indicative of the former presence of a doorway (between these two areas) that had been burnt down. A stone-filled drain ran from the corner of the northern smithy wall through this opening and northwards into the area east of the adjacent building. This initially appeared as a metalled surface and may have served the dual function of pathway and shallow drain. Such features were a requirement for blacksmiths, as water was required to cool tools during the forging process. This water would normally have been contained in a trough or barrel close to the hearth area. Later forges had a pumped water supply, but this was not the case here. A small area of possible iron-working was located against the eastern baulk of the trench, 2m from the original smithy entrance. Here, sections of a shallow 4m-wide pit were excavated and found to contain a considerable amount of clinker, as well as a large bloom that was 50cm long and 40cm wide. This was set against a linear masonry feature projecting 60cm from the baulk (7017). A large deposit of burnt orange sand/clay filled the pit, indicative of in-situ burning.

A road surface running east–west was immediately apparent in the southern end of the trench. It consisted of irregular-shaped stones laid flat to create a rough and uneven surface. It is likely that a deposit of compacted clay would have been laid down on and between the stones to create an even surface. A number of features were contained in this road surface, including a large stone at the southeastern corner of the blacksmith's workshop that acted as a jostle-stone preventing carts running against the corner of the structure. A small shallow gully lay along the southern edge of the road abutting the adjacent smithy. Again, stone arrangements set into the road surface marked features such as junctions and property boundaries, clearly showing that the road and settlement were deliberately planned and laid out. At the structure's southwestern corner, a row of four larger stones marked the start of this road, while a corresponding inset of large flat stones marked the top of the north–south running road. An area of general rubble collapse was located across the central portion of the site, running eastwards under the shell midden and northwards from the east-running road. This consisted largely of stone with mortar and slate interspersed throughout, and represents collapse associated with the former walls of the workshop.

Discussion

The blacksmith's art had developed since antiquity and had become one of the most necessary trades in late medieval society. People depended on the smith for the production and maintenance of their tools, equipment and other items made from iron. As such, blacksmiths' workshops became central places in towns and villages across the land and were vital parts of urban or agrarian communities. The term itself comes from the craft of shaping heated or black metal through a variety of means. In a useful discussion of how blacksmiths' shops appear in the archaeological record, Light (1984) identified four primary areas within a smithy: work; domestic; refuse; and general storage. A number of key features would also have been present, including a forge, bellows, an anvil, a quenching tub, a work bench, tools and fuel.

The forge was of central importance in the blacksmith's shop. At Dunluce, this consisted of a paved hearth set into the west side wall with an associated chimney. This was fired using coal and probably charcoal. A raised masonry structure over the hearth would have contained the hot coals and embers that the blacksmith worked with. A set of hand-operated bellows would probably have been set against this to allow the smith maintain a working temperature. In order to heat the metal to allow it to be shaped, it was initially put in the forge before being removed using tongs. It was then placed on the anvil, which provided a hard surface on which the hot metal could be shaped through hammering. A quenching tub would have been used for hardening the metal through rapidly cooling it in a bucket or barrel of water immediately adjacent to the forge. This was likely just to the left of the forge at Dunluce, as the anvil and working area were located to the right. The spatial arrangement of this workshop indicates that the smith was right-handed. Storage took place along much of the north wall, where a concentration of hanging nails was located. Much of the refuse or clinker was pushed against the western portion of the south wall, where some storage also took place.

Blacksmiths' shops would also have constituted a social area within a community. Each household and inhabitant would have needed this facility and the blacksmith's services would have been in constant demand. As such, it became a central place in the town and an integral part of its social fabric. This would have been a place where people met, gossiped, discussed business and politics and generally passed the time of day. There are clear archaeological indications of this social role. A cluster of small flat slate gaming discs were found in the open space to the northeast of the entrance and in the disturbed contexts along its northern wall. In the open space, two of these discs were found associated with a small conical piece, indicating that two separate board games were played (fig. 6.23). Four further pieces were found in the disturbed contexts immediately to the west. Seventeen pipe bowl fragments were also recovered from the trench, seven of which dated to the period 1620–60, with two carrying the initials 'RB' on the heel and bowl respectively. Two bowls were dated to 1650–80, while a final one was from the period 1680–1710. The remaining examples were too fragmentary to date with precision.

Comparative sites

A number of blacksmiths' workshops or smithies from this period have been excavated, but comparative evidence remains limited. At the Avalon colony in Newfoundland, a forge was constructed in 1622 (Carter 1997). Here, a 5.2m by 3.4m wooden structure was built into a small hill in order to create a level area. The foundations of the forge partially survived, while post-holes supporting a bellows and the location of the anvil stump were identified. A second, probable seventeenth-century, workshop was discovered at Hart near Liverpool, where a smithy with a brick hearth, clay floor, pits and post-holes associated with a working bench were identified (Daniels and Jackson n.d.). Other later examples from the eighteenth and nineteenth century have also been investigated, including an example on the Mount Vernon estate in the US and in Australia (Hyett 2002). All of the sites maintain an almost identical layout that appears to have changed little into the early part of the twentieth century.

Church

The church at Dunluce has already been referred to in chapter 3 in relation to its use during the later Anglo-Norman period. The current building is, however, late medieval and was probably rebuilt in the early seventeenth century by the MacDonnells (fig. 6.24). Following the remodelling of the cathedral of Connor in 1609, *Sancto Cuthberto Dunlups* was listed as a member of the new chapter (Reeves 1847, 263). It is positioned within an irregular enclosure wall that has been reconstructed in recent centuries, just east of the stream. In the nineteenth century, the course of the stream was straightened. Originally, it would have flowed further to the east and the church

6.24 Photograph of the church from the south. The building was refurbished a number of times since the late sixteenth century before its eventual abandonment in the early nineteenth century.

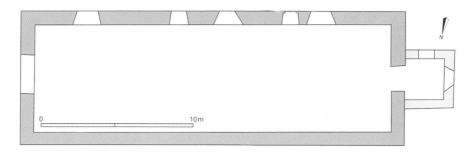

6.25 Plan of the church.

was positioned on a small promontory-like piece of land surrounded by the watercourse on three sides. Earthworks in the field to the south of church show the original line of the system, as well as indicating stream-edge structures. It is tempting to envisage a mill in this area. The church itself is a rectangular masonry structure measuring 23.15m long by 6.75m wide internally (fig. 6.25). It is currently entered through a small porch at its western end, but this is a later eighteenth-century addition and the building would originally have been entered through two doors on its southern side wall, both later blocked up to create windows. It is unclear whether these were contemporary, but the example at the western end of the wall was of a finer build. It had external sandstone surrounds with an internal rebate. Red brick was also used in its western side, but this may be a later fill. The use of sandstone in this manner dates to two primary horizons in the castle – the 1580s and the period 1609–20 – while the use of brick is related to the latter period. A sandstone window also survives high in the western gable. The second, slightly wider (1.28m), doorway was positioned 9m west of the east gable. Traditionally, this has been referred to as the MacDonnell family entrance, while the lower door was a public entrance. The key problem with this interpretation is that the MacDonnells were Catholic and this was a Protestant church, built to cater primarily for the needs of the Scottish settlers, in both the town and the surrounding area. Three windows were contained in the south wall. Both of the eastern splayed examples measured 1.7m wide internally and ranged between 1.86m and 1.96m high. The third window was wider at 1.88m and was 1.92m high. The ground level appears to drop off from the eastern end as the height of the first window was 84cm above present ground level, while the westernmost example was 1.22m above the surface. This is likely related to later collapse and burial activity, rather than indicating a sloping floor level. A large window was contained in the eastern gable wall, but its decorative stonework has long vanished. It would have been *c.*2.2m wide at its base and was nearly 3m high. The ridge for the roof trusses is 2.7m above ground level at the eastern end, but is present across both gables and on the north wall. A number of these structural timbers were removed from the church during the 1820s and used in the new St Cuthbert's in Bushmills, while the majority seem to have been reused in the large barn next to Dunluce House. A number of grave-stones and markers survive. Immediately opposite the original western door, a limestone memorial plaque with sandstone surrounds is set at chest level in the north wall. It reads

> Here under lyeth the body of Florence McPhilip alias Hamilton, late wife of Archbald McPhilip of Dunluce, mercht and daughter to Captaine Robert Hamilton of Clady who departed this life the 20th of July 1674. Death can dissolve but not destroy. Who sowes in tears shall reape in joy.

A second grave-stone in the southern section of the graveyard close to the southeast corner of building reads 'Here lyeth the children of Walter Kid, marchnat of Dunluce, burges if Irvvin. He made this stone tenth of March in Anno Domin 1630'. No other seventeenth-century memorial is currently visible, but it is likely that more are buried across the site. In particular, there has been a significant build-up of soil against the southern wall that is currently over 1m above the internal ground level of the church. Other less prominent grave-markers would have included simple stones marking the ends of the graves.

Summary

This settlement, founded in the first two decades of the seventeenth century, was established by Randal MacDonnell as a mercantile entrepreneurial venture. He brought to the town a number of Scottish merchant settlers, who maintained their familial and business connections with western Scotland. A number of Gaelic settlers also established residence in the town and it would be a mistake to regard it as a solely Scottish settlement. Detailed planning went into its construction and its houses, streets and associated buildings represented the emerging architectural norms of the day. Of special interest is the fact that this town appears to have been laid out and built prior to the re-established settlements of the official plantation west of the Bann. Randal was thus demonstrating considerable ambition in developing Dunluce at a slightly earlier date and showed that he was in tune with official government thinking of the day. His inability to break with his ancestral home and his continued partial medieval mindset, however, resulted in the building of a town in an unsuitable location, one that was to result in its eventual failure and abandonment. Following his death in 1636, the fortunes of the town were subject to a considerable downward spiral.

CHAPTER 7

Revolution and abandonment: 1641 and beyond

Randal, 2nd earl of Antrim

Randal, 2nd earl of Antrim, was born in 1609. Jane Ohlmeyer (1993) has written an excellent biography and there is little need to go over this here. Instead, the brief pertinent facts relating to his tenure as earl and at Dunluce are recounted. Having been educated on the Continent and served in the military, he married Katherine Villiers, widow of the duke of Buckingham, in April 1635. Both engaged in a lavish lifestyle and, following a rocky start, became an integral part of the London court scene. Following the death of his father in 1636, the 27-year-old inherited the baronies of Dunluce and Kilconway, as well as the castle at Dunluce (fig. 7.1). His brother, Alexander, received Glenarm, but handed this back to Randal following payment of a sum of money. By the end of the 1630s, the couple had built up debts in excess of £40,000 through gambling and the furnishing of their homes at Dunluce and elsewhere (Ohlmeyer 1993, 61). We know from an inventory written in 1645, when Katherine transported the house's goods to England for safety during the rebellion, that Dunluce was lavishly furnished and decorated (McDonnell 1992). Tapestries covered the walls and curtains were hung both around beds and across the windows. The house featured oriental carpets, ornamental cabinets and numerous chairs and armchairs, many of them covered with silk, satin or lace. Paintings and large mirrors decorated the walls, while the house also contained a library, globes, an Irish harp and even a telescope, illustrating the new emphasis on cultural and learning in society. A visitor would be struck not only by the wealth and style of the occupants, but also by the contrast between this house with its new form of architecture and its medieval castle precedents. Lifestyles and house interiors of this class did not come cheaply, and in order to meet the cost of servicing some of their debt the couple left their English quarters and retreated to Dunluce, taking up permanent residence in 1638. To economize, a contemporary recorded that 'they contract themselves into a narrow room' (Ohlmeyer 1993, 75), a probable reference to the main room in the manor house.

For much of 1640 and the opening months of 1641, Randal was away from Dunluce, probably in Dublin, and left the castle in the charge of a Captain Digby. With the outbreak of hostilities in 1641, Digby initially organized a force of between

7.1 Randal MacDonnell, 2nd earl of Antrim. Both Randal and his first wife, Katherine, lived a lavish lifestyle in England before moving to Dunluce. Randal lost the Antrim estates in the 1640s, but regained them following the restoration of Charles II to the English crown. He subsequently moved from Dunluce to Ballymagarry, before Glenarm was finally adopted as the chief family residence (image reproduced courtesy of the McDonnell family, Glenarm).

Randal MacDonnell

Randal MacDonnell was born in 1609, the eldest legitimate son of Randal, 1st earl of Antrim, and his wife, Alice O'Neill. He was partly educated in France from 1625, before being presented at the court of Charles I in 1627. In 1635, he married Katherine Villiers (née Manners), widow of the duke of Buckingham, and was appointed 2nd earl of Antrim in 1636, following the death of his father. The couple enjoyed a lavish lifestyle in England before moving permanently to Dunluce in 1638 because of debts. With the outbreak of conflict in the 1640s, Randal initially supported Charles I against the covenanting armies and was created marquis in 1644, but was later twice imprisoned. Katherine died in 1649, and Randal later married Rose O'Neill in 1653. During the 1650s, he managed to win favour with the Cromwellian regime but lost his estates following the restoration of Charles II. After an extensive legal battle, he won the estates back and effectively withdrew from public affairs. He died childless in 1683 and was succeeded by his brother Alexander.

six hundred and seven hundred men to defend the Antrim estates. The causes of this rising across Ulster were complicated and multifaceted and included religious tensions, social animosities, political hostilities and an assortment of ambitions. Within a short period, the rebellion had spread across Ireland and was to last for nearly ten years. Both Alasdair MacColla and Tirlough Oge O'Cahan had initially played a leading role within the militia organized by Digby, but they were later to join the rebellion with James MacDonnell. In January 1642, they attacked Portnaw, a fording point just south of Kilrea on the Bann, killing over sixty Protestant soldiers before marching on to Ballintoy, Dunluce, Clogh and Coleraine. The events of the 1640s later became the focus of a major enquiry charged with examining the impact of the rebellion on mostly Protestant individuals, their property and land. In 1653, a branch of the enquiry focused on the events following Portnaw and the evidence collected contains some valuable information relating to the castle and surrounding landscape.

1641 depositions

In February 1653, Alice, the countess dowager, was interviewed at Coleraine by Major Richard Brasier and Colonel Thomas Coote (TCD dep. 838022r017, fos 22r–23v). In her evidence, she stated that at the outset of hostilities she was staying in the castle at Ballycastle until Monroe's Scottish forces had arrived in the Route and taken her son Randal hostage at Dunluce, at which point she had fled across the Bann. She contested the assertion that she had refused entry to certain British residents of the town and that her servants had prevented their entry to the house, the tower that would originally have stood at the northern side of the Diamond in Ballycastle, just east of the church (fig. 7.2). It was further suggested that shelter was provided for the miller, a carpenter and their families in order to protect the family's interests in the area, while others were removed from the house, castle gate and bawn and murdered. Further allegations concerned a Jennett Speir, who begged for her life while hanging off the countess' gown, before being taken away and murdered behind the stables as she and others were owed money by the countess. In a separate examination, Gilduff O'Cahan of Dunseverick was examined at Coleraine in March 1653 (TCD dep. 838024r018, fos 24r–26v). He testified that on Sunday 24 October 1641 he came from his house at Dunseverick to the town of Dunluce with a footboy to hear mass. No service was available, so he retired to the house of James Stewart in the town to drink wine (fig. 7.3). Henry McHenry, Manus O'Cahan and others were also present, and a number of bottles were consumed before an armed band arrived to declare that the Irish in Tyrone had risen in rebellion. The leader of the band, Captain McPheadress, instructed the Scots in the town to arm themselves and gather in the 'new pavement in the inner court next the drawbridge and outer gate of

7.2 Painting of 'an October market' (1853), showing the partially standing remains of the castle at Ballycastle (image reproduced courtesy of the Causeway Museum Service).

Dunluce Castle'. This is an interesting reference to the recently cobbled yard and the erection of a cross-wall north of the brew-house down to the bridge. The fact that it was regarded as 'new' in the early 1640s provides further evidence that the construction of these elements may have taken place in the 1620s.

While the events outside the castle were unfolding, a highland Scots resident of Bushmills came to inform the drinking party that a large force of Argyle's men had arrived at Bush Bridge, a mile from Dunluce, and they were intent on taking the castle (which later proved to be a false alarm). O'Cahan left his sons drinking and made his way into the castle, where he 'bolted the outer gate' before he received the key for the inner gate (possibly the internal north door of the gate house) and entered the castle proper. Later, his sons, Captain Digby and eight of the earl's men entered the castle but refused entry to the Scots. That night, the earl's brother, Alexander, and Archibald Stewart arrived to the area of the 'new pavement near the castle gate, the bridge of the castle drawn up and the gate locked'. O'Cahan went into an 'upper room' over the gate, ascertained who they were, and let the drawbridge down to allow them to enter. He then held the castle with Captain Digby for a week before a letter from the earl stood him down.

The testimony then moved to the murders at Portnaw on 3 January 1641. After this event, the insurgents, led by James and Alister McColl MacDonnell and others, marauded through the Route before unsuccessfully besieging the small garrison of Scots at Ballintoy House. They subsequently encamped at Craigballinoe before

7.3 Photograph of a sample of glass bottles recovered from the excavations at Dunluce.

7.4 The harbour at Ballintoy, with the seventeenth-century church visible in the middle ground above the port. Limited traces of Ballintoy House survive immediately south of the church (image reproduced courtesy of Nigel McDowell, UU).

making their way to Dunluce. Captain Digby refused to yield the castle, after which time a number of the insurgents acting without orders 'set a house on fire, whereby the whole town was burnt'. To the witness' knowledge, only one man, William Gault, was killed near the 'new buildings in the court next the castle'. On the same night, the commanders and their men quartered at Ballymagarry with O'Cahan and his sons-in-law, the McHenrys, before marching to Old Stone (Clogh). O'Cahan returned to his own home at that point. He also recounted that Alister McColl MacDonnell had instructed him to attack the soldiers stationed in Ballintoy Chuch, which he duly did (fig. 7.4). An initial attack was repulsed, after which they returned and attempted to knock a wall with pickaxes before killing a man and boy at the spring near the church. The house at Ballintoy was attacked with cannon as part of the same campaign, but its defenders also managed to repulse the assailants.

Henry McHenry testified in Coleraine on 11 March 1652 that he had made his way from his dwelling at Ballymulvannagh to Dunluce on the morning of Sunday, 24 October 1641 (838027r019, fos 27r–28v). He met his father-in-law, Gilduff O'Cahan, who was drinking wine in his son's (Roger O'Cahan) house, except for the time when mass was celebrated by a priest called Neill McLam. When pressed as to where mass was actually said, McHenry claimed not to be able to remember. The differences in testimony are interesting here, with some parties denying that mass ever took place and others failing to remember where it was conducted. The difficulties that Catholics still faced in the 1650s are apparent in these discrepancies. After 1pm, Captain McPheadress arrived in the town with fifteen mounted men. A little later, a highlander arrived in the house where the O'Cahans and McHenry were drinking, and whispered something to the elder O'Cahan, at which point he left and entered the castle gate. Later, Captain Digby arrived and entered the castle gate with McHenry. McPheadress demanded entry from the court before the castle but was refused. At 10pm, the earl's brother, Alexander, and Archibald Stewart arrived and were identified by O'Cahan, who held a candle in a window at the entrance. Subsequently, they were allowed in and had a discussion in the 'hall' before departing for Coleraine. O'Cahan, Digby and a small number of warders then held the castle for four to five days before O'Cahan returned to Dunseverick.

It was later claimed that, following the murders at Portnaw, James and Alister McColl MacDonnell, Tirlough and Manus Roe O'Cahan and other insurgent leaders with five hundred men gathered at Craigballinoe, a mile from Dunseverick, and forced the McHenrys and Gilduff O'Cahan to join them before marching to Dunluce the following day. James McColl instructed Digby to surrender Dunluce, which he refused to do and, as a consequence, a number of the insurgents set fire to the town. The examinant and others were standing on the hill 'a little above the town' during this episode (fig. 7.5). Brian Modder McHenry O'Cahan of Maddybenny was examined on the same day (838029r020, fos 29r–30r). He testified that he lived near the Bann, about two miles from Coleraine, and following the outbreak of the

7.5 View of Dunluce Castle from the base of Gallows Hill. During the late medieval period, a gallows would have stood here as a reminder of the power and authority of the castle residents.

7.6 Late medieval structures at Dunseverick Castle, with Islay visible on the horizon.

rebellion he removed his family and goods to Dunseverick Castle, the house of his father-in-law, Gilduff O'Cahan (fig. 7.6). When the insurgents came to Craigballinoe, they told him that they had killed O'Cahan's tenant, John Roe Spence, his wife and others who lived at a 'town' about one mile from Dunseverick. Brian Modder was at pains to point out that few of the insurgents had gained entry to the castle at Dunseverick while others had taken a drink at the gate. He took no further part in the rebellion, but when the Scottish forces arrived in 1642 he fled across the Bann and was granted land in Upper Ossory in the Queen's County by the earl of Antrim.

Donnell Gorm MacDonnell of Killoquin in the parish of Magheresharkin [Rasharkin] testified on 11 March 1652 that he believed Alister McColl MacDonnell and Tirlough Oge O'Cahan had had command of two companies and were primarily responsible for the murder of the thirty British soldiers at Portnaw a mile from his house, on land owned by the examinant's father and Henry O'Hagan (fos 30r–30v). The rebel force then moved to Ballymoney, which they burned, before travelling to Ballintoy and Dunluce. The testimony of Coll McAlister on the following day (838032v024, fos 32v–33r) supported the statements of MacDonnell regarding the Portnaw murders of Christmas 1641. He claimed to have little involvement in the events of the early 1640s, and knew little of the various atrocities committed including the murder of British individuals at the 'salt pans' of Ballycastle (fig. 7.7). A number of seventeenth-century pans are still visible along the shore to the north of Ballycastle and these consist of rock-cut troughs close to the high-water mark. Donnell Spence, a labourer from Billy parish, was interviewed on 1 March and gave evidence that Turlough O'Cahan and a number of his men had murdered his parents at a house in Billy before the defendant fled to Dunluce (838054v080, fo. 54v). Fergus Fullerton, a maltman from Billy and a soldier with the English forces, further testified that Irish rebels had burned the town of Ballymoney before marching to Ballintoy and on to Craigballinoe (838056r086, fos 56r–56v). They then made their way to Ballymagarry near Dunluce and wrote a letter to Captain Digby, requesting that he surrender the castle or they would burn the adjacent town. When they were met with a refusal, Gilduff O'Cahan and John Mortimer were responsible for setting fire to the settlement.

One of the most important testimonies in the context of Dunluce came from one of the town's residents, Hugh Colume (838058r090, fo. 58r). In his evidence, he stated that Gilduff O'Cahan of Dunseverick, his son-in-law Brian Modder McHenry O'Cahan and his sons Manus and Connor Reagh O'Cahan and Brian Ballagh O'Cahan's two sons had been drinking with others in Matthew Stewart's house around midday on Sunday, 24 October 1641. They had made their way into the castle, where only one man was stationed, and later that afternoon heard that the Irish had risen in rebellion over the Bann. That night, Alexander MacDonnell, Archibald Stewart and Captain Digby came to Dunluce and the following day Digby and a number of Scotsmen garrisoned the castle. About four nights after the murders at

Portnaw, Irish forces commanded by James McColl MacDonnell, Alexander Coll MacDonnell, Gilduff O'Cahan, John Mortimer, Brian Modder McHenry O'Cahan, Henry McHenry O'Cahan and Coll McAlister came to the town. The British residents fled to the castle and 'the rocks thereabouts'. The Irish subsequently murdered William Gault in the town, another in the 'bowling green' and a third near the 'counting house'. (This counting house was probably an administrative office or building within or close to the castle complex that facilitated the collection of rents and dues. Small offices of this nature were often located near the gate lodges of the large eighteenth- and nineteenth-century estates. Tenants would come and pay their rents at these offices and therefore had no need to venture near the big house of the landlord.) According to the witness, two unknown men were knocked down and thrown over the rocks (presumably dumped over the cliff edge). At the same time, they 'set on fire and burned the town of Dunluce'. A second resident, James Widderoe, a baker, testified that Gilduff O'Cahan and others were drinking on the morning of 24 October in James Stewart's house before O'Cahan and a number of his men entered the castle (838058v092, fos 58v–59r). The man stationed in the castle, known only as Anthony, then made his way to Captain Digby's house, a mile from the castle, to inform him of the intrusion, possibly at Ballymagarry. Digby, Stewart and MacDonnell duly arrived that same night and an agreement was made whereby Digby and a number of Scots took charge of the castle the following day. He further stated that the inhabitants of the town lived 'peaceably' until the murders at Portnaw, after which the rebel forces tried to take the castle but failed and duly burnt the town and killed William Gault and four others around the town and rocks.

Willaim McPheadress of Loughguile gave evidence on 8 March 1653 (838072r129, fos 72r–72v). He testified that on 24 October 1641 Archibald Stewart came to Derrykeighan Church and informed him that the Irish in Tyrone had risen in rebellion and requested that Dunluce Castle and its cache of arms be secured (fig. 7.8). McPheadress made his way to Dunluce and instructed five or six men of the town to watch the castle gate before Anthony (Digby's man) locked it with its key. As they came away, however, they were stopped on the street by Gilduff O'Cahan, who took the key and entered the castle. McPheadress and others remonstrated with O'Cahan and were called rogues.

Antrim intervenes

The earl travelled north in April 1642 in an attempt to negotiate a truce between the two sides in north Ulster. Major General Robert Monro agreed to meet him at Dunluce at the end of May, but arrived with a large force at the castle and duly imprisoned Antrim at Carrickfergus before installing a new garrison at Dunluce. The duchess shipped their furniture and belongings back to England, where they were

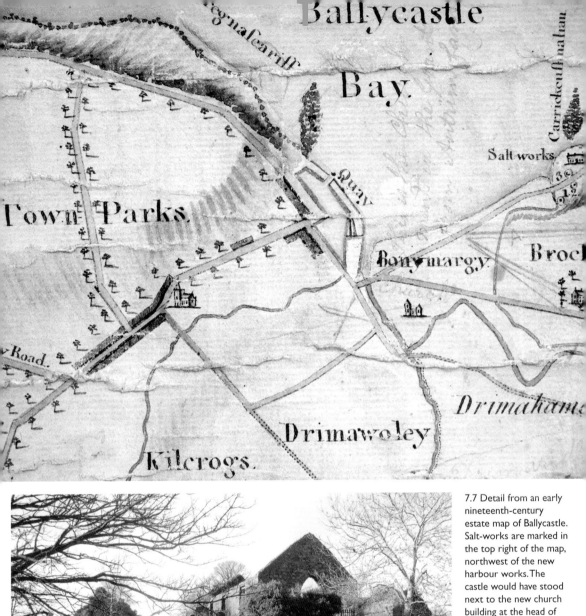

7.7 Detail from an early nineteenth-century estate map of Ballycastle. Salt-works are marked in the top right of the map, northwest of the new harbour works. The castle would have stood next to the new church building at the head of the main street in the town (image reproduced courtesy of the Causeway Museum Service).

7.8 Derrykeighan Church, with a replica of the Derrykeighan stone in the foreground. This is an important piece of early stone sculpture and is indicative of the significance of the site.

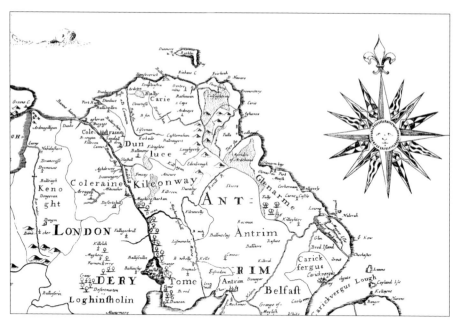

7.9 Detail of the study area from William Petty's 1685 *Hiberniae delineatio*.

7.10 Lord Mark Kerr's 1811 sketch of a standing bawn corner tower then used to house a bell at Ballymagarry House, 2km west of Dunluce. This was the last remaining structure associated with the seventeenth-century house at Ballymagarry, where the MacDonnells had taken up residence in the middle of the seventeenth century (after McDonnell 2004a).

later sold off. Randal escaped at the end of October, disguised as a cripple, and joined his wife at York. He returned to Ulster the following year, but was again arrested and imprisoned at Carrickfergus, before escaping once more in November. In 1644, Randal was created a marquis and spent the remainder of the war attempting to develop a military career and enhancing his reputation. At the end of the war, he effectively sided with Cromwell initially, but his estates were confiscated and he was granted lands in Co. Mayo. In 1653, he married Rose O'Neill, daughter of Henry, chief of the Clandeboy O'Neills, Katherine having died in the late 1640s. Most of his former estates were subsequently granted to Cromwellian soldiers, or adventurers, in return for their contribution to the war effort after 1649. Daniel and John Cooper, Henry Johnson and Thomas Price were among those who secured lots in Dunluce barony.

The status of Dunluce Castle and town throughout this whole period remains unclear. MacDonnell does not appear to have been resident there, although his wife, Rose, does give her address as Dunluce in 1656 (Ohlmeyer 1993, 250). Glenarm appears to have been adopted as the primary residence of the family, with Petty depicting the castle there as the 'earl of Antrim's house' on his barony map (fig. 7.9). Sir John Clotworthy, 1st viscount Massereene (c.1600–65), had also received and bought extensive lands across the Antrim estates and was to lead the case against MacDonnell being regranted his estates following the Restoration. His appeals were to no avail, and Randal MacDonnell was regranted estates in 1663 and officially restored in 1665. This process led to a degree of social unrest across north Ulster, as the new Cromwellian settlers feared for their land acquisitions. This came to a head at the Dunluce fair on 13 November 1663, when a Cromwellian landowner, Tristram Beresford, attempted to collect the dues ahead of Antrim's agent. The scene threatened to get ugly as other Cromwellian supporters gathered around Beresford before the situation was diffused by the constable of the castle.

Population

One of the major difficulties with examining settlements of this date is assessing the population levels of the towns and of the surrounding landscape. The so-called 1659 census of Ireland, probably compiled by William Petty, lists forty-six people resident at Dunluce town (Pender 1939). Fifteen were classified as English while thirty-one were Irish. These were the leading members of each household, suggesting that there were at least forty-six houses in the town at this time. It is unclear whether people of low social standing were included in the survey, so hovels and families on the periphery of the settlement were probably not represented. If we take it that there were at least six people in each household, then the minimum population of the town in the late 1650s was 276. The assignation of an English identity in the survey should not be taken too literally, as the Scots and English were usually grouped under the same ethnic tag. Across the baronies of Dunluce, Cary and Kilconway, a total of 4,078 persons were listed, 1,138 of whom were labelled English and 2,940 Irish.

In 1662, a hearth tax was introduced shortly after the Restoration. This was to be imposed on all houses that paid over 20s. in rent, so hovels and other temporary shelters were excluded. Two shillings were to be paid on each hearth or stove in a house and the tax collected for Antrim was published in the hearth money rolls of 1669 (PRONI T307) (Carleton 1991). Excluding Lord Antrim, thirty households were listed at Dunluce town, sixteen fewer than a decade earlier. Nine of these were widows, reflecting the aging nature of the demographic within the town and possibly the loss of life during the Cromwellian wars. Nearly all of the surnames in the town by this date appear to be either Scottish or English, suggesting that most of the Irish had departed (table 7.1).

Table 7.1 Individuals from the hearth money rolls listed as resident in Dunluce town (PRONI T307).

	Surname	Forename		Surname	Forename
1	Allexander	John	16	Lastly	Capt Wm
2	Antrim	Lord	17	Martin	Robert
3	Bane	Widow	18	Martine	Hugh
4	Bany	Uny?	19	Mathews	John
5	Blacke	John	20	McBretty	Widow Phel
6	Browne	Robert	21	McCanlis	David
7	Calvell	David	22	McCanlish	David
8	Crilly	Pat	23	McKaghin	Daniell
9	Delman	Widow	24	McGawan	Daniell
10	Dicky	John	25	McKay	ffranc
11	Egilsonne	Thomas	26	Kenny	Wm Sen.?
12	fallertune	John	27	Kenny	Wm Jun.?
13	Grodes	Widow Granyny	28	Moore	Widow
14	Hamilton	Widow	29	Nickell	John
15	Kenkelin	Widow	30	Ranell	Widow
			31	Woodrune	Widow?

The final days

Dunluce had effectively ceased to be Antrim's primary residence long before his restoration in 1665. Much of his time was now spent at Randalstown, while he stayed at Ballymagarry when on the north coast (fig. 7.10). He died 'at his dwelling near Dunluce' in early 1683, presumably at Ballymagarry, and was buried at Bonamargy in March. He died without children, and so his brother, Alexander, became the 3rd earl of Antrim and adopted Glenarm as his principle residence (fig. 7.11). Randal had retained a symbolic connection to Dunluce and still conducted business there and brought visitors to it. Writing in 1671, the archbishop of Armagh, Oliver Plunkett, wrote that he had spent three days with MacDonnell 'at his house at Dunluce; it is a noble building, the palace is perched on a high rock, which is lashed on every side by the sea' (Hill 1873, 345). As his involvement with the castle waned, the fortunes of the town dipped accordingly. Such a mercantile settlement would have greatly depended on the patronage and continued enthusiastic engagement of its benefactor. With Randal's removal from the public sphere, the town's inhabitants, now greatly reduced following the Cromwellian period, gradually departed, leaving the town desolate and abandoned by the 1680s. The main house was by that time roofless and much of its stonework appears to have been robbed during the Cromwellian period and early 1660s. Some of the settlers took stone from the building and many of the quoins and window stones must also have been taken at this date, rendering the site a ruin.

Dunluce fair

Following the abandonment of the site at the end of the seventeenth century, only one major activity took place in the castle's environs – the annual Dunluce fair. While we have little historical detail of this event, extensive traces of fair activities were uncovered during the excavation. This would have been a typical fair of the period, where many hundreds of people came from across the surrounding regions to sell produce, purchase materials and peruse the various commodities on display. They were apparently raucous affairs, with much drinking and general merriment. At Dunluce, this seems to have eventually got too much and it was stopped by the 1740s due to excessive drunkenness and debauchery. It appears that the primary location of the fair was the by-now deserted merchants' street. Evidence for a number of booths selling beer, shellfish and other foodstuffs was found in abundance in the excavation trenches in this area, whereas there was very limited evidence for such activity immediately outside the castle.

In Trench 5, the stone foundations for a temporary booth were found around the entrance to the seventeenth-century house (fig. 7.12). It was clear from the excavation evidence that this house was in ruins by the 1690s, and the stall would have been set up in the limited shelter of the west wall. The seller would have utilized the door for shelter and the internal area would have been used for the temporary storage of goods. This stall was primarily for the sale of shellfish, which were also

7.11 William Bartlett's 1830s view of Glenarm, with the castle and walls prominent. Glenarm Castle remains the seat of the McDonnells to this day.

7.12 Excavating the shell midden in Trench 5. The rough foundations for a crude structure are visible in the centre foreground. This is all that remains of a booth that would have sold shellfish and beer during the eighteenth-century Dunluce fair.

apparently consumed at the location, as a large accumulation of limpet shells, with occasional periwinkles, had built up around the foundations. Some animal bone was also recovered from this midden, including cattle and fish bone, as well as cat remains. Large quantities of late seventeenth- and early eighteenth-century ceramics were also recovered, including Staffordshire ware beer mugs and the ubiquitous blackwares. A quantity of glass was also found, including a portion of a late seventeenth-century onion bottle. Beer and wine appear to have been sold at this booth, which effectively served the equivalent beverage and food functions of an inn. Is it any coincidence that this house ruin was chosen as a place for the sale of alcohol? At the end of the street, it was in a relatively peripheral area where individuals could drink in an era of increasing temperance.

The trench also contained further evidence of temporary activity. A small hearth was located against the external wall of the south gable of the house. Its context clearly associated it with a post-occupation phase and it likely represents either fair attendees seeking shelter against the wall or another travelling individual or group who sought temporary refuge among the town's ruins. The deposits suggest that this was a peat fire with the fuel likely sourced from the nearby bogs to the south.

Excavations in Trench 7 uncovered very similar evidence of the fair. A large deposit of shell (7003) was exposed under the sod in the western sector of the trench, lying over the north-running road. This deposit was spread over an area 3m by 2.6m and was up to 10cm thick. It consisted predominantly of periwinkle and limpets with some dogwhelk. Bone fragments were found towards the base of the deposit, including cattle, sheep and fish. The clay pipe fragments and Staffordshire slipware date the deposit to the late seventeenth and early eighteenth century. This deposit represents another midden associated with the fair and the location of a booth or stall set against the rear wall of the smithy, between the workshop and the southern gable of the house that was partially exposed in the trench. The deposit was formed within the ruins of the smithy. One slight contrast between this booth and that uncovered in Trench 5 was that it contained less ceramic and glass material associated with alcohol consumption. As with Trench 5, large numbers of clay pipe stems were found. Interestingly, no such middens were uncovered from Trench 8, but small quantities of similarly dated ceramics and glass were found in later disturbed contexts, indicating that people were at least wandering over to this area. The quantities were very low, however, supporting the hypothesis that this remained a relatively exclusive area and the main focus of the fair was on the merchants' street. Once the fair stopped, all cultural activity in the town field ceased. No ploughing took place and the removal of stones was prohibited by the earl. There were documented cases where the earl's agents pursued and prosecuted people for removing stones. Grazing did take place at a later date, and the prolonged impact of cows walking across the site led to further structural collapse and the spreading of rough angular stones around the extant structures. Over the course of the eighteenth and nineteenth centuries, the structures grassed over and the houses and streets were slowly buried beneath wind-blown sands and soils. By the time the first Ordnance Survey map was produced in the 1830s, foundations from the town were still visible but were not remarkable enough to include on the maps. All above-ground traces seem to have disappeared by the 1860s, with only the earthworks bearing testament to the town's former presence.

CHAPTER 8

Tourism, conservation and development, 1800–2000

Tourism beginnings

In 1693, Richard Bulkeley, of Trinity College Dublin, published the first scientific paper with the Royal Society on the Giant's Causeway and introduced this geological wonder to the world. Susanna Drury's two gouaches produced in 1739 popularized the site in a universal way and dramatically illustrated the beauty of the landscape. Numerous individuals can be seen examining various parts of the feature in her drawings, demonstrating that the causeway had already become a tourist attraction. By the end of the eighteenth century, Dunluce also became a must-see attraction on this new coastal destination. Both Portrush and Portstewart capitalized on this, redeveloping themselves as Victorian seaside towns in the later part of the century. A number of early visitors to the castle have left mementoes of their trips in the form of personal graffiti. Much of this is on the internal walls of the north range, but carved names can be found all over the site. George Boothe of Omagh carved his name on the mural stairs in the northeast tower on two occasions, on 21 August 1831 and in 1837. He probably visited with M. Boothe and S. Patter(son?) in 1831 (fig. 8.1). Both C. Walkinshawn and W. Buick visited the site in 1849 and carved their names and the date of their visit above the collapsed section of wall along the western cliff edge. One possible 1820s date appears in the north range. Apart from the Boothe date, this is possibly the earliest carved date on the walls. Numerous other names and symbols appear across the site and provide an interesting connection with past visitors. The surname 'Petrie' is also present among these names, and it is just possible that this is George Petrie (1790–1866), the antiquarian, music collector and landscape painter. Petrie certainly collaborated with other antiquaries, including Bartlett, who drew the site, so it should not be surprising that his name appears. Sometime, probably in the early 1820s, Petrie must have visited the site and produced a watercolour of the castle. An engraving of the site by Petrie appeared in an 1823 guide of the Giant's Causeway (Wright 1823) (fig. 8.2). Given Petrie's keen and accurate attention to detail, we can take his drawing of the site to be an accurate representation. A number of features warrant mention, including his inclusion of a doorway at the southern end of the external wall of the western range in the inner court area. Two apparent drain outlets are visible on the wall directly opposite the manor house, where the large chasm now exists and where the name Petrie is carved above the opening. The presence of these

8.1 Photograph of the Boothe graffiti in the northeast tower. Many visitors have etched their names in the castle walls.

8.2 An engraving of the castle by George Petrie, published in Wright's 1823 *Guide to the Giant's Causeway*.

two openings and the erosive nature of the cliff face at this point probably led to the larger collapse at a slightly later date. Petrie also depicted a possible window at attic level in the south gable of the manor house. This appears in a number of drawings of the site, and the twentieth-century masonry patching of this feature is clearly noticeable. There is no internal indication of this feature, however, so it may be indicative of a rebuild of the chimney or represent the loss of masonry at some point.

Artists and the castle

By the close of the eighteenth century, the castle began to attract the interest of painters. James Nixon (1741–1812) produced one of the earliest known images of the site, a watercolour dating to sometime between 1761 and 1794 (fig. 8.3). He drew the castle from a position low on the foreshore below the western side of the site and included an oversized man crossing the bridge. Among the many interesting elements of this piece, an engraving based on which was later published in volume II of Francis Grose's 1794 *Antiquities of Ireland*, is the fact that the collapse of the curtain wall opposite the manor house is shown, indicating that this had occurred during the eighteenth century. This contradicts Petrie's later drawing. The accuracy of both drawings is not in question, and so the likelihood is that repairs were conducted on the site in the early part of the nineteenth century. This is significant, as there are certain features across the site that had defied dating, including elements of this wall and the inserted masonry in the manor house doorway. It appears that the MacDonnells undertook some repair work and upkeep during their tenure of the site, a deduction supported by the fact that they protected the surrounding fields and maintained property boundaries and external walls. The entrance to the gate tower had collapsed by this date, but its western wall stands higher than it does today. It is also clear that the cliff face has eroded considerably since that time, as Grose shows at least 2m of grassed area outside the walls, most of which has now eroded away. A high wall is also present, running along the northern edge of the cliff. It appears to be a hurried sketch, as a number of major features are missing, including chimney stacks and some buildings. A second very informative sketch was published in 1802 by Captain William Smith in volume 1 of *Original drawings and paintings of Ireland and Scotland*. It is a fine, crisp drawing showing the south face of the castle and the bridge and is the earliest highly accurate view of the site (fig. 8.4). Lord Mark Kerr, born in 1776, the third son of the fifth marquess of Lothian, in 1799 married Lady Charlotte MacDonnell, daughter of the 6th earl of Antrim. He produced a series of accurate sketches of the castle in August 1809, many of which were published by Hector McDonnell in his *History of Dunluce* (McDonnell 2004a). Kerr also shows a doorway on the western range and indicates the collapse of the wall opposite the manor house. Most significantly, his drawings do not show crenellations on the walls, while later

8.3 A version of James Nixon's 1794 illustration of the site from the west published in Grose's *Antiquities*.

8.4 William Smith's 1802 illustration of Dunluce from the south
(image reproduced courtesy of Trinity College Dublin).

drawings do, including Petrie's. Could Kerr's visit have spurred the MacDonnells to engage not only in repair but also in fanciful reconstruction in the second decade of the nineteenth century? This certainly seems likely.

In 1817, the Manchester painter W. Watts exhibited three paintings of Dunluce at the Royal Academy. One oil-on-canvas shows a male and a female figure emerging from the cave beneath the castle carrying nets and oars. This was on the market again in 2011 valued at £5,500. Agustus Earle (*c.*1793–*c.*1838) was a travel artist who famously travelled with Charles Darwin abroad the *Beagle* before he had to return home due to ill health. He produced an accurate representation of the south facing front of Dunluce Castle probably in 1835, when he visited this part of the coast (fig. 8.5). Earle painted a number of figures precariously crossing the narrow bridge, while others emerge from the cave below. Goats are shown grazing in the foreground, while ships can be seen passing on the horizon. The watercolour by Fermanagh artist William Bourke Kirwan (1814–52) depicts three figures standing on the foreshore, with the castle in the background. It clearly shows the north range standing. An etching by J. McGahey, printed in a Christian evangelical text *Youth's instruction* (Mason 1830), illustrates the castle from the east in a dramatic style, with the northern building range intact and the southeast tower crenellated. Similarly, David Frederick Marham's 1848 sketch of the castle has the north range intact. All of this combines to counter the tale that this range fell in 1639.

In one of the best-known illustrations of the site, William Henry Bartlett (1809–54) produced a dramatic drawing in his own distinctive style in the 1830s (fig. 8.6). His drawings were noted for their relative historical accuracy and were widely copied. The Dunluce image was reproduced in a number of antiquarian works, including *The scenery and antiquities of Ireland* (1840). An 1834 print was based on an original by T.M. Baynes (Wright et al. 1834).

Andrew Nicholl (1804–86) was born in Belfast and lived in Church Lane near Queen's Bridge. He was a founder member of the Belfast Association of Artists in 1836 and exhibited at the Royal Hibernian Academy (RHA) in 1848 and later at the Royal Academy in London. The RHA elected him as a member in 1848. He is probably best known for his depictions of Sri Lanka, or Ceylon, as it was then known, where he spent time as an art teacher, but he also produced a series of watercolours along the north Antrim coast (fig. 8.7). In 2002, one of his pencil and watercolours of the castle sold at Christies, London, while his study of wildflowers with the castle in the background sold in Dublin in 2005. Abroad, the castle was also attracting attention, and a number of European artists produced interesting images of the site during the middle of the nineteenth century. Many of these were embellished, showing impossible details including harbours and housing at the base of the cliff. Franz Emil Krausse's (1836–1900) landscape paintings gained popularity across Britain in the later part of the century and, in one oil painting, held by the Bury Art Gallery, Museum and Archives, he illustrated a number of fishing boats drawn up on

8.5 Augustus Earle's 1830s painting of Dunluce Castle from the south.

8.6 William Henry Bartlett's dramatic 1830s illustration of Dunluce Castle from the east.

the shore beneath the castle, with women standing by lobster pots. The castle's popularity had not waned by the end of the century, when Albert Dunington (1860–1928), for example, then living at Great Western Street in Manchester produced an oil-on-canvas of the site (1891).

With the advent of mass tourism and the arrival of the railways, a number of companies began to use images of the castle to promote their products. One such well-known example is a 1924 travel poster by Albert Julius Olsson, produced for London, Midland & Scottish Railway (LMS) to promote rail travel to Northern Ireland. It is now held at the National Railway Museum in York, England. A series of postcards appeared at a later date, as well as stamps and other memorabilia.

Photography

As photography developed in the later nineteenth century, a number of local photographers developed a keen antiquarian interest. These included R.J. Welch (1859–1936), his apprentice W.A. Green (1870–1958), A.R. Hogg (1870–1939) and the Belfast antiquarian F.J. Bigger (1863–1926). The Lawrence Collection of the National Library of Ireland contains a number of pictures of the castle, while the Welch Collection, held by the Ulster Museum in Belfast, includes a number of images of the interior. One of the most interesting shows two gentlemen standing against the southeast tower, with the reconstructed loggia in the foreground (fig. 8.8). A second image shows the external front wall of the manor house and indicates that the doorway was partially blocked up with masonry. These and other images were taken on 15 May 1929, soon after the clearance was undertaken. The Green Collection is held at the Ulster Folk and Transport Museum and contains valuable general external views of the castle, as well as feature shots of the gate tower and examples showing the electric trams. Many of Hogg's photographs are held at the Ulster Museum and some are images of the castle probably taken in the 1920s and early 1930s. During the period before the Second World War, the RAF flew a number of reconnaissance missions along this coast, and the photographs they took remain a valuable record for the state of the monument at that time. Among the most useful are shots taken on 25 November 1930 (fig. 8.9). The images clearly show the area in front of the castle gate before it was landscaped, where additional masonry buildings and other features are visible. House platforms and associated plots are clearly delineated in the town field, while further, previously unidentified, settlement features are also visible in the eastern cliff edge field. Another aerial photograph, taken in September 1948, provides a fine view of the landscape setting of the castle and shows the outer mainland court area before the new visitor buildings were added and the walls heightened. Dunluce House and associated farm buildings are clearly visible in the background (fig. 8.10).

8.7 One of Andrew Nicholl's paintings of the castle (image reproduced courtesy of the Ulster Museum).

8.8 Welch's 1929 image of the southeast tower and loggia, following the clearance work of 1928. Over 2m of debris had accumulated in this area following the castle's abandonment.

Writers

A number of writers and poets clearly drew inspiration from Dunluce Castle. It is often cited as the inspiration for the mythical castle 'Cair Paravel' in C.S. Lewis' *Chronicles of Narnia*. As a native of Belfast, Lewis had been a frequent visitor to Dunluce and the castle must have left a significant impression on this highly imaginative writer. A number of poems feature Dunluce, including Edward Quillinan's epic four-part *Dunluce Castle*, published by Johnson and Warwick in 1814. This long rambling romantic tome had some impact when published, but it is largely forgotten today, outside specialist circles. Edward Lear produced a short rhyme in 1872 in the volume *More nonsense, pictures, rhymes, botany &c*:

> There was an old man of Dunluce,
> Who went out to sea on a goose;
> When he'd gone out a mile,
> He observ'd with a smile,
> 'It is time to return to Dunluce'.

The American poet Sarah Orne Jewett (1849–1909) later published a shorter poem, also entitled *Dunluce Castle*. Jewett had visited Ireland during the summer of 1882 and published the piece in November of the following year in *Harper's Magazine*, accompanied by an illustration of the castle by Charles Graham (1852–1911):

> To-day from all thy ruined walls
> The flowers wave flags of truce;
> For time has proved thy conqueror,
> And tamed thy strength, Dunluce!
> Lords of the Skerries' cruel rocks,
> Masters of sea and shore.
> Marauders in their clanking mail
> Ride from thy gates no more.
> Thy dungeons are untenanted.
> Thy captives are set free;
> The daisy, with sweet childish face,
> Keeps watch across the sea.
> Thy halls are open to the sky.
> Thy revelry has ceased;
> The echoes of thy mirth have died
> With fires that lit the feast.
> What keepers of thy secrets old
> Flit through the wind and rain!

8.9 RAF aerial photograph of Dunluce taken at 13:00 on 25 November 1930.

8.10 Aerial photograph of the site from the south, taken in September 1948. This image is very useful as it shows how the castle looked before the modern buildings were added to facilitate visitors and the works depot.

What stern-faced ghosts have come by night
To visit thee again!
Grim fortress of the Northern sea.
Lost are they power and pride;
Within thy undefended walls
The folded sheep abide.

Many other writers and poets have made reference to the site, but these are beyond the scope of the present book. It is to be hoped that another researcher will contextualize Dunluce's place and impact within the broader arena of cultural studies.

A conservation history: 1928–2000

Malcolm Fry (2005) has written a detailed account of the emerging role of monument protection in the new Northern Ireland government from partition in the 1920s. From an inauspicious start, the management of built cultural heritage quickly became integrated into the programme of government, and sites such as Dunluce were taken into state care because of their national importance and cost of upkeep. Conservation principles at the time were guided by the preservation, consolidation and weatherproofing of remains, without any attempt at reconstruction. Unused areas were to be grassed over and fallen masonry and vegetation were to be removed. In the period after Dunluce was taken into care in 1928, a programme of site conservation and stabilization was initiated. The so-called government 'B-files' (B2093/1928; B2093/1975) held by the DoENI document this process, often including the most banal and smallest of details. They make for fascinating reading and were the source for the following section. Most of the work across Northern Ireland was directed by Dr David Alfred Chart (1878–1960), a historian employed as deputy keeper of public records in the new Stormont administration (Fry 2005), with the support of the architect T.F.O. Rippingham. Approval was granted for the commencement of the repairs in July 1928 and a mason and 'foreman' named Harry Campbell was put in charge, with an overall budget of £1,025. In August, a work programme was drawn up, following discussions with the earl of Antrim, and included the erection of a gate and wire fencing to enclose the site, 'reasonable clearing to restore original levels', the cleaning and weather pointing of wall-tops and the securing of their bases. This was not an inconsiderable job, as it was found that there were over 2m of masonry and general build-up in places. By September, Campbell had begun recruiting men and he collected their wages each Thursday at Bushmills Post Office. The clearing work involved six or seven labourers over six weeks, while the masonry work was undertaken by Campbell, a second mason and one or two labourers over an eight-week period. Much of the clearance work reported

8.11 The 'funnel' area looking southwards towards the lodgings.

8.12 An early twentieth-century photograph showing (probably) Miss Simpson at Dunluce House, which then functioned as a tea-room. She served as the site caretaker and guide for many years before retiring to Bushmills.

on in the 1928 report (appendix, below) was undertaken during this schedule from September through to December, when work ceased until the spring due to inclement weather.

Following a visit on 3 April 1929, Chart reported that the work of consolidating the fabric was proceeding and that one of the labourers was clearing out the souterrain. He stated that

> this is now found to go deeply beneath the northeast circular tower, and it is necessary to go cautiously and to prop. Several pieces of flint found, though none perfectly shaped. These and other items are being kept. Three chambers of the souterrain are now cleared, and the last opened is by far the largest. Miss Simpson keeps the place very well, but is asking for a lawn mower.

Simpson had been appointed as the caretaker of the site and appears frequently in the records. At the same time, the government's architect wrote a memo to Robert Cochrane, contractor, Causeway Street, Portrush, expressing his surprise that 'no start had been made with the bridge and fencing' (B2094/28, 5 July 1929) (fig. 8.11).

On 18 February 1931, Simpson wrote to the ministry of finance in relation to the stones that had fallen in the kitchen. A note on file two days later sadly stated that it was two months since the death of Campbell. By October of the same year, a minute recorded that the

> ministry [was] in possession of the castle on the rock and not the mainland field above it. We discovered some time ago that underneath the field surface lay an extensive paving of stones. We uncovered sufficient of this to serve as a pathway to the Castle, and it has been very useful in providing a dry road in wet weather.

This was the pathway leading from the road down to the castle. Grazing was taking place in the field to the west of the path and in the area in front of the castle. The grazing tenant was noted as Sir Malcom Macnaghten, recorded as an 'English high court judge', who suggested the erection of fences to control the cattle and protect the site. Macnaghten, from the Macnaghtens of Dundarave House in Bushmills, was originally appointed a barrister in 1894 and later became an MP for North Londonderry in 1922 and for Londonderry county and city between 1922 and 1928. He served as a judge of the king's bench division of the high court of justice from 1928 to 1947, before becoming a privy councillor in 1948. He married Antonia Mary Booth in 1899 and died in January 1955. Subsequent concerns were raised that Antrim might disagree with Macnaghten's plans. Antrim later wrote to Dr Chart, agreeing to the fencing but making it clear that he was not giving up his rights to this area, which was still in his ownership (24 October 1931). A letter in the same month from Macnaghten suggested a series of improvements, including lines of fencing and new gate access to various areas and fields. He had obviously developed an intense interest in the site by this time and was later to write expressing an interest in displaying the finds recovered from the 1928 clearance work at the site. Both the fireback and the coins were recorded as being in the possession of Dr Chart. The fireback was later noted as being 24 inches high, 27.75 inches wide and 2 inches thick, with a coat of arms inscribed on it. This was stored at Carrickfergus.

By April 1931, Macnaghten had bought and renovated the farmhouse and installed the caretaker Miss Simpson as housekeeper. It was being run as a tea-house, with plans to develop it as a small hotel (fig. 8.12). Later that month, Chart wrote to Macnaghten, stating that he could display the objects in the house, but a suitable cabinet should be built for them. Macnaghten, whose address was given as 18 Elden Road, London, W8, was also planting shrubs and creating an area for car parking. The artefacts were delivered to Miss Simpson in November and included a 'brown Bellermine jug, 8 fragments, a fragment of a coloured tile, dark glazed pottery (2 pieces, one being a handle), window glass. 2 pieces, 1 clay pipe, 1 fragment of bronze'. A suitable case had also been made. An official visit in July 1937 noted that three hundred visitors had paid the six-penny rate and 150 had paid half price during the month of June. Banks of flowering plants had been established under the shelter of the walls, with colonies of rock plants on wall-tops. A caretaker's hut was present and a ladder was to be provided for access to the southeast tower. A suggestion was also made that the exhibition be placed in the northeast tower, which should be floored, and that the souterrain should be covered by boards. That same month, a D. Carson, now caretaker of the castle and later referred to as a 'disabled ex-serviceman' with only one arm, wrote to Chart that he would lay the floor in the east tower, place trapdoors over the souterrain and put up steps to the southeast tower at a cost of £1. In April of the following year, all of the above had been completed and Carson was removing weeds from cobbles. A certain Mr McAleese, who apparently lived with Simpson, had also submitted a claim for looking after the finds.

In February 1939, work on the northeast tower, including making it watertight, adding a new door and window and fitting an oak trapdoor, had been completed. Nonetheless, the weather was still causing considerable problems across the site. On 8 February 1940, a new caretaker, Mrs James Johnston, reported that part of the cliff adjacent to the entrance of the castle had fallen away. Carson was also working on the site at the time. The following April, it was reported that about three tons of rock had become 'disintegrated' from the cliff under the southeast corner of the gate house. In January 1942, Johnston made yet another worrying report, stating that 'part of wall, on west side of Dunluce Castle, has fallen into the sea'. This portion was later found to be the southwest corner of the inner court. A subsequent inspection found that 'a right angle in the wall is gone down, taking with it about 7 feet of the northward-running component of the angle and about 5 feet of the westward running component'. Elsewhere, despite the general shortages and financial difficulties associated with the Second World War, a battery had been installed in the tower to illuminate the exhibition of finds now stored in the building. Unfortunately, the fireback had split when a visitor lifted it and accidently dropped it, and it was also rusting badly. Dunluce House was no longer a tea and guest house, as Miss Simpson had gone to live with a brother in Bushmills and Sir Malcolm had let the house to a private individual. Mrs Johnston was living in the 'cottage' and acted as warden of the Youth Hostel Association premises, as well as issuing entry tickets to the castle. The hostel was housed in the large north–south running barn in the farmyard adjacent to Dunluce House. By the 1950s, the objects listed on display at the site included 'ancient window glass, clay pipe, Bell armine (sic) jug, pottery fragment, portion of ship's pumps, door key, 2 crested buttons, 1 plain button, bullet, old weight with figure of teapot, cannon-ball'. The coins from the original work had been collected from a bank vault and were now lodged in the assistant secretary of the finance ministry's office. In 1955, Patrick McKinley purchased Dunluce House from the Macnaghtens and started farming the immediate surrounding landscape.

By the 1960s, a new wing of the ministry of finance, the ancient monuments branch, took charge of the site. Much of the work throughout the following decade was carried out under the supervision of Mr Meek. The last few months of 1963 were especially busy. Joists on the northeast tower were pointed, as was the southern curtain wall and around window openings. Stones in the 'bake oven' were 'firmed up' and tarmacadam was laid down in December on the path leading to the castle. Sealing work was also undertaken on the doorway, where 'stonework is broken down in the northeast wall'. Early in January 1964, paving stones for the path were laid in the gallery (loggia) and rubbish was being removed from the base of the southeast tower to facilitate the paving. A wall was also being built in the gallery and missing stones were being replaced where the 'wall adjoins the southeast tower on the south wall'. The whole of the southeast portion of the castle was the focus of work in the summer months of 1964, with extensive pointing and stone replacement undertaken. In October, a new top was built on the wall of the northeast tower, which was extensively repointed, and a sill was reset in a door and window. By November, part of the curtain wall was taken down and rebuilt where it bonded into the tower. A new top was also built on it.

In the opening days of 1965, the workmen at Dunluce were listed as S. Patterson (Billy, Bushmills), D. McMullan (Billy, Bushmills) and W.J. Elliott (28 Woodvale Terrace, Bushmills). During the early part of that year, work focused on the kitchen area. In January, masonry was removed from the top of the chimney flue of the oven fireplace and the wall top was sealed. During April and May, the east wall top was resealed and pointed and work was also undertaken on the 'latrine'. Work ceased on 3 June and transferred to Beaghmore stone circle. Two years later, a letter dated 18 September 1967 to Miss Lonsdale expressed concern about the security of the coin collection, housed in the northeast tower. At this time, the door of the chamber was secured by a ground bolt and could easily be opened. A new caretaker's hut was also required, as the existing one was over thirty years old. This was erected in June 1969. A break-in occurred that year, and the coins were transferred to a bank for safe keeping on the advice of the police. By this time, there was an increased interest in filming at the castle, from the BBC and others. Dunluce was now open to the public from Monday to Saturday, 10am to 6pm (closed 1 to 2pm) and on Sunday from 2 to 6pm. During the winter months, it was open 10am to 4pm on Saturday and 2 to 4pm on Sunday.

Towards the end of 1969, work focused on the bridge and railings. By October, a wall had been built at the west entrance to the castle, measuring 24 feet long and 4 feet high. A grille was fitted on the souterrain and a pillar was rebuilt at the southeast tower. Work was also undertaken on the wall at the east side of the entrance, and three new flagstones were laid in the castle entrance, following the removal of broken ones. By November, the emphasis had shifted to bringing cobbles up from the shore for laying at the castle entrance. This became the major focus of activity in the opening months of 1970, when a total of 680 man-hours was spent 'wenching' cobbles up from the shore, presumably for use in the cobbling of the inner yard and elsewhere. For two further months in 1971, one man was employed picking building stones at the castle (fig. 8.13).

The impact of natural deterioration was constant, and in February 1971 stone fell from the south gable of the hall. That year also saw the state purchase the outer ward from the earl of Antrim, who was concerned about the impact grazing sheep were having on the masonry in that area and did not feel that the family had the resources to protect it. In a letter dated 4 June 1971 from the superintendent of works, Patrick McKinley was to be told that he no longer had any right to graze this area, which was being tidied up by a Miss Kenny to 'establish neat grass'. That same month, George Robinson (superintendent of works at the Moira depot) and the archaeologist Dudley Waterman visited the castle as a result of the purchase and proposed that the 'entire compound … be made secure'. New entrances were proposed and the refurbishment of bay windows and replacement of masonry from fallen chimneys to proceed. The monthly reporting process also changed at this date, with less detailed information now being returned to central government. Robinson had joined the ancient monuments branch in 1962 after serving in the RAF and retired in 1985, when he was awarded an MBE for services to local history.

By November 1971, the men were engaged in levelling the ground at the mainland buildings and had begun to dig a verge around the rooms of these buildings. In January of the following year, they were removing sods and topsoil from the new car park area and levelling the ground there. In February, the grounds around the castle were levelled off and soil and grass seed were put down. Building of the wall around the car park was also started. This wall was still being built by August, by which time gates had been erected into the castle grounds and a new path laid out from the car park to the castle entrance. Railings were erected around the top of the cliffs in the grounds. The final job that year seems to have been the laying of a water main to supply the castle. The opening month of 1973 saw more cobbles brought up from the shore for the 'floors in the castle grounds'. January was a busy month, with the lifting of stone flags in front of the 'banquet hall', ground levelling and cobble-laying in sand and cement. Stone flags were also lifted *in* the banquet hall, and the ground was levelled off for their relaying. In the 'courtyard in front of entrance into castle', cobbles were lifted and relaid. Cobbles from the shore continued to be collected and winched up to the yard in the castle, using a motor winch. During March of the same year, walls were being built to the east and west of the mainland into the outer yard area and this continued until the summer. Steps were also built in front of the entrance to the 'banquet hall'. Throughout that year, a series of drains were laid across the site and stone steps were made down to the cave. Consideration was now given to opening the site during the winter months, a proposal outlined to Miss Kenny, the site caretaker (fig. 8.14).

By March the following year, the construction of a pier under the bridge was nearly complete. A new bridge was also built and this was nearly complete by August. Additionally, twenty-seven square yards of flagstones were laid. During April, the walls around the construction yard were built up in order to secure this area. Stone was sourced from an old house at Ballylough, something that appears to have happened quite frequently during reconstruction work at the site and elsewhere. That year also saw a BBC outside broadcast from the castle in June. Finally, during December, the cobbles of the inner courtyard were lifted and the area was recobbled. The hearths in the main hall were also 'fixed' with slates. Early in the New Year, new lintels were erected over two doors and 'built up around with stones at the northeast end of the castle grounds'. Cobbling of the 'main yard' continued intermittently to the end of the year. A list of objects on display at the castle in January 1976 included 'ancient window glass, clay pipe, Bellarmine jug, pottery fragment, portion of ship's pumps, door key, 2 crested buttons, 1 plain button, bullet, old weight with figure of teapot, cannon-ball'. Little structural work took place during the year, aside from general caretaking, and consideration was given to making a new display case for the coins.

The files make it clear that from the mid-1970s the men at Dunluce were involved in works throughout the district, at sites like Bonamargy, Mount Sandel, Dungiven and Dooey's cairn. The files also reflect the changing political circumstances of the time. In May 1977, the men were on strike as part of the United Unionist Action Council campaign, called by Unionists and Loyalists, including men like Ian Paisley (who emerged as one of its leaders), who were in favour of returning devolved simple majority rule to Northern Ireland. The strike was also an attempt to force the British government to impose stronger security measures against the IRA. The fact that the men were all on strike is strongly suggestive that they were associated with the Unionist tradition. Sometime late that year, the site custodian was asked to 'pack up the few odds and ends in the show-case in the round tower for transfer to Moira'.

1978 saw the advent of health and safety concerns. In June, a letter to Mr Robinson from A.J. Kennedy, safety supervisor, stated that the well in the cliff area was several feet deep and unguarded and was to be filled with rough gravel. The new caretaker, Mr N.L. Patterson, detailed an accident in September, in which a member of a school group fell into the souterrain. After this event, the files become pretty pedestrian. The archaeologist Marion Meek now had responsibility for the site and in September, Mrs E. Patterson, of 41 Main Street, Bushmills, was appointed as guide at the site. Little of note is contained in the B-files after this date, but it is clear that significant conservation work continued to be undertaken. Some of this work proved to be controversial. Stonework for a new window was inserted into the southern bay in 1987. Originally, this was meant to have been inserted in the central bay, but measurement mistakes resulted in its insertion in the southern bay instead. A small quantity of primary stonework was removed to facilitate its placement. Masonry from the doorway was also removed around this date, and a series of temporary frames were inserted to replace the stone. While the removed masonry was probably nineteenth or early twentieth century, its removal has led to the unsatisfactory temporary shoring up of this feature with ugly steelwork. Of equal concern was the insertion of an incorrect arch over the door in the east wall of the house, providing access to the kitchen area. Other areas of concern include the covering of the masonry steps in the northeast tower for health and safety reasons and continued landscaping that impacted on the surrounding archaeology. Undoubtedly, many conservation mistakes were made during this period and it is unfortunate that a far more rigorous recording programme did not accompany these changes.

As Dunluce's popularity grew, it became necessary to develop improved visitor facilities. 1988, for example, saw 25,000 people visiting the site, and in June 1990 the DoE requested that their works service draw up plans for a visitor centre. A building incorporating a toilet block at the southeast corner had been rebuilt, while the new visitor centre was subsequently built in the southwest corner. The site was later opened seven days a week, and guiding staff were employed during the summer months to improve the visitor experience. By 1997, visitor numbers had increased to 36,282, 1,463 of whom were classified as educational visitors. This relatively low number was viewed with a degree of concern, and more effort was to be invested in attracting school and college groups, similar to initiatives then being undertaken at Carrickfergus. In 1998, the safety and structural integrity of the bridge was causing concern and, following an inspection late that year, a programme of maintenance was undertaken. This began in November 1999 (a programme of work and conservation of the gate house had commenced in October) and finished at the end of May 2000. Cobbling at the bridge was also carried out, and a programme of repointing was conducted throughout 2000, as well as the rebuilding of walls associated with the bridge, parapet and buttery, that continued into 2001. The following decade saw far

8.13 Conducting ground-penetrating radar survey in the cobbled yard of the castle
(image reproduced courtesy of Chris McGonigle, UU).

8.14 Early twentieth-century Robert Welch photograph of Dunluce from the east
(image reproduced courtesy of the Ulster Museum).

more informed intervention, mostly associated with protecting the structural integrity of the monument and the cliff. In particular, a major programme of cliff-face stabilization was undertaken. The process of protecting the monument continues unabated and will no doubt carry on for many centuries.

Table 8.1 1950 list of coins found on the site in 1928 (DoENI file B2093). The current location of these coins is unknown. The other finds from the site appear to have ended up at DoE's Moira depot, where several were discarded

Date	Type	Detail
1632	Scottish	Charles I, turner (copper coin), numeral II
Charles I	Scottish	Uncertain variety of turner (copper coin)
17th century	Irish	Worn copper St Patrick farthing
17th or 18th century	Irish	Irish copper halfpenny. Overstruck. Undertype not clear but may be half penny of James II (or gun-money shilling)
17th century	Irish	Rev. St George and dragon
1816–20		George II (1760–1820). Worn sixpence of last coinage
1633–9		Charles I (1625–49). Tower mint, sixpence, m.m. crown (1633–6)
After 1637?	Scotland	Charles I (1625–49). Silver forty-penny piece. Struck after 1637? Engraved by Nicholas Briot
1642	Scotland	Charles I. Copper turner or (=2*d.* English), Bodle, 3rd issue, 1642 and after. Obv. CAR.D.G.SCOT.ANG.FRA.ET.HIB.R. Crowned CR. Rev. NEM MEIMPUNE LACCESSIT Thistle
1620	France	Louis XIII double tournois. m.m. G= Poitiers
1620	France	Louis XIII double tournois 1620. m.m. G= Poitiers
1629?	France	Copper double tournois; mint of La Rochelle
1639	France	Louis XIII double tournois 1639
1630s?	France	Double tournois (illegible)
1630s?	France	Double tournois (illegible)
1630s?	France	Double tournois; uncertain date and mint
	France	Louis XIII?
1630	France	France (Louis XIII). Principate of Dombes. (Gaston 1627–50), copper double tournois dated 1630. Rev. 3 Fleurs-de-lis with label of difference
	France	France (Henry IV?). Copper double tournois, struck at Henrichemont. Rev. fleurs-de-lis round arms of Be'thune
1860–70	England	Victoria, playing counter or medalet. Prince of Wales model sovereign

CHAPTER 9

Dunluce: a chronology

Dunluce Castle has played a hugely significant part in the socio-economic and political life of the communities of north Ulster and the Western Isles of Scotland for many centuries (fig. 9.1). While there is evidence that there was early medieval settlement on the headland and then Anglo-Norman activity in the thirteenth century, the castle itself was built very late in the fifteenth century. By that date, its builders, the MacQuillans, were the dominant family grouping across the region and became lords of the Route. Their subsequent loss of the site to the MacDonnells in the 1550s consolidated the castle as the centre of power across the north coast of Ulster and the southern Western Isles. This was a maritime world, firmly rooted in the Gaelic tradition and embedded in the social conditions of the time. It was a local world dominated by the power of the medieval lords sharing Catholicism, a common language and a common sense of cultural traditions across the region. This was not, however, the idealized Gaelic world of the imagination of late nineteenth-century writers, but instead a world marked by almost continual conflict, political ambitions and inter-clan aggression. Economy was rooted in agrarian practice and fishing. Daily

9.1 Dunluce Castle viewed from the south. Note the netting protecting the cliff face immediately below the castle walls.

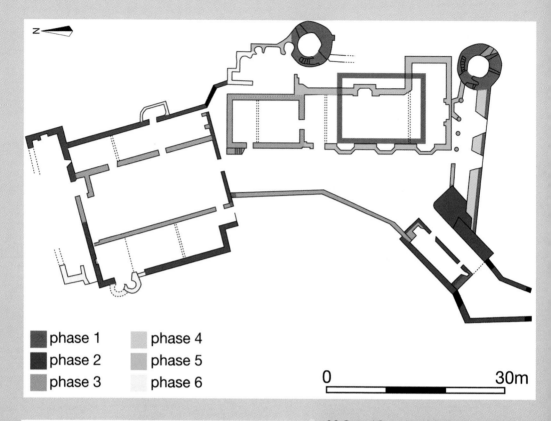

N

phase 1
phase 2
phase 3
phase 4
phase 5
phase 6

0   30m

9.2 Ground-floor plan of the castle illustrating the major phases of development.

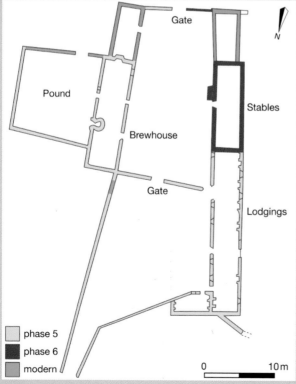

Gate

N

Pound

Stables

Brewhouse

Gate

Lodgings

phase 5
phase 6
modern

0   10 m

9.3 Plan showing the phases of development of the mainland ranges.

Chronological development of Dunluce (fig. 9.2)

Phase 1, c.1490–1510
The earliest architectural horizon of the castle dates to the closing decade of the fifteenth and opening decade of the sixteenth century. On the promontory, the MacQuillans constructed a fortified chiefry centre consisting of a large rectangular building surrounded by a curtain wall with at least two corner towers, both of which survive along its eastern side. Entry into this castle was across a narrow bridge to a gate house set in the southwest corner of the curtain wall.

Phase 2, 1555–1655
In the middle of the 1550s, the MacDonnells took the castle from the MacQuillans and embarked on a programme of castle refurbishment. They erected a large gate tower above the existing gate house and extended the castle environs by creating a walled enclosure at the northern end of the promontory, containing a rectangular building at its northeast corner.

Phase 3, late 1580s
A generation later, in the 1580s, a second major MacDonnell refurbishment was undertaken, in line with contemporary Renaissance trends. The old MacQuillan building was levelled and a loggia was inserted inside the southern section of curtain wall. First-floor additions to the northern enclosure wall resulted in the development of two ranges – one on either side of a yard used for domestic functions and providing both lodgings and a small hall for the occupants. The upper floors of both corner towers were also modified at this date, and access to the wall-walk associated with the southern curtain wall was reconfigured. It is also probable that the buttery building was constructed during this phase, albeit at a slightly later date than work on the northern ranges.

Phase 4, 1590s
Phase 4 involved the refortification of the site during the course of the Nine Years War. Two large embrasures were inserted into the southern wall to facilitate the placement of guns.

Phase 5, 1608–13
In the opening two decades of the seventeenth century, Randal MacDonnell engaged in a major programme of building and castle refurbishment. He erected a new Jacobean house over the site of the original MacQuillan building. The southern gable of the house was connected to a covered range along the southern curtain and the buttery building was incorporated into the northern gable. Immediately east, a kitchen was added. New buildings were established on the mainland, including stables and an enclosed courtyard. A second building stood opposite the stables across the yard to the east. In the immediate environs of the castle, a town was established.

Phase 5, late 1610s–20s
As the 1st earl's (Randal MacDonnell) power and wealth grew, he further invested in the site. A large lodgings block was erected along the western side of the mainland courtyard and a brew-house was developed opposite the stables (fig. 9.3). This mainland area was further subdivided by a cross-wall, creating further access to the inner portion of the castle. Sections of the town continued to develop through this period.

Phases 6–7, mid- to late seventeenth century
These phases mark the gradual decline and abandonment of the site. While a number of the castle buildings went through minor refurbishment, including new tiled roofs in the 1630s, the conflict of the 1640s and 1650s saw the manor house being burned and its stonework robbed. Much of the town was also destroyed in 1641 and it never recovered.

9.4 Rough seas beneath the cliffs at Dunluce, looking eastwards towards the Giant's Causeway.

life must have been a constant struggle for those who lived in the harsh and often challenging environment at the edge of the Atlantic. The Plantation of Ulster heralded significant change across the region, but the MacDonnells weathered this new social storm and emerged intact, developing ambitious building and mercantile schemes across their estates. Archaeological investigation is now exposing the full and impressive extent of their ambitions that were previously a mere side-line in later written histories. By the outbreak of the 1641 rebellion, the fortunes of Dunluce had declined and, following initial abandonment in that decade, the site never really recovered. The castle itself featured only as the figurative centre of the Antrim estates, with the earls moving first to Ballymagarry and later to Glenarm. Around the castle, the town died a slow death before it was effectively forgotten beneath the soils of time. While the castle was subject to extensive conservation work throughout the twentieth century, it has only recently been subject to the intensive form of investigation reported upon here.

9.5 Satellite image of north Ulster and Scotland (Landsat ETM+ mosaic courtesy of the Global Landcover Facility (GCLF)). This was the local maritime world of the people who lived at Dunluce Castle, where boats facilitated quick and easy access across the region.

The castle's future

The archaeological findings and architectural analysis at the castle have been both important and exciting. For the first time, a more informed picture of the site's cultural development is emerging. Much remains to be done, and it is hoped that future work at the site will further expand and fine-tune our understanding of this major site. The beginning of this work has, however, highlighted both major challenges and opportunities. Continuous conservation intervention is required to protect Dunluce from the climate of the north coast (fig. 9.4). As our winters become harsher and more storm events are forecast, these conservation efforts need to be intensified. The underpinning of the rapidly eroding cliff has been a significant undertaking, but constant monitoring and proactive intervention are still required. Considerable opportunities are also present. There is an urgent need to develop sustainable visitor facilities and allow the castle to continue to be used as a centre for educational engagement. Such ventures require significant investment, but it is clear that sustainable heritage enterprises can be developed that play an integral role in Northern Ireland's economic and social future. Dunluce can inform us about our difficult past and help develop a greater sense of awareness and understanding between the various communities and traditions of this region. The castle highlights the sense of interconnectedness that exists between this part of Ulster and parts of western Scotland (fig. 9.5). It will continue to be our most iconic archaeological monument and we look forward to the site revealing further secrets over the coming years.

CONFIDENTIAL/53503/
Dunluce Castle – interim report:
work during September–December 1928

Meeting of the Advisory Committee, 9 January 1929

Except from certain of the outer slopes of rock-stack, the clearing of accumulated debris, soil and vegetation has been completed, and the buildings and sites are now exposed down to the levels of the later pavements. In cases where the pavements were found to be missing, the levels below were exposed by trial-holes, and in some cases earlier pavement levels were found. Such disturbance has been very slight and in all cases the filling has been carefully replaced and the later levels preserved. This report will give details of such exploration, but, generally, will be confined to an account of the clearing down to the levels now exposed. The various buildings and sections will be dealt with in the order in which they were cleared, and an account will be given of the nature of the debris removed, of the articles found in the debris, and the evidence adopted to determine the levels to be exposed.

(I) Outer yard

After a few trial-holes had revealed the presence of a disturbed bedding of mortar but no paving except loose fragments, it was decided to work down in layers. The accumulation of loose soil and slate was removed in this manner over the central area of the yard. A few small flagstones were found actually bedded, but over the greater area nothing was found except the broken-up bedding of mortar lying on the higher levels of the uneven rock surface. The absence of filling in the hollows of the rock would seem to indicate that the paving had been removed at an early date, i.e. before the roofs had shed their slates, and that there was a period of exposure during which the filling had been washed away. In the angles of the southern end of the yard, covered by fallen masonry, small areas of paving were found in situ. The levels of these pavings were adopted for the level of the grass with which the unpaved area has now been covered. Soil from other clearing was used for filling, and a system of field drainage was laid in the hollows with the dual object of reducing percolation through the rock-stack, and keeping the new lawn in condition. The subsidence against the centre of the west curtain was bridged in concrete, covered with soil, and grassed over the same level as the yard. Objects found in this area include a clay pipe, and a silver-plated spur. All were found in shallow soil and probably trodden in. Some leaded window glass was found outside the north window of gate house chamber.

At the northern end of the yard, the removal of a foot or so of loose soil (containing a few broken slates) revealed a complete paving of cobbles laid in clay and with a fall to a central channel running through into the Inner yard. The line of junction with the stone flagging of the southern half of the yard is very clear. A coin of 1639 (Louis XIII) was found in the cobbles.

At the southern end of the yard, against the gate house, a mound of fallen masonry 10' high was found to cover a flight of four sandstone steps, much decayed, leading up from the gate house passageway. The whole of this masonry had apparently fallen at one time, the loose mortar being washed to the bottom. The top covering of soil was 2' thick. Nothing of interest was found except a carved apex stone with herring-bone pattern on one face.

(II) Passage and chamber of gate house

Accumulation here averaged 3' at outer entrance and 10' at inner entrance to yard. The order of debris (both chamber and passage) as follows:

> a foot or so of soil;
> heavy deposit of stone and loose mortar, the mortar washed to the bottom;
> shallow layer of soil and broken slate;
> layer deposit of stone and mortar and little decayed wood.

Nothing of interest found in debris of passage, but in chamber the following:

> Coin of 1639 (Louis XIII) in hearth of fireplace;
> Two cast iron fire-backs with arms of James I (union) found at S. end and presumably fallen from upper floors.
> Two cylindrical objects of cast iron 2' long (very like modern drainpipe) with wood attached to outside (these were found at bottom of debris);
> A quantity of iron spikes and other iron.

Removal of debris exposed a complete paving of sandstone flags in passage, and in chamber trace of wooden flooring along base of wall plaster. The level of this chamber floor was a foot or so above the rock surface. To preserve the floor level, the loose mortar of debris has been left up to the level of the wood floor. It is proposed to grass this area next spring.

(III) Elizabethan hall etc.

In a trial excavation along inside of walls, traces were found of scraps of decayed wood flooring adhering to plaster at base of walls. The 1- to 3-feet-deep accumulation of soil, slate and plaster and decayed wood was, therefore, removed to this level, which corresponds with the level of stone hearth as seen against the jamb of fireplace. The excavated material was riddled and the soil used to fill the hollows in yard outside. An immense quantity of slate was found; many of the slates being unbroken and showing large peg holes. Several pieces of green glazed ridge tile also found, and a quantity of window glass in tinted diamond panes. At the east side in a maze of fallen masonry, some plaster ribs (? of ceiling or chimney ornament) and several carved stones of chimney-piece. In the southeast, some burnt wood, leaded window glass, a portion of a brass candle stick, pieces of pavement tile and blue-and-white delf.

Preparation has been made for grassing this area next spring. A system of field drains will be laid between floor level and the rock surface below.

(IV) Buttery (so called on Lynn's Plan)

Removal of two feet of soil and slate exposed a complete pavement of rough stone. On top of stone pavement was a layer of fallen plaster. Articles found include a broken stem glass, a piece of coloured bottle, and some diamond panes of thin greenish window glass. The floor paving shows the chase for wood partition near north end. The floor is laid immediately upon the rock surface.

(V) Kitchen etc.

Accumulated debris here about 2' deep, consisting of fallen masonry, decayed wood and some broken slates, deeply overlaid with silted soil and mortar washed down from neighbouring higher levels of debris. Clearing exposed a pavement of rough stone, part of which has sunk under weight of fallen mass of walling. This suggested the presence of filling below the floor; a trial hole was made and the rock found beneath a foot of filling and sandstone rubbish. The sunken area of pavement was relaid. Nothing of interest found here, except a few scraps of window glass and pottery. The drains of sinks along west wall have not yet been cleaned. Decayed wood of sills and post found in situ in this north wall of kitchen indicate a timber-framed construction. On the south end of the kitchen two stone steps exposed leading up to cobbled yard behind Elizabethan hall.

(VI) Yard behind Elizabethan hall

Generally this area was overlaid to a depth of two to three feet with stone and slates. Between hall door and chimney projection, a large area of burnt wood and bones lay at bottom level. The clearing of the whole yard exposed a paving of cobble, finishing against patches of outcrop along the cliff edge. These patches of outcrop represent the line of the cliff edge upon which the latter curtain wall was built. The northern end of this curtain remains, and the stone stair giving access to the rampart has been uncovered. The earlier curtain can be traced six or seven feet lower down the cliff face, where several foundation stones are still affixed to the rock. It seems clear, therefore, that the earlier curtain was not lost as a result of subsidence of rock face, but as a result of pressure from the filling that had been backed behind it to level off the yard. The depth of this filling must have been about eight feet if we accept the outcrop as the original level of the yard.

At the southern end of the yard, against the east wall of the Elizabethan building, a range of outlets into a drain running below the cobble pavement has been exposed. The cleaning of the drain has not yet been done. Some window glass and pottery found here.

In clearing this area, a small section of cobble pavement was found bearing on a very loose material. Investigation showed that an extensive hollow existed below the pavement. The loose sunken cobbles were then lifted and found to be set upon a filling of clay and rubbish thrown into a void in the rock. This was first thought to be a well or a drain. When cleared it was found that the clay and rubbish had been packed into the hollow so that the pavement could be repaired, for other cobbles lay beneath the filling. The filled hole was found to be about 4' deep, with a passage opening from one side. The passage had silted to a foot in depth. The clearing was continued, a quantity of pottery, burnt wood, bones and shell being found in the deposit. The passage was then found to develop into a small low ceiled chamber, roughly elliptical in plan with a second outlet leading into another similar chamber. The whole has not yet been cleared, but it is apparently a rock-cut souterrain. The original entrance may be at the unexplored end. The thickness of rock cover is not more that 6 inches, and it will be necessary to prop before the clearing out can be completed.

(VII) Northeast tower

Silted soil removed to a depth of 18 inches revealed a compacted filling probably the bedding of a stone floor. No finds.

(VIII) Southeast tower

Similarly silted. Clearing revealed a rock cut floor with a curious square hold 12" deep cut in the centre. This suggests the seating of a post or column to support (or perhaps strengthen) the floor above.

(IX) Covered way (later gallery) inside south curtain wall

In this narrow space, extending from gate house to southeast tower, lay the heaviest accumulation of debris. The average depth was eight or nine feet. For the greater part, the clearing was done in layers, caution being essential due to the presence of detached columns in situ buried in the debris. The order of the excavation was as follows:

> Thin covering of soil;
> Plaster, stone and slate and very small quantity of decayed wood;
> (at the east end a considerable quantity of brick very much broken);
> at bottom level, lying on the levelled surface of rock, a thick mortar bedding overlaid with a deposit of burnt wood (6" thick along centre of area, less at sides).

Articles found included green glazed pottery, iron spikes, window glass and pieces of decorated glazed tile. Masonry included a few parapet and coping stones and a finial fallen from south wall of Elizabethan hall.

Parallel to the south curtain and seven feet from its inside face, a five-bay arcade of sandstone columns was unearthed. These are built up of small stones, two to each course, and are very much decayed. All were incomplete and the debris yielded no material which would be identified as belonging to this feature. Later adaptation (at a period when brick was used) has enclosed the openings to form a chamber. The columns had then been plastered over and their bases concealed by a wood floor at a slightly higher level. A fireplace with a brick hearth has been contrived in the easternmost bay. To preserve the latest floor level would involve the covering up of the column bases. It was, therefore, decided to grass this area at the level of the column bases.

(X) Inner yard

Except for some fallen masonry along east and west walls the accumulation was slight, less than a foot of soil and slate. Clearing exposed a complete pavement of cobbles laid with a distinct fall towards the northeast corner. Here was found an outlet into a built drain beneath east range of buildings. Several coins were found between the cobbles; some early seventeenth-century French and two of our King Charles I. An iron key was beside north door of northeast range.

(XI) Building along east side of inner yard

The debris here was as follows:

A few inches of soil with a few slates and very little stone;
Layer of fallen plaster, apparently from ceiling, but with no wood.

Clearing exposed random stone pavement in the northern half of range. The southern half was similarly floored fro trace was found of a pavement bedding. Drainage and other preparation has therefore been made for grassing at the level of adjoining stone pavement.

At the north end of range, the drain carrying surface water from the northeast corner of the yard was found in a collapsed state. The covering pavement was lifted, the drain cleared out, reconstructed, and the pavement relaid. The outlet from the drain is on the north slope of rock-stack. A coin (Irish) was found here. With the exception of a few scraps of pottery, nothing else was found in this east range. The exploration in the region of the drain revealed that a considerable depth of filling exists between paving and rock surface at this end.

(XII) Buildings along west side of inner yard

The accumulation here as in east range. Clearing exposed complete paving of random stones, with chases of two partitions, and towards north end, a dishing of the pavement to an outlet through west wall on to external slope of rock-stack. The following found in outlet of drain:

A fragment of bronze;
Several pieces of a brown glazed pottery flagon decorated with a mask and medallion.

(XIII) Buildings to north of inner yard

The debris here very slight, except for a mound of fallen masonry inside porch, and at east end lying over the broken wall tops. Clearing exposed plaster at base of walls with evidence of wood floor level, as in Elizabethan hall.

Below this level there is considerable depth of deposited filling. It is highly probably that the loss of the outer north wall, founded perilously near the edge of the vertical cliff, was due to the pressure of this deposited material. An effort will be made to secure this filling so that the site may be grassed over at the level of the original floor.

(XIV) Northern section generally

It is important to note that the volume of stone debris found in the clearing of the inner yard and its buildings represents only a fraction of the material that would be necessary to raise the existing low walls between yard and chambers to the level of the eaves.

(XV) Approach road

A cobbled roadway has been uncovered leading down from the field gate at public road. The excavation varied from the thickness of a sod at the upper end to three feet at the lower end. At the lower end, a French coin of early seventeenth century found at bottom of excavation and a tunic button bearing a crest found near the surface. The width of the clearing is 9', but this does not represent the full width of the original road. The incline is steep. Between mainland buildings and drawbridge, the cobbles have disappeared. The forecourt between drawbridge and gate house has a paving of cobbles lying a foot above an earlier similar paving. The direction of the earlier paving differs from the later one, and points to the existence of an earlier entrance northwest of the present gate house. The whole of this forecourt has not yet been cleared, but it is evident that the gap was bridged at a higher level than at present, and that the filling behind platforms on either side of the gap has disappeared.

* * *

After the lower levels of ground floor pavements had been cleared and exposed, the upper levels of ramparts, wall tops and vaults were freed from accumulation of vegetation, soil, and in some cases the debris of higher masonry. Rampart levels were uncovered along top of south curtain wall and at the upper levels of southeast tower. In both, the paving was found to be missing, but the bedding of the pavement remains along the top of the south wall. The tower rampart appears to have been included in a later higher chamber, for the jambs of a fireplace can be seen above the level of the earlier rampart.

In the northeast tower, the upper surface of the vault over the ground floor chamber retains traces of an early pavement bedding. On all the levels, the patches of bedding have been left without treatment, but the masonry where exposed has been cleaned and will be weather pointed.

The south curtain, totalling 6' 6" in thickness, is built of two distinct walls. The outer is the earlier; the inner has been built against the outer to provide sufficient width to accommodate a rampart. Both were built off the unlevelled surface of the natural rock; and, as a result of later levelling inside are now elevated upon a vertical face of rock-cut wall. This rock-cut face shows evidence of early decay, and a small area of medieval underpinning done in small cobbles can be seen. More of this underpinning may be covered by the plaster, which survives on the inner face of wall. The decay has continued during the three centuries or so of burial under debris, and the stability of the wall was threatened. It has, therefore, been necessary to cut away the soft rock to a depth of about 2', and to replace with a material capable of supporting the weight of the wall above. Concrete, with a facing of old slates, laid horizontally was adopted as a method of ensuring stability, and at the same time giving a face which is not assertively modern, but can be distinguished from the original medieval underpinning.

The same method of underpinning has been adopted below the southeast tower, where the levelling mentioned above has had the effect of elevating the foundation to a height of five feet above the general level of the yard.

The precariously suspended masonry between the upper and lower windows of the Elizabethan oriels has been made secure by the insertion of a reinforced concrete beam completely hidden in the thickness of the walling.

The work is now suspended until April or May 1929, when the remaining necessary works on the fabric, together with fencing, new entrance bridge and the cleaning out of drain and souterrain, with the undertaken.

(Intd) TFOR, 14 January 1929. Works Branch, 113 Royal Avenue, Belfast.

Bibliography

Abbreviations

AFM	*Annála ríoghachta Éireann: annals of the kingdom of Ireland by the Four Masters from the earliest period to the year 1616*, ed. & trans. John O'Donovan (7 vols, Dublin, 1851; repr. 6 vols, Dublin, 1990)
AU	*Annála Uladh, annals of Ulster: otherwise annála senait, annals of senat: a chronicle of Irish affairs, 431–1131, 1155–1541*, ed. W.M. Hennessy & Bartholomew MacCarthy (4 vols, Dublin, 1887–1901)
BBC	British Broadcasting Corporation
BL Add. MS	British Library Additional Manuscripts
CAF	Centre for Archaeological Fieldwork
CCM	*Calendar of the Carew manuscripts preserved in the archiepiscopal library at Lambeth* (6 vols, London, 1867–73; I: 1867; II: 1868)
CDI	Calendar of documents relating to Ireland, I, II, V (5 vols, London, 1875–86; I: 1875; II: 1877; V: 1886)
CMA	Centre for Maritime Archaeology, University of Ulster
CPCR Charles I	*Calendar of patent and close rolls of chancery, Charles I, 1625–33*, ed. J. Morrin (London, 1863)
CPRCI James I	*Calendar of patent rolls of chancery in Ireland, James I*, ed. J.C. Erck (Dublin, 1846)
CPRI	*Irish patent rolls of James I: facsimile of the Irish Record Commission's calendar prepared prior to 1830*, foreword by M.C. Griffith (Dublin, 1966)
CS, X	*The Civil Survey, AD1654–56*, ed. R.C. Simington (10 vols, Dublin, 1931–61; X: 1961)
CSPI	*Calendar of the state papers relating to Ireland*, I, II, III (24 vols, London, 1860–1911; I: 1860; II: 1867; III: 1877)
dGPS	differential Global Positioning Systems
DoENI	Department of the Environment, Northern Ireland
ETM+	Enhanced Thematic Mapper Plus
Fiants Eliz.	Calendar and index to the faints of the reign of Elizabeth I, *appendix to the 11th–13th, 15th–18th and 21st–22nd reports of the deputy keeper of public records in Ireland* (Dublin, 1879–81, 1883–6, 1889–90)
GIS	Geographic Information System
GLCF	Global Land Cover Facility
GPR	Ground Penetrating Radar
GPS	Global Positioning Systems

IMC	Irish Manuscripts Commission
JRSAI	*Journal of the Royal Society of Antiquaries of Ireland* (Dublin, 1892–)
LiDAR	Light Detection And Ranging
LMS	London, Midland & Scottish Railway
MBE	Member of the British Empire
MP	Member of Parliament
NIEA	Northern Ireland Environment Agency
OD	Ordnance Datum
OS	Ordnance Survey
PRIA	*Proceedings of the Royal Irish Academy* (Dublin, 1836–)
PRONI	Public Records Office Northern Ireland
PSAMNI	*Provisional survey of the ancient monuments of Northern Ireland* (Belfast, 1940)
QUB	Queen's University, Belfast
RAF	Royal Air Force
RCAHMS	Royal Commission on Ancient and Historic Monuments, Scotland
RHA	Royal Hibernian Academy
SMR	Sites and Monuments Record
TCD	Trinity College, Dublin
TCD dep.	TCD: 1641 Depositions Project, online transcript January 1970 (http://1641.tcd.ie/deposition.php?depID<?php echo 838030r021?>)], accessed November 2011
UJA	*Ulster Journal of Archaeology* (Belfast, 3 ser.: 1853–62, 9 vols; 1895–1911, 17 vols; 1938–)
UU	University of Ulster
YHA	Youth Hostel Association

Unpublished sources

Brannon, N. 1987 'Archaeological excavations at Dunluce Castle: summary report'. SM7/ANT2:3–SM. Unpublished DoENI file.
Muhr, K. Note in DoENI Dunluce SMR file ANT002:003.

Ayr Burgh Archives, Scotland

B6/11/4: Monument conservation.

British Library, London

BL Add. MS 4756: Entry book of reports of the commissioners for Ireland, 1622.
BL Add. MS 4794: James I to Chichester, 3 May 1613.

Department of the Environment, Northern Ireland

DoENI file B2093: Dunluce Castle.
B2093/1928: Dunluce Castle.
B2093/1975: Dunluce Castle.
B2094/28: Dunluce Castle.

Public Record Office, Northern Ireland

PRONI D2977/3A/2/36/1: Antrim papers.
PRONI D2977/5/1/1/1: Antrim papers.
PRONI T811/3: 'A report of the voluntary work done by servitors ... within the counties of Antrim and Monaghan'.
PRONI D/1759/3C/3: Muster rolls, Antrim, 1630–1.
PRONI T307: Hearth Money Roll, Antrim.

Published sources

Arlincourt, C.V.P. 1844 *The three kingdoms: England, Scotland, Ireland*. London.
Bardon, J. 1996 *A history of Ulster*. Belfast.
Bell, J.L. and T.E. McNeill 2002 'Bonamargy Friary, County Antrim'. *UJA* 61, 98–116.
Benn, G. 1877 *A history of the town of Belfast*. London.
Bigger, F.G. 1905 'Some historical notes about Dunluce and its builders'. *UJA* 11:4, 154–62.
Breen, C. 2005 *The Gaelic lordship of the O'Sullivan Beara: a landscape cultural history*. Dublin.
Breen, C., Forsythe, W., Raven, J. and Rhodes, D. 2011 'Excavation and survey at Dunstaffnage Castle, Argyll'. *Proceedings of the Society of Antiquaries Scotland* 140, 165–78.
Breen, C. and Raven, J. forthcoming 'The castle at Ballylough, Co. Antrim'.
Caldwell, D. 2008 *Islay, the land of the lordship*. Edinburgh.
Carter, M. 1997 'A seventeenth-century smithy at Ferryland, Newfoundland'. *Avalon Chronicles* 2, 73–106.
Case, H.J., Dimbleby, G.W., Mitchell, G.F., Mitchell, M.E.S. and Proudfoot, V.B. 1969 'Land-use in Goodland townland, Co. Antrim, from Neolithic times until today'. *JRSAI* 99, 39–53.
Canny, N. 2001 *Making Ireland British, 1580–1650*. Oxford.
CARARE 2012 *http://carare.eu/rum/Community/Gallery/Gdansk-plan-of-brewery*, online resource, accessed Jan. 2012.
Carleton, T. (ed.) 1991 *Heads and hearths: the hearth money rolls and poll tax returns for Co. Antrim 1660–69*. Belfast.

Charles-Edwards, T.M. 2011 'The province of Ulster in the early middle ages'. In Lynn, C.J. and McDowell, J.A. (eds) *Deer Park farms: the excavation of a raised rath in the Glenarm Valley, Co. Antrim*. Belfast, 39–60.

Clinton, M. 2001 *The souterrains of Ireland*. Bray.

Curl, J.S. 1986 *The Londonderry Plantation, 1609–1914: the history, architecture and planning of the estates of the city of London and its livery companies in Ulster*. Chichester.

Curtis, E. 1938 'The MacQuillan or Mandeville Lords of the Route'. *PRIA* 44C, 99–113.

Daniels, R. and Jackson, S. n.d. *The blacksmith's shop, Hart*. Hartlepool.

Day, A. and McWilliams, P. 1992 *Ordnance Survey memoirs of Ireland, parishes of County Antrim V, 1830–5, 1837–8*. Belfast.

De hÓir, S. 1982–3 'Guns in medieval and Tudor Ireland'. *Irish Sword* 15, 76–87.

Dobson, D. 2004 *Scottish emigration to colonial America, 1607–1785*. Athens, GA.

Douglas Simpson, W. 1976 *Dunnottar Castle, historical and descriptive*. Edinburgh.

Dubourdieu, J. 1812 *Statistical survey of the county of Antrim*. Dublin.

Duffy, S. 2004 'The lords of Galloway, earls of Carrick and the Bissetts of the Glens: Scottish settlement in thirteenth-century Ulster'. In Edwards, D. (ed.) *Regions and rulers in Ireland 1100–1650*. Dublin, 37–50.

Fletcher, J. 1975 'The medieval hall at Lewknor'. *Oxoniesia* 40, 247–53.

Fry, M.F. 2005 'Preserving ancient historic monuments and sites in state care in Northern Ireland, c.1921 to c.1955'. *UJA* 64, 160–71.

Gillespie, R. 1985 *Colonial Ulster: the settlement of east Ulster, 1600–1641*. Cork.

Gillespie, R. 2006 *Seventeenth-century Ireland*. Dublin.

Glasscock, R.E. 1993 'Land and people, c.1300'. In Cosgrove, A. (ed.) *A new history of Ireland, II, medieval Ireland, 1169–1534* (second ed.), Oxford, 204–39.

Grose, F. 1794 *Antiquities of Ireland*. Vol. 2. London.

Gwynn, A. and Hadcock, N.D. 1970 *Medieval religious houses: Ireland*. London.

Hadfield, A. and Maley, W. (eds) 1997 *Edmund Spenser: A view of the present state of Ireland*. Oxford.

Hill, G. 1873 *An historical account of the MacDonnells of Antrim*. Belfast.

Hogan, E. 1878 *A description of Ireland, c.1598*. Dublin.

Horning, A. 2001 '"Dwelling houses in the old Irish barbarous manner": archaeological evidence for Gaelic architecture in an Ulster Plantation village'. In Duffy, P., Edwards, D. and FitzPatrick, E. (eds) *Ireland, 1300–1650: land, lordship, and settlement*. Dublin, 375–96.

Horning, A. 2004 'Archaeological explorations of cultural identity and rural economy in the north of Ireland: Goodland, County Antrim'. *International Journal of Historical Archaeology* 8:3, 199–215.

Hyett, J. 2002 'Variation on a theme: the archaeology of an Australian blacksmith's shop'. *Australasian Historical Archaeology* 20, 92–5.

Ivens, R.J. 1988 'Notes on medieval coarse pottery in the Ulster Museum'. *UJA* 57, 127–31.

Jope, E.M. 1951 'Scottish influence in the north of Ireland, castles with Scottish features'. *UJA* 14, 31–47.

Kew, G. 1988 *The Irish sections of Fynes Moryson's unpublished itinerary*. Dublin.

Kingston, S. 2004 *Ulster and the Isles in the fifteenth century*. Dublin.

Lane, A. and Campbell, E. 2000 *Dunadd: an early Dalriadic capital*. Oxford.

Lawlor, H.C. 1935–7 'Dunluce and its owners prior to the Norman invasion'. *PRIA* 43C, 307–11.

Lewis, H. 2010 'From prehistoric to urban Shoreditch: excavations at Holywell Priory, Holywell Lane, London, EC2'. *London Archaeologist* 12:9, 249–54.

Lewis, J. 1996 'Dunstaffnage Castle, Argyll & Bute: excavations in the north tower and east range, 1987–94'. *Proceedings of the Society of Antiquaries of Scotland* 126, 559–603.

Lewis, S. 1837 *A topographical dictionary of Ireland* 2 vols, London.

Light, J.D. 1984 'The archaeological investigation of blacksmith shops'. *Journal of the Society for Industrial Archaeology* 10:1, 55–6.

Lynn, W.H. 1905 'Notes on the ruins of Dunluce Castle'. *UJA* 11:3, 97–107.

Mac Cionnaith, L. 1938 (repr. 1969) *Dioghluim dána*. Baile Átha Cliath, no. 89.

MacCoinnich, A. 2007 'Siol Torcail and their lordship in the sixteenth century'. In *Crossing the Minch: exploring the links between Skye and the Outer Hebrides*. Skye, 7–32.

McDonnell, H. 1987 'Glenarm Friary and the Bissets'. *The Glynns* 15, 34–49.

McDonnell, H. 1992 'A seventeenth-century inventory from Dunluce Castle'. *JRSAI* 122, 109–27.

McDonnell, H. 2004a *A history of Dunluce*. Belfast.

McDonnell, H. 2004b 'Surviving Kinsale, Scottish-style: the MacDonnells of Antrim'. In Morgan, H. (ed.) *The Battle of Kinsale*. Bray, 265–78.

McGladdery, C.A. 2005 'The Black Douglases, 1396–1455'. In Oram, R. and Stell, G. (eds) *Lordship and architecture in medieval and Renaissance Scotland*. Edinburgh, 160–87.

McGuigan, J.H. 1964 *The Giant's Causeway tramway*. Lingfield.

McLeod, W. 2007 'Images of Scottish warriors in later Irish bardic poetry' in Duffy, S. (ed.) *The world of the Galloglass*. Dublin, 169–87.

McNeill, T.E. 1980 *Anglo-Norman Ulster*. Edinburgh.

McNeill, T.E. 1983 'The stone castles of northern County Antrim'. *UJA* 46, 101–28.

McNeill, T. 1997 *Castles in Ireland*. London.

McNeill, T.E. 2004 'Excavations at Dunineny Castle, Co. Antrim'. *Medieval Archaeology* 48, 167–204.

McVeigh, J. (ed.) 1995 *Richard Pococke's Irish tours*. Dublin.

Mallory, J.P. and McNeill, T.E. 1991 *The archaeology of Ulster*. Belfast.

Mason, J. 1830 *Youth's instruction*. London.

Maxwell, C. 1923 *Irish history from contemporary sources, 1509–1610*. London.

Murphy, M. and O'Conor, K. 2008 *Roscommon Castle*. Boyle.

Murray, P. 2004 *George Petrie (1790–1866): the rediscovery of Ireland's past*. Cork.

Robinson, P. 1984 *The plantation of Ulster*. Dublin.

Nicholls, K. 1985 'Abstracts of Mandeville deeds'. *Analecta Hibernica* 32, 3–26.

Nicholls, K. 1993 'The development of lordship in County Cork, 1300–1600'. In O'Flanagan, P. and Buttimer, C. (eds) *Cork: history and society*. Dublin, 157–212.

Nicholls, K. 2007 '*Scottish mercenary kindreds in Ireland, 1250–1600'*. In Duffy, S. (ed.) *The world of the Gallowglass: kings and warriors in Ireland and Scotland, 1200–1600*. Dublin, 86–105.

Ó Clabaigh, C. 2012 *The friars in Ireland, 1224–1540*. Dublin.

O'Conor, K.D. 2002 'Housing in later medieval Gaelic Ireland'. *Ruralia* 4, 197–206.

Ohlmeyer, J.H. 1993 *Civil war and restoration in the three Stuart kingdoms: the career of Randal MacDonnell, marquis of Antrim, 1609–83*. Cambridge.

Ohlmeyer, J.H. 2004 'A laboratory for empire? Early modern Ireland and English imperialism'. In Kenny, K. *Ireland and the British Empire*. Oxford, 26–60.

O'Keeffe, T. 2000 *Medieval Ireland: an archaeology*. Stroud, Gloucestershire.

O'Laverty, J. 1887 *An historical account of the diocese of Down and Connor ancient and modern*. Vol. 4, Dublin.

Orpen, G.H. 1920 *Ireland under the Normans*. Vol. 4, Oxford.

Otway-Ruthven, A.J. 1968 *History of medieval Ireland*. London.

Pearson, L. 2010 *The brewing industry*. Stratford-upon-Avon.

Pender, S. 1939 *A census of Ireland, c.1659*. Dublin.

Perceval-Maxwell, M. 1973 *The Scottish migration to Ulster in the reign of James I*. London.

Power, D. et al. 1992 *Archaeological inventory of County Cork, vol. 1: West Cork*. Dublin.

Price, S. 2007 *Newsletter of the Worcestershire Archaeological Society* 76, 11–12.

Quinn, K. 2002 'Archaeological study of Dunluce Castle'. MA, QUB.

RCAHMS 1984 *Argyll, vol. 5: Islay, Jura, Colonsay, Oronsay*. Edinburgh.

Reeves, W. 1847 *Ecclesiastical antiquities of Down, Connor and Dromore, consisting of a taxation of those dioceses*. Dublin.

Reeves-Smyth, T. 1999 *Irish gardens and gardening before Cromwell*. Barryscourt Lectures IV. Cork.

Reeves-Smyth, T. 2007 'Community to privacy: late Tudor and Jacobean manorial architecture in Ireland, 1560–1640'. In Horning, A., Ó Baoill, R., Donnelly, C. and Logue, P. (eds) *The post-medieval archaeology of Ireland, 1550–1850*. 289–326.

Robinson, P. 1984 *The plantation of Ulster*. Belfast.

Tabraham, C.J. 1997 *Scotland's castles*. London.

Tabraham, C.J. and Good, G.L. 1981 'The artillery fortification at Threave Castle, Galloway'. In Caldwell, D.H. (ed.) *Scottish weapons and fortifications, 1100–1800*. Edinburgh, 55–72.

Treadwell, V. 2006 *The Irish Commission of 1622*. Dublin.

Webb, M. 1860 'The clan of the MacQuillins of Antrim'. *UJA* 8, 251–68.

Wilcox, R. 1980 'Castle Acre Priory excavations, 1972–6'. *Norfolk Archaeology* 37, 231–76.

Williams, B.B. and Robinson, P.S. 1983 'The excavation of Bronze Age cists and a medieval booley house at Glenmakeernan, County Antrim, and a discussion of booleying in North Antrim'. *UJA* 46, 29–40.

Wilson, H.E. and Manning P.I. 1978 *Geology of the Causeway coast*. Belfast.

Wright, G.N. 1823 *A guide to the Giant's Causeway*. Dublin.

Wright, G.N., Petrie, G., Bartlett, W.H. and Baynes, T.M. 1834 *Ireland illustrated: from original drawings*. London.

Young, R. 1885 'Dunluce Castle'. *Journal of the Royal Historical and Archaeological Association of Ireland* 7, 133–46.

Glossary

Ballybetagh	Gaelic landholding unit constituting and estate. In general, four quarters made up a Ballybetagh
Barrel vault	Semicircular vault in the shape of half a barrel, split lengthways
Bastle	Fortified farmhouse with thick stone walls, of a type distinctive to the troubled sixteenth-century Anglo-Scottish borders
Bawn	Walled courtyard or enclosing wall that surrounds or is located beside a castle or fortified house
Bonnaghts	Group of soldiers or armed men serving for pay
Carucate/ ploughland	Amount of arable land usually tilled in a season (usually 120 acres, but varied because of the nature of the local terrain)
Centring	Frame used to support an arch under construction
Chamfer	Made by cutting off the edge of anything right-angled, but especially angles on stonework
Chancel	Eastern end of a church in which altar is placed
Chiefry	Office or territory of a Gaelic-Irish lord
Corbel	Stone block projecting from a wall to carry structures, especially floor beams
Crenellation	Notched stone battlements
Diocese	District under the jurisdiction of a bishop
Embrasure	Recess for a doorway, window or arrowloop
Gabion	Wicker basket filled with earth and/or stone, used in fortifications
Garderobe	Latrine
Jamb	Straight side of an archway, window or doorway
Light	Opening between the mullions or jambs
Lintel	Horizontal beam (slab) over a door or window
Loophole	Small narrow light of various forms in wall from which to shoot arrows etc.
Moiety	Half division of something
Mullion	Vertical stone or timber dividing window lights
Mural stairs	Stone stairs in wall
Nave	Main body of a church, assigned generally to laity
Parish	Subdivision of a diocese, having its own church and clergyman
Ploughland	see carucate
Pintle	Pin or bolt, usually inserted into a gudgeon, which is used as part of a pivot or hinge
Quarter of land	Three ploughlands or carucates/a quarter of a ballybetagh
Quoins	Stones, frequently dressed, used in the angles of buildings

Rubble	Wall construction using rough, unsquared stones
Seneschal	Official with responsibility for administering justice
Sept	Branch of a Gaelic-Irish family
Splay	Angled embrasure
Transom	Horizontal stone or timber dividing a window into separate lights
Yett	Iron grille that could be placed in front of an entrance

Index